THE BABY
AND CHILD CARE

QUICK REFERENCE

ENCYCLOPEDIA

Dr. Margaret I. Wood

Main entry under title:
The Baby and Child Care Quick Reference Encyclopedia

Bibliography: b
IBSN 0-9695420-0-3

Editor: Kathy Fremes
Cover Photo: Mark Wright/Elephant Boy Productions

IBSN: 0-9695420-0-3
Written, Printed and Bound in Canada

Family Communications Inc.
37 Hanna Avenue, Unit 1
Toronto, Ontario M6K 1X1 (416) 537-2604

THE BABY AND CHILD CARE

QUICK REFERENCE

ENCYCLOPEDIA

Dr. Margaret I. Wood

A Family Communications Inc. Publication

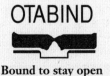

OTABIND

Bound to stay open

Publisher's Note

Otabind (Ota-Bind). This book has been bound using the Otabind process. You can open this book at any page, gently run your finger down the spine, and the pages will lie flat.

Acknowledgements

The publisher would like to thank the pediatricians at The Hospital for Sick Children for their assistance in scientifically reviewing and approving the text and illustrations in The Baby and Child Care Quick Reference Encyclopedia.

Our thanks to author Dr. Margaret Wood for her tireless effort to ensure that the book contains the most up-to-date and accurate information.

Thanks also to the editor, Kathy Fremes, for coordinating the work of Dr. Wood with that of the pediatricians at The Hospital for Sick Children.

A special thanks to our corporate sponsors. It is through their generosity that this book is available at no cost to families across Canada. Our gratitude is extended to all companies who participated, but we must single out those companies whose significant financial contribution helped the publishers launch the book.

Johnson & Johnson
INC
McNEIL

Fisher-Price

DONALD G. SWINBURNE
Publisher

Preface

Child health care has been studied intensively in recent years. Prevention of accidents and illnesses has become an integral part of the care of young children. The Hospital for Sick Children has always given superb care to the sick or injured child but has also contributed through research and education to the care of the child in the community. The Canadian Pediatric Society and The American Academy of Pediatrics have also supported this work.

The Baby and Child Care Quick Reference Encyclopedia is not an all-inclusive encyclopedia but one which addresses the more common problems and needs of the infant and child to the age of 10 years as seen in a pediatric practice. It is meant only as a guide and as a supplement to child health care in the community. As it is impossible to incorporate all the thoughts expressed by those involved in this book, it has been necessary to simplify some areas where there is currently much discussion.

This book has evolved over many years from a small practical book. I have used it for over 45 years and have been privileged to be involved with the writing of the contents for 36 years, drawing upon my experience as a pediatrician and mother. The interest and concerns of parents and those involved in the care of children have been most helpful. It has been gratifying to me to reflect on the changes which have taken place.

I am indebted to many staff members of The Hospital for Sick Children for help, advice and recommendations. The support and assistance of my husband, Dr. Ross Johnson, also a pediatrician, has been particularly appreciated.

Thanks are due to the editor, Kathy Fremes, and staff of Family Communications who have made this book possible.

Margaret I. Wood, MD FRCP(C)
The Hospital for Sick Children
Toronto, Canada

In this book your child is called he or him because that is more convenient. You will understand that girls are thought just as highly of as boys and that suggestions usually apply to both sexes. Similarly, the doctor will be addressed as she or her for simplicity.

The advertisement of any product or service in this book does not imply endorsement, whether direct or indirect, by either The Hospital for Sick Children, the contributors or the author.

Table of Contents

Action Charts

Dedicated to Norma Carr Swinburne, a mother who knew caring for children was 75 percent love and 25 percent patience.

Nutrition
The Foundation
of Health

It seems miraculous that a tiny fertilized ovum – invisible to the naked eye – develops into a perfect baby some seven pounds in weight in only nine months. It is one of the marvels of nature.

Except for identical twins (which develop from one ovum), every baby is different. A mother passes on to her baby just as many but no more inherited characteristics as the father. The parents share equally in this regard even though the infant spends the important first nine months of his life within the mother's body. The mother, in turn, inherited half her inborn traits from each of her parents, and the father did likewise. Thus a baby inherits some of his characteristics from his grandfathers and grandmothers and so on back down the family trees.

Some traits are dominant and express themselves, at the same time concealing the weaker and recessive trait. It isn't surprising that babies, even from a very early age, show different kinds of behavior. Some are rather quiet and placid, others are jumpy and tense; the rest are somewhere in between.

You will find that you modify your care according to the responses of your baby. As he grows you do this almost automatically, unless you are set on carrying out a rigid schedule. However, such a schedule is unnecessary and makes life harder for both you and your baby. If you are flexible, you'll find that in a few weeks your baby will have established a schedule of his own.

It's exciting to watch a child grow in size and awareness. Before long he will know you and will smile when you come to him. As he becomes older he will learn to do many things, partly of his own accord, and partly as a result of what you and others do for him. We hope this book will help you to care for your baby comfortably and to enjoy him.

YOUR PRENATAL DIET
Food For Growth

During his stay within your uterus, your baby obtains his food supplies from you. In addition, your uterus, its other contents, the volume of your blood and your breasts are also increasing in size. For the health of both you and your child it's especially important to eat well during pregnancy; select foods rich in proteins, minerals and vitamins. The healthy eating habits you develop during pregnancy will stand you in good stead when you prepare well balanced meals for your growing family.

All nutritional experts recommend that a mother consume about 4 cups of milk, (32 ounces or 900 millilitres) each day during the last half of her pregnancy. This may be a great deal more than you are accustomed to, but it is a good idea to get into the habit of drinking milk and using it to prepare meals. Milk is an unusually nutritious food, before, during and after pregnancy. It provides a very large percentage of the calcium, vitamin B2 (riboflavin) and first-class protein in well-planned meals, as well as several other useful nutrients. During the prenatal period you need to eat at least 50 percent more calcium than you did before you became pregnant. To make both bones and teeth, your unborn baby needs plenty of calcium. Four cups of milk provide 75 percent of the amount of calcium recommended in the latter part of pregnancy. The only common food that rivals milk in calcium is cheese. If you are not fond of milk, you can replace some of it with cheese, which we will talk about later on.

Four cups of milk will also give you almost as much excellent protein as two good servings of meat. Your baby needs proteins for developing all his organs and tissues, not just his muscles. The proteins in milk are so good that they can supplement or greatly improve the poorer proteins that you eat in foods made of flour or other grains. Milk adds valuable amounts of vitamin Bl or thiamine, as well as phosphorus, which also plays an essential role in bone and tooth formation.

Ounce for ounce, skim milk has a little more than half the calories of homogenized or whole milk and two percent milk has roughly 80 percent of the calories. Skim milk contains all the ingredients of whole milk, except for the fat. Vitamin A, which is removed in the skimming process, is replaced by the dairyman. Reconstituted dried skim milk is much cheaper and just as nutritious as the liquid milk.

Add milk to soups, sauces and casseroles. Use extra skim milk powder in muffin, tea biscuit or other recipes. Half a cup of ice milk can replace the same amount of skim milk but the "ices" are four times higher in calories. Substituting calcium tablets or syrup for milk is expensive and has only a fraction of the calcium in milk.

Vitamin D

All commercial milk – homogonized, evaporated or dried – has been fortified with Vitamin D. Check the label. What function does this vitamin play? It helps you to absorb into your bloodstream the calcium found in foods. Therefore, this vitamin is especially useful during pregnancy or when you are breast-feeding. If you use the recommended amounts of vitamin D-enriched milk you will not need vitamin D supplements

Some brands of margarine have also been fortified with small amounts of vitamin D. As margarine is high in calories, you probably will not eat much of it, but it is a good idea to add a little to your yellow or green vegetables because it helps you to absorb the yellow carotene from them. Carotene is turned into vitamin A in our bodies. Butter has a similar action but contains very little vitamin D. Four hundred IU of vitamin D and about 4,000 IU of vitamin A are recommended daily.

Cheese is sometimes called solid milk, although it doesn't quite deserve that name, since much of its B vitamin is lost in the whey. However, one ounce (30 grams) of one of the firmer whole milk cheeses (such as cheddar or process) can take the place of seven ounces (196 millitres) of milk in calcium and protein. Unfortunately, all the common cheeses of this type are higher in calories than skim milk. If you are having to watch your calories closely, you would do well to choose a skim milk processed cheese – one ounce (30 grams) has fewer calories than seven ounces (200 millilitres) of skim milk but just as much or more calcium and protein as cheddar. Cottage or cream cheese is far lower in calcium than the other types of cheese.

Fruits and Vegetables

This group of foods can provide you with enough vitamin C (ascorbic acid), a great deal of vitamin A and useful amounts of both iron and cellulose (roughage) if you are selective. A minimum of an orange, half a grapefruit or a juice glass (about four ounces) of fresh, packaged, diluted frozen or canned citrus or vitaminized apple juice is recommended daily. After opening or squeezing, citrus juice retains its vitamin C for several days in the refrigerator. On the other hand, the amount of vitamin C in vitaminized apple juice drops after the can is opened, even though it is refrigerated. After one day's storage, 20 percent of this vitamin has disappeared. Therefore, small cans (19-ounce or 530-millilitre) which you can finish in a couple of days are better buys for small families than large cans.

A double dose of tomato juice or of fresh or canned tomatoes is a good alternative to the citrus products. A serving of cantaloupe or of fresh or frozen strawberries is equally valuable. New potatoes and all the vegetables of the cabbage family, including turnips, are also quite rich in this vitamin. If they are cooked in small amounts of boiling water until tender, they retain a large percentage of their vitamin C. As vitamins leak out into the cooking water, it is worth using as a soup or sauce stock. Cooking potatoes in their jackets further reduces the loss into the water; baking them is even better. Eat potatoes shortly after cooking them and avoid mashing them to maximize their nutritional value.

The yellow-fleshed vegetables and fruits and the green vegetables provide carotene, the precursor of vitamin A. The deeper the color the higher their vitamin A value. If you are using skim milk, plan to have one of these products or tomatoes, which also contain carotene, every day. Fortunately carotene withstands boiling or baking without harm. All the fruits and vegetables add a little iron to your meals, especially the mature legumes such as peas, beans and lentils. They all provide some cellulose, which remains in the digestive tract and helps to prevent constipation – often bothersome during pregnancy. Prunes or prune nectar and figs are especially effective in relieving this trouble.

Raw fruits make excellent low calorie desserts. Those canned in syrup or frozen with added sugar provide about twice as many calories per serving. The additional calories are in the sweet liquid, which you would be wise to pass on to some slender member of the family. At least two servings of fruit (one high in vitamin C) and three servings of vegetables are recommended daily during pregnancy.

Cereal and Cereal Products

The dark whole grain cereals that you cook at home provide iron, cellulose and considerable thiamine (vitamin B1). The cellulose, present in the bran fraction of the cereal, is useful for preventing constipation. Unenriched white or yellow cereals, such as semolina, farina (white wheatlets) or corn meal, on the other hand, are low in these three food factors. Many of the ready-to-eat cereals have been enriched with two or more of the B vitamins, and many, such as bran flakes, have had outstanding amounts of iron added. You'll find this information on the label. As your needs for iron (both for your own and for your baby's use) are at their highest when you are pregnant, you would be wise to choose the iron-rich types. Those made of all bran may be too laxative for a few. The special baby cereals are well reinforced with both iron and B vitamins. If you like them, they would be excellent in your meals.

Non-sweet baked goods such as bread and rolls, are a good deal lower in calories than cakes, cookies and sweet biscuits, but all of them are actually "fillers" which you can safely reduce if you are gaining too fast.

Meat, Poultry and Fish

At least one good serving of one of these foods each day is recommended and even more is an advantage. They all add good amounts of excellent proteins as well as iron and B vitamins. If you choose lean cuts and do not eat any fat that you can see, you reduce their calories, sometimes by as much as 50 percent. Liver of any kind is the most nutritious food – it contains outstanding amounts of vitamins A, riboflavin and iron, as well as plenty of protein and thiamine. You would do well to have it once a week. Heart and kidney are almost as valuable and economical. This food group is one of your main sources of protein, iron and B vitamins.

Eggs

Eggs contain fair amounts of excellent protein, iron, vitamin A and the B vitamins, but some nutritionists suggest that relatively sedentary people should not eat too many egg yolks because of their cholesterol content. Nearly all the experts would agree that three eggs a week are fine for everyone.

Sweets and Fats

Sugar, candies, syrup, honey, jams, jellies and marmalade add nothing, or practically nothing, but calories to your meals. Fat-rich foods like corn oil, margarine, butter, commercial mayonnaise and shortening are, ounce for ounce, even higher in calories than sugar. They add little else. Thus you would be wise, especially if you are having to watch your weight gain closely, to use all these foods and others high in sugar or fat sparingly.

Salt

Iodized salt is the type recommended during pregnancy, as your needs for iodine are higher than usual at this time. However, during the last few months before your baby is born, some physicians cut down your use of salt for other reasons. In that case you can obtain additional iodine by eating sea fish, either fresh, frozen or canned.

2

Baby's Room, Equipment and Clothing

W hen a baby is expected in your family, planning a space for him will occupy much of your thought and probably necessitate several shopping trips. Baby, ideally, should have his own room, preferably one that has a large window so that it can be well ventilated. If you have a choice, pick a room that is as cool as possible in the summer because really hot weather is rather hard on babies. On the other hand, especially in his first few weeks, his room needs to be reasonably warm and easy to heat. As he grows older, his room may be relatively cool at night – 60-65 Fahrenheit (16-18 Celsius). A room thermometer may be hung about 3 feet from the floor in his room.

Furnishings

Your baby will soon develop into a child, so the furnishings should be chosen with this in mind. Furnish his room with easily washable items. Many germs that don't bother adults can make an infant sick; partly because he has no immunity to them (he has never met them before) and partly because his body reacts vigorously against them. To save him as much as possible from germs, cleanliness is important.

Dark drapes and blinds help to keep out the early morning sun and the mid-day heat in summer. Screens will be necessary during the summer months. Flies carry germs on their bodies and may infect your baby by alighting on his food, rattles or other things that he puts in his mouth.

Many spills will occur in his room, so a water and stain-resistant flooring will make the care of his room easier. Wall-to-wall broadloom is hard to keep clean and scatter rugs with no rubberized underpads or backs are dangerous.

You will need a good overhead light and some sort of night lamp, as you will want to check him while he is asleep without disturbing him. You may have to remove the night lamp when he becomes a busy, inquisitive toddler.

Baby's Bed

For the first three or four months a small crib or cradle with casters will make baby's bed mobile. This is helpful because if he becomes sick you may want to have him closer to your own bed. Also, such a small crib can be pushed from room to room, so that when he is awake he can watch what you are doing.

If you select a cradle of the rocking variety, ensure that it swings no more than 20 degrees from the vertical – the maximum set by Canadian federal legislation.

Other parents prefer a bassinet, lined if its sides are rough, with possibly a small folded-up cotton blanket as a mattress. Pillow cases or even cloth diapers make good covers for small mattresses, which means you won't have to wash crib sheets. A newborn is easier to look after and probably happier in a little bed than in a large crib. However, at about four months you will want a regular-sized crib for his room, so it is more economical to skip the bassinet and put him in a crib which he will use until he is at least two.

A baby should always have his own bed. He does not need a pillow. Crib guards (bumper pads) may be purchased to protect him from banging into the side of the crib or from putting an arm or leg through the slats of the bed. They are plastic-covered foam cushions that are fastened to the sides and head of his crib.

Standards for cribs were updated in 1986. A new crib, made in Canada, will meet these standards. Ensure that there are no sharp edges or areas where fingers or toes may be pinched. The slats should not allow a 2 1/2 x 4 x 4-inch (6 x 10 x 10-centimetre) block to pass between them. Mattress supports on cribs should be bolted to the frame securely. (Some babies treat their mattresses like trampolines!) An adjustable position of the mattress will make caring for baby easier; as will a drop side. If you have any questions about the safety of your crib or the one you wish to purchase, contact Consumer and Corporate Affairs Canada, Place du Portage, Hull, Que., K1A 0C9.

Infant/Child Car Seat

In Canada, parents are required by law to use a car seat when transporting small children. For more information on this essential piece of equipment see Chapter 19.

 NOTE *All infant car seats must face the rear of the automobile.*

Change Table

Choose a change table that is high enough to work at comfortably and position it out of the reach of blind cords or anything hazardous that might be grabbed by a tiny hand. Pockets for holding baby's toilet articles on the side of the table are useful and a nearby shelf for clean linen and clothes will be necessary.

 Never leave baby alone on a change table. Use the safety straps and keep one hand on the child at all times. Many parents, quite rightly, don't trust change tables and use other alternatives.

Baby Baths

A plastic or inflatable baby's tub on a low table or a specially designed baby's bath that fits over a kitchen sink or across the bath tub, can all serve the purpose. It is easier to stand or sit than to kneel when bathing an infant – an important consideration when you select your baby's tub.

A small tub or basin is also handy when you are changing him after he has had a bowel movement. The water should be 90 fahrenheit (29 Celsius).

 Never leave your baby unattended when bathing him.

Rocking Chair

Rocking chairs have been a traditional part of the nursery. Rocking a restless baby will often soothe him and give you a rest at the same time. If there are no arms on the chair, it is often called a "nursery" rocker because baby can be supported on your lap while he nurses. Some rockers are designed with padded, low arm rests to facilitate holding an infant.

Chest of Drawers

Baby will need a whole chest of drawers for his clothing and bedding supplies. If chosen with care, this piece of furniture can be used for many years.

Other Equipment

An infant lounger (inclined plastic seat) in which baby sits in semi-reclining position with the aid of straps is a handy rig for carrying him for short distances and setting him down where he can see what is going on. He is safe in this until his back becomes strong enough to topple the seat – between four to six months old.

 Some infant car seats can double as infant loungers, but infant loungers don't double as car seats.

As baby grows he will need other furnishings for his busy life. You can think about these additional items and shop for them gradually. An open toy box will help considerably in keeping his room tidy, and open shelves will make it easy for him to put away his own books, toys and animals.

A vaporizer may be necessary during the winter months when the air is often dry. As a result, the lining of the nose becomes irritated and produces thick mucus. If your baby catches a cold, it is important to keep his nasal secretions (mucus) thin and liquid. Putting moisture into the air will help.

Baby Carriage, Stroller and Front Carriers

New baby carriages can be very expensive but you can buy, rent or borrow a second-hand one. Babies like the feeling of motion and you will both enjoy going on outings together.

Strollers are smaller, lighter, collapsible and less expensive than carriages – ideal for shopping or travelling. In this country strollers are requird by law to have reliable brakes and locking devices, seat belts and sturdy frames.

Infant front carriers are useful as they free the hands of the carrier and allow baby the extra closeness of personal contact.

If your baby (after he is a month or so old) sleeps out of doors in good weather it may stimulate his appetite and give him rosy cheeks. It may make him sleep more soundly at night as well.

 Fit the carrier to the larger parent and ensure that it has good head support for the infant.

PACIFIERS THAT DON'T PASS**

Although these regulations prevent most hazards caused by pacifiers, parents should check the condition of their child's pacifier regularly.

- The pacifier should be designed with sufficient strength and durability to withstand reasonable force, even after repeated boiling, and it should not break down into easily-swallowed components.
- The guard or shield should be large and rigid enough to prevent the child from inserting the nipple too far into his mouth.
- Any cord attached to the pacifier should be short enough to prevent the pacifier from being hung around the neck.
- All materials used in the pacifier should be non-toxic and, at the time of sale, sterile.
- Any ring or handle should be hinged, collapsible or flexible so that the pacifier cannot be forced into the mouth if the baby should fall or roll on his face.

** *These tips are from Consumer and Corporate Affairs Canada*

Baby's Clothing

The clothing a baby needs is an expandable list. During his first year he grows so quickly that he can't possibly wear out all the clothing you have on hand. So whenever possible buy a size ahead to let him grow into the garment. Think of the season of the year, and if it is towards the end of one season, try to buy a size that he will be able to use the next year. Serviceable secondhand infant clothing can be an economical option.

- 3-4 dozen cloth diapers and safety pins or disposable diapers
- 3-6 undershirts
- 4 nightgowns for new babies
- 4-6 stretch sleepers (second size which fits up to 6 months)
- 3 knitted or flannelette jackets or sweaters
- 3 small bibs
- 4 pairs plastic pants
- 4 pairs of cotton or wool soakers
- 2 bonnets

- 1 sleeping bag or snowsuit (sometimes called a "walker") that converts into a sleeping bag
- 6 crib sheets (2 fitted for the bottom)
- 2 cotton blankets
- 2 flame-proof quilts
- 6 quilted cotton and/or rubberized flannelette sheets
- sun hat
- warm hat
- mittens

Diaper Care

Terrycloth, gauze, flannelette or bird's eye cloth diapers have become more popular recently with the rising concerns about the environment. Consequently there have been a number of new manufacturers who have "reinvented" the cloth diaper and the results are encouraging. The new diaper designs are more absorbent, easier to clean and better fitting than the ones of yesteryears.

There are two basic "new" varieties of cloth diapers: the traditional diaper with pins or velcro fasteners but now they come pre-folded; and the two-part diaper that has a liner inside of cloth covers (training pants). The liner allows urine to pass through, keeping the bottom drier, but catches faeces, preventing the outer diaper from becoming too soiled. With all soiled diapers, scrape or flush off the bowel movement into the toilet, rinse and place diapers in a pail of water which can be treated with specific disinfectants for cloth diapers. If you are using an automatic washer, set it at hot, for both wash and rinse. Dry the diapers in the sun whenever you can, but the dryer is more convenient.

You would be wise to use mild soap flakes or unscented laundry detergent for the first month or so, especially if your baby's buttocks were red when you brought him home from hospital. This doesn't mean that the hospital was lax, but it is a warning that his skin is easily irritated.

There are two alternatives to washing your own diapers – you can use either a diaper service or disposable diapers. The convenience of a diaper service is a great boon to a new mother. Incidentally, the diapers they provide are safe as they have been sterilized. Disposable diapers are also worth considering, although an occasional baby cannot wear them because they irritate his skin. It is reassuring to have a package on hand for emergencies or for days away from home. If by chance your baby develops loose stools (diarrhea), disposable diapers will minimize their handling and thus make the spread of harmful germs less likely. They will also lighten your work and give you more time to care for your baby when he is sick.

Undershirts

Undershirts made of cotton knit can be purchased in summer or winter weights. They may be long sleeved, short sleeved or sleeveless. Unless you are living in a cold part of the country or have a drafty house, the short sleeved ones are the most useful. You will probably buy the 3-month size for your new baby. Some mothers find the pullover type easier to use than the cardigan style. With the latter, those with the snap (dome) closures are less trouble than the buttoned types. The 2-year size will often fit a chubby 6-month baby and a lean 3-year old.

Diaper Pins

The special safety pins that have an extra guard at the top are the best kind to buy. They rarely come undone and they are harder for little fingers to open. Velcro fasteners are commonly used instead of pins.

Nightgowns

Nightgowns that tie up the back are the simplest garments for new babies. Legged garments are not necessary as newborns usually lie curled and only make the frequent changes that small babies need more time-consuming. Nightgowns are made of flannelette or woven cotton, and for the first month or so baby wears them both night and day. Some mothers buy the type with mittens attached, which prevent baby from scratching himself.

Sleepers

When baby is one month, stretch terry cloth sleepers for both day and night wear are the most popular choice. All sleep wear will be made of flame resistant fabrics before too long. The domed opening which extends from his toe to his neck makes it easy to dress and undress him and yet he is well covered and warm. They are also easy to launder.

Sweaters and Jackets

Baby will need two or three jackets or sweaters. The machine-washable jackets of orlon or flannelette are more practical than the wool ones. However, you may want a knitted wool sweater and bonnet set, even though it does involve more care. Mittens and warm hats that cover the ears are necessary in winter as are heavy socks or booties. A wide brimmed hat is essential for summer sun protection.

Bibs

A few small waterproof bibs to save his clothing from becoming wet when he drools are useful.

Cotton Soakers and Plastic Pants

During the newborn period you will not want to use plastic pants, as a small baby's skin may irritate easily. Instead, soakers made of terry cloth, of many layers of cotton sewn together or of wool will not only keep him warm but will also absorb much of the irritating urine. Often the cotton pants can be used as training pants later on. After baby's skin has become less sensitive you will want to use plastic pants to keep his clothing dry. Both pull-on and snap types are available and many mothers feel that the latter are more comfortable for baby. You would be wise to wash the plastic pants at least once daily.

Changing Baby

Some babies don't seem to mind being wet; others are unhappy when they are. However, you will have much less trouble with diaper rash if you change him every time you find him awake and wet. If he has had a bowel movement, gently remove as much of it as you can, working from the front backward, with a clean part of the diaper. Then wash him off with warm water, dry him and put a little bland powder in his creases and diaper him again.

There are a number of commercial baby wipes on the market (beware of the scented variety as they may irritate). You can also clean him with some olive or baby oil on a piece of absorbent cotton or soft toilet paper if this is more convenient but remember to wipe off the excess oil.

Bedding

The bedding we have recommended is for a crib made in the conventional way. A waterproof flannelette and/or quilted cotton pad is used to cover the mattress – this will prevent it from becoming damp and eventually smelling. Baby lies on a cloth fitted sheet and is covered by a flame-proof, washable quilt or cotton blanket.

Some babies are so restless when they sleep that they will need sleeping bags to keep

Sleeping bag

them covered and warm. A young baby does best in a conventionally made bed. If he is fretful, wrapping him snugly in a small cotton receiving blanket may quiet him.

Sleeping Bags

If you are able to buy either light or heavyweight sleeping bags, choose the type most suitable for the season and the warmth of your rooms. When baby goes out it is much easier to carry him in a warm sleeping bag than to cope with blankets that may be kicked off. Some legged snowsuits are convertible into sleeping bags. Sleeping bags are excellent for baby when he sleeps outside in his carriage, although he may need covers as well.

BABY-PROOFING YOUR HOME

- Ensure that dangling cords and tablecloths are out of reach.
- Put child safety locks on cupboards containing dangerous cleansers and other household substances that could cause harm.
- Retrieve small objects that drop to the floor, such as coins, nuts, pins etc. These objects can become lodged in baby's throat if he attempts to swallow them.
- Store sharp objects safely out of baby's reach.
- Cover outlets that are not being used.
- Remove furnishings with sharp edges.
- Check that baby's furnishings, car seat and other store-bought items meet current safety standards.
- Review your home for any potential hazards (broken steps, etc.) and repair them immediately.

Your Child's 3
Medical Care

T he physician in charge will check your baby over very soon after he is born. No doubt your first question will be, "Is he all right?" The chances are very high that the answer will be "Yes." If a family doctor is taking care of you, she will examine your baby very thoroughly before you come home and advise you on his early care and feedings. She will also tell you when to bring your infant to her office for the first of his regular visits. If an obstetrician has delivered your baby, it is common practice to have a child specialist (pediatrician) examine him soon after birth and at regular intervals later on. Both arrangements are excellent. During the first year, protective immunization and advice on feeding and development will be discussed. The important point is to have a doctor see your baby frequently during his first year even though everything is going well.

During baby's second year these regular visits will be less numerous. From the second to the sixth year, if your child is healthy, twice a year will be sufficient. From then until your youngster has stopped growing you would be wise to take him to your physician once a year to ensure that he is in good physical condition. Most parents keep in close contact with their physicians for the first two years, but then they default and do not attend regularly for well child visits. One of the results of this is that a number of children may enter school suffering from some physical, mental or psychosocial deficit that reduces the level of their optimal health and well-being. When your doctor and your dentist have a chance to see your child at regular intervals, they can discover these defects at an early stage and can usually remedy them before they interfere with the child's progress. Your doctor will mention many of the normal changes in your child's behavior that commonly occur as he grows older and will help you to cope with his care in other ways. You would be wise to make a list of the questions that you want to ask the doctor during your visit. An experienced pediatric nurse who works with your doctor may be able to answer most of your questions and she may also give your baby his immunizing needles. Regular visits to your doctor will settle your concerns for your child, and of course, will help to keep him healthy. This book cannot take the place of these visits.

Immunization – A Tremendous Boon

Immunization can protect babies and children from many dangerous and crippling diseases. If you think about the harm that smallpox, diphtheria, polio, whooping cough, measles, mumps and rubella (German measles) used to cause, you realize how grateful we all should be to the medical scientists whose labor has made these preventive measures possible.

Many of these acute infectious diseases are now rare in Canada and some people look on them as illnesses of the past. As a consequence, they don't bother to have their youngsters adequately immunized. Unless a very high percentage of the population has been rendered immune, these diseases could break out again. For example, diphtheria became common and severe in certain countries in Europe during the last war because their immunization programs had broken down. And more recently massive epidemics of whooping cough occurred in Japan and the United Kingdom when immunization programs were temporarily discontinued. Even now on this continent, a few youngsters develop a preventable disease because they have not been adequately protected by available immunization.

Some people may be casual about immunization because they think, mistakenly, that if by an odd chance their non-immunized child did contract one of these diseases, an up-to-date physician would be able to cure him. For the virus diseases such as polio, this certainly is not true. Besides it is far safer and surer to prevent a disease than to allow it to occur and then struggle to reduce its damaging effects. Smallpox is currently considered eliminated in all countries of the world. Intensive immunization through the World Health Organization and co-operation between countries has brought this serious illness to a halt, hopefully permanently. Smallpox vaccination is no longer considered necessary.

How Immunization Works

Normal children and adults are able to produce an antibody (a neutralizing substance) when an unnatural or foreign substance makes its way into their body. Any specific foreign substance stimulates the body to produce a matching antibody. A different foreign body will result in a different matching (specific) antibody. The bacteria and viruses that cause disease are unwelcome foreign bodies and our immune system reacts against them by making antibodies as a means of eliminating the invading factor.

The purpose of immunization is to stimulate the individual to produce antibodies without having to suffer an attack of the disease. To achieve this end, scientists have either changed some product made by particular bacteria or viruses, or have so altered the bacteria or viruses themselves that although they do not cause disease, they still provoke the body to make the appropriate antibodies. Thus, when a child has been completely immunized against diphtheria, he has an adequate supply of the specific antibody (diphtheria antitoxin in this case) on hand, ready to immediately neutralize or render harmless any diphtheria bacteria that happen to make their way into his throat or elsewhere. Canadian parents should be reassured that all immunization procedures have been thoroughly tested and found to be both safe and effective. Finally, the injections cause a baby or child little discomfort.

Immunization Schedules

A mother passes on to her baby some of her antibodies against several diseases even before birth. As the baby hasn't made them himself, they are called passive antibodies. However, they don't survive for long in the body and by the time baby is two or three months old, he can begin to make antibodies for himself, if he is stimulated to do so. Therefore it is customary to start immunizing him at about that age to give maximum protection. Two common methods used in immunizing babies and children will be outlined. Some physicians use different schedules and immunizing materials but all act in a similar manner. The important point to remember is to take your child to the doctor's office or clinic on the day when the next immunization procedure is due. Very often your baby is given a regular check-up at the same visit.

In one commonly used program, the two to three-month-old baby, is given a small injection into the muscle of his thigh of a mixture containing diphtheria toxoid, whooping cough (pertussis) vaccine, tetanus toxoid and polio vaccine. This mixture is often called **DPT + Polio.** The injection causes baby to produce antibodies against all four of these diseases at the same time. However, he doesn't produce much after this first needle. After the second immunization, which the baby usually gets two months later, the body responds by making considerably more of these antibodies. After the third injection, which follows after another two-month interval, the response is even better. Babies don't make antibodies against whooping cough as well as they do against the three other diseases. Yet about 80 per cent of immunized babies won't catch whooping cough and the others, if they do develop it, will only have a mild attack. This vaccine is very helpful, as severe whooping cough can damage a baby's lungs.

If baby has a slight cold or sniffle but seems otherwise well, he can still have a needle. However, if he is feverish or very sick, he shouldn't be immunized. As soon as he is better take him to the doctor for the missed injection.

The infant's thigh, where the "shot" was given, may become slightly red and swollen. If he seems fretful or a little feverish, most physicians will tell you to give him acetaminophen baby drops. Your doctor may suggest another dose four hours later. Your baby probably won't need more than these two doses and possibly none at all. Some doctors may suggest that acetaminophen be given as a precaution at the time of the needle, even before symptoms develop, to offset any reaction.

The baby has now produced four different antibodies – one against each disease – these antibodies will gradually decrease as he becomes older. Because of this decreasing level the child may receive a booster injection when he is 18 months old and he will need a booster when he starts school (between four to six years). In his mid-teens, he will need another booster but this time whooping cough is not included.

The second type of schedule is similar except that the polio vaccine is given by mouth instead of being included in the injected mixture.

Measles, mumps and rubella (German measles) or **MMR vaccine** is given to a one-year-old. Since some cases of modified measles have been occurring in children who have been immunized for measles, many doctors recommend a booster in the pre-teen period.

Haemophilus influenzae type B or *HIB* vaccine is recommended for all children at 15-18 months of age. Children up to five years should be considered for immunization . This organism can cause serious illnesses in young children, in particular meningitis. With many children now in day care, epidemics do occur. It is important to protect your child.

There is no vaccine available for chicken pox, but much work has been done in the development of such a vaccine for future use.

Ask your doctor what she has given your child each visit and record it right away. If you move to another area, or change doctors, or if your child has an accident and requires anti-lockjaw (anti-tetanus) treatment, this record will help your new doctor.

Before starting school, it is now compulsory in many areas of Canada for a child to be immunized against diphtheria, whooping cough, tetanus, polio, measles, mumps, and rubella.

Many other factors play important parts in keeping youngsters in excellent health. In order for them to grow and develop normally, they must have healthy, well-cared-for bodies, suitable food, sufficient sleep, enough exercise, fresh air and plenty of affection and attention. We will discuss these later on.

4

Bringing Baby Home

W hen you get a really good look at your first new baby, he may seem rather different from what you expected. You may observe several of the harmless little lumps, spots and seemingly unusual characteristics which many newborn babies exhibit. Your doctor may not have thought to mention them to you; but you, with your hawk-like eyes, discover them promptly. After all, those baby pictures in magazines are perfect!

Newborns seem floppy and very small at first. Although he is usually about 20 inches (50 centimetres) long, he tends to lie in a curled position as he did in the womb. He probably weighs between seven to eight pounds (3200-3600 grams), although a few babies weigh in at 10 pounds (4500 grams) or even more. Boys tend to weigh a little more than girls.

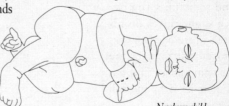

Newborn child

Those under 5 1/2 pounds (2500 grams) are "low birth weight" infants, and may need very special care, most often in a hospital. A baby born under 37 weeks gestation, (or more than three weeks ahead of the due date),is considered premature. A "low birth weight" infant may be born after 37 weeks gestation but is not considered premature. Your doctor will examine him thoroughly for any problems.

For the first few days, normal babies lose weight and some are slower in regaining this loss than others. By two weeks of age all healthy infants are gaining beyond their birth weight and most have started to do so earlier.

Head

As human beings have proportionately larger and more complicated brains than any of the other mammals, it is not surprising that even at birth a baby's brain and head are large. The brain grows and develops a great deal, especially in the first and second year. The skull is specially designed to allow for this growth and also to permit his rather large head to be born safely.

You may notice that his head is a little out of shape or that he has a soft lump on it, most often on the top. Both are the result of the temporary pressure exerted on his pliable skull when he was passing through the birth canal. They will disappear quite soon.

With such a large head and weak neck muscles, you will always need to support the back of his head with your fingers, and his neck and upper back with the rest of one hand when you pick him up. With your other hand you support his lower back and seat (buttocks). You may be a little awkward at first unless you have held babies often, but this way of carrying him soon becomes second nature.

Actually a new baby's skull bones are not tightly locked together; there are some spaces between them that are filled with very tough membranes. These allow his skull bones to overlap a little while he is being born, and sometimes you can see slight ridges on his head where one bone has moved a little over the adjoining bone. This too is quite all right and will soon disappear.

The biggest patch of membrane – between four of his skull bones – is on the top of his head. It is commonly called the soft spot, or more technically, the anterior fontanelle

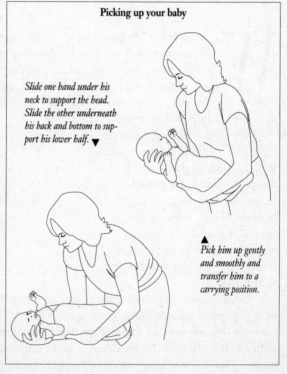

Picking up your baby

Slide one hand under his neck to support the head. Slide the other underneath his back and bottom to support his lower half. ▼

▲
Pick him up gently and smoothly and transfer him to a carrying position.

(see illustration in Chapter 13). Although it is softer than bone, its membrane is very strong. It is perfectly safe to wash over it thoroughly with soap and water. Some mothers are afraid to do this, and that may be one reason why greasy brownish scales, called cradle cap, often appear. Cradle cap can be remedied easily (see page 30).

As your baby grows older the skull bones on all four sides of the fontanelle grow into it, and eventually all the skull bones interlock tightly together. Your baby's skull bones are relatively soft, and if you always put him to bed with his head on the same side, his head may temporarily become a little lopsided. It is wise to vary the side on which he lies frequently. He soon likes to lie so that he faces the light, but if you turn him in his crib after each feeding, he will then lie on each side of his head alternately.

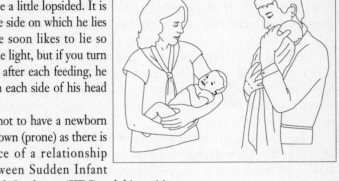

Both holding positions illustrate how to support the infant's head.

It is best not to have a newborn sleeping face down (prone) as there is some evidence of a relationship between Sudden Infant Death Syndrome (SIDS) and this position.

IMPORTANT

Babies should not be given pillows.

Skin

Your doctor examines your baby carefully soon after he is born. She notices the color of his skin: whether it is very pink, which is normal in newly born babies; or whether it is pale or yellow (jaundiced). If she finds anything wrong, she will have tests done to discover the cause so that she can treat it effectively. Such abnormalities are rare and nearly all of them can be corrected.

Don't be upset if your baby's skin develops a mild jaundice when he is two or three days old, because this is common. What causes it? When he is born a baby has an unusually large number of foetal red cells in his blood. He needed all these cells when he was living in your uterus, but after birth, when he begins to breathe air, many of these foetal red cells are unnecessary. As they break down the liver is temporarily unable to handle the changes necessary for the excretion of the yellow pigmented substance. It gives his skin a slightly yellow tinge. Usually the color is fading by the fifth day of life. If it persists longer, if it seems to be getting darker or if he develops jaundice later on, be sure to inform your doctor.

A newborn baby often has a coating of fine hair on his face and even more on his back. In fact, the pinkness tinged with yellow on his downy face resembles a peach!

often across his nose. These are likely tiny blocked sweat glands. They soon become unblocked and disappear without treatment. He may also develop a few patches of a light, blotchy rash on his body but this, too, soon clears up of its own accord.

A good many babies with dark skin, and a few with light, have a deep blue patch, usually on their lower back. The blueness is due to an excessive amount of pigment in that patch of skin. It is not caused by bruising. It may become less marked as he grows older and is of no significance.

You may see one or two tiny red spots on the white of his eye. These soon disappear and they are not of any consequence. He may have a very small red spot on his eyelid at the corner. This may persist for a few weeks but it almost invariably goes away. Similar spots are even more common at the nape of his neck and the glabella – a point midway between the two supraorbital ridges. The former are more likely to persist but his hair grows over them in time. The popular name for these spots used to be stork bites. Your doctor will have noticed any birthmarks (haemangiomas), of which only a few may need treatment later on. The others gradually disappear. None of them are the result of frights or emotional shock during your pregnancy as many people once believed.

Some babies are born with quite a thatch of hair – yours may have very little. Most of his first hair will fall out and he will eventually grow more hair which may be somewhat different both in color and texture. If he lies on his back a lot, the back of his head may become temporarily bald.

Face

Your new baby's nose and chin seem small and he moves his mouth a great deal. He purses his lips, he makes sucking motions, and often his mouth quivers or trembles, usually when he is partly awake. If he happens to get his hand in his mouth he will suck it vigorously. Babies are born with a very strong sucking instinct.

A newborn's eyes are closed most of the time at first, but if you hold him up and move him gently back and forth, his eyes may pop open much like a doll's. If his skin is relatively fair, his eyes will be blue-grey but they may change and it could be some months before their permanent color will be known. Dark-skinned babies have brown eyes from birth.

When you turn on the light in a baby's room, he will likely flinch or he may sneeze for no apparent reason even though he probably can see little or no detail. His sight will improve within a few weeks. Although his eyes may water a little, he probably will not shed true tears for a month or six weeks. Some babies are born with a blocked tear duct. This is described in Chapter 5.

Body

Many parents are a little worried about the stump of the umbilical cord. Before birth the vein and arteries in this cord carried food supplies to the baby and removed his wastes. Soon after he is born, the physician ties or clamps off the cord and cuts it a few inches from baby's body. This causes the baby no pain. From then on the stump of the cord gradually dries up, becomes black, and, one to two weeks after birth, drops off.

The area where the cord was attached to baby may remain moist for another two or three days. Usually all you need to do is to keep it dry and clean (put his diaper on a little lower). You can swab the area with rubbing alcohol. Until this spot becomes dry, give your baby sponge baths.

Sometimes the navel bulges out – especially when baby struggles or cries – because there is a small space between the muscles of the front of his abdomen. This bulge is called an umbilical hernia. It causes baby no harm or discomfort and, usually by the time he is three, it has disappeared. Occasionally it persists in diminishing size until the age of five or six years. Only rarely do such hernias persist so long that they need to be repaired by a surgeon.

In the first few days after birth the breasts of either a boy or a girl baby may become enlarged. A little fluid may even leak out of the nipples. This is perfectly normal and requires no treatment. It usually clears up in a week to 10 days, although sometimes it lasts longer. If the breasts are rubbed, massaged or squeezed, their tissues may be injured or they may become infected. So just wash them as you do the rest of him and do nothing more. This breast swelling is due to the fact that before birth a hormone from your body has passed across to your baby.

Genitals

Sometimes the external sex organs are a little puffy and enlarged soon after birth, but this is of no consequence and soon disappears. Occasionally a girl baby may have a little white discharge from her vagina for a week or two after birth. This too is caused by hormones which have travelled from you to her before she was born. You may not even notice this discharge unless it is tinged with blood. This too is quite all right and it will clear up naturally.

Sometimes a baby boy's testes are not down in his scrotum, or they may slip back into his abdominal cavity when he is chilled or the scrotum is touched. This is not abnormal at an early age. If the baby's testes can not be brought into the scrotum, the baby will need to be seen regularly by his doctor to assess the situation. Occasionally the scrotum may continue to look swollen. Tell your doctor about this. It may be due to a little sac of fluid (hydrocele) that will disappear as he grows, but it may be due to an inguinal hernia that requires early treatment.

Whether you want your boy to be circumcised or not is generally a matter of family or religious preference. Once in a while circumcision is needed because the covering over the penis is too tight. Circumcision is a simple procedure which is most often done before the baby leaves hospital. Folded sterile gauze covered with a petrolatum jelly is kept wrapped around the penis for a time after the circumcision is performed. A bit of blood may ooze now and then, but if the penis really bleeds, inform your doctor.

kept wrapped around the penis for a time after the circumcision is performed. A bit of blood may ooze now and then, but if the penis really bleeds, inform your doctor.

No special care of the uncircumcised penis is necessary. Cleansing with soap and water at bath time is all that is required. Gradually over two to three years, the foreskin will become retractable but in some boys it will not be fully retractable until puberty.

Hands and Feet

His hands and feet seem rather red and large at the ends of his somewhat skinny arms and legs. His limbs soon become more plump. At first he keeps his hands clenched, with his thumbs neatly tucked inside. Sometimes he hasn't all his fingernails; they will soon appear. His legs may seem a little bowed – this is the result of the curled-up position which he customarily assumes before he is born. His feet may seem to toe in a little, but that too is due to positioning. Both disappear as he grows older.

What Baby Can Do

He can do all the prime essentials very well – eating, sleeping, breathing, eliminating and crying. He can taste and hear. Loud noises close by disturb him, although some babies are more sensitive to them than others. He tends to focus on large objects about a foot away from his eyes – such as his mother's face. Other objects further away or closer are probably blurred.

He likes to be held firmly and moved gently because he is frightened or stressed if he feels that he may be dropped. When he gets that sensation, he reflexively throws out his arms as if to clutch hold of something and either looks startled or gives a sharp cry. Thus you can save him such alarm if you hold him firmly and don't move him too abruptly. You naturally handle him cautiously at first, but sometimes a new baby is not as fragile as he looks. He likes to be carried snugly.

At first he will probably cry more than you like, but if his relatively simple needs are met, he thrives, and he is quite unaware that you are inexperienced. Both you and your partner will enjoy it when you cuddle him and do take time from your busy routine to do just that – enjoy him. You can't spoil a young baby.

Help at Home

If you can count on your partner, a relative or a congenial neighbor to help you with and sleep. Many mothers feel that they cannot sleep during the day. If you relax and lie down on your bed in a darkened room, you might be surprised at the result. During your baby's first month he will waken five or more times in each 24-hour period, and his longest sleep is apt to be only five hours. With this in mind, don't be too ambitious. Plan the simplest meals possible and limit visitors.

Baby Blues

Quite likely you will have a few spells of the "blues" before your first-born is two weeks old. Such spells are very common. Do not feel ashamed. Probably a combination of factors causes them, including fatigue and some normal anxiety. The latter may be a remnant of the instinct, which for unnumbered centuries, has driven mothers to care for and defend their young. The complete revolution in your household and the natural letdown that follows the nine long months of waiting are partly responsible for these upsets. Of course you are pleased to have your baby but he's not an unmixed blessing.

Your partner may also be bothered by the same sort of feeling. He too may feel inadequate to meet his new, increased responsibilities. It's a good idea to let him share in some of baby's care from the start. Perhaps he would prefer to let you manage baby until he becomes less fragile looking and floppy, and will choose to help out as much as he can around the house. Work together as much as possible and even in the rather disorganized first few weeks, try to find some time to relax with your partner.

Sibling Rivalry

If you already have a child, he too will inevitably have some frustrations. Try to imagine how an only child feels when a new baby invades his home. Of course, you will have told him months before that he is going to have a new baby brother or sister. He has been looking for a playmate; instead you have brought home a wrinkled, squalling little creature with whom you spend a great deal of your time. He has never had to share your love and care before, and instinctively he resents the new baby.

5

Bathing Your Baby and Skin Care

M ost babies are bathed daily before their morning feeding, but if another time suits you and your baby better, that is fine. Always give him his bath before, not after, a feeding because he nearly always goes to sleep following these two major events.

Sponge Baths

When your baby comes home from hospital, sponge baths are recommended until the cord drops off at one to two weeks of age. Choose a comfortable position for yourself, either standing at a table or counter or sitting at a low table. Have the following necessary articles you need for the bath, close at hand:

- large soft bath towel (a linen hand towel is handy for a new baby)
- two small, soft washcloths
- pure, unscented soap in a dish
- talcum powder or cornstarch
- mineral oil or baby cream (if recommended by your doctor)
- sterile absorbent cotton
- baby brush and comb (not needed for sponge baths)
- clean clothes
- apron

Spread a large bath towel on your lap, undress baby and wrap him in it. Wash his face with water only. As he doesn't like this part, especially when he is older, make it brief. Then you wash, gently, one small part of his body at a time, with little soap. Rinse. Pat the area dry with the hand towel (especially in the creases) and powder lightly. Try to keep the rest of his body covered with the towel to avoid chilling, and, of course, the room should be warm with no drafts. Sponge baths are slower than tub baths, but keep on giving them until the navel is entirely dry. You don't want any harmful germs to reach that area. Before the cord falls off, you can dab its base with absorbent cotton soaked in rubbing alcohol. After it has fallen off and the skin is healing, you can keep on applying the alcohol at bath time, until it is healed.

You may prefer to give him his sponge bath standing up beside a higher table or the kitchen or bathroom counter. Put a pad or a small towel on the table or counter and proceed as we have just described. Be sure to keep a hand on baby all the time – even a small baby may roll off a counter or table. If the phone or doorbell should ring when you are tending baby, either take him with you, place him in his bed, or ignore the interruption.

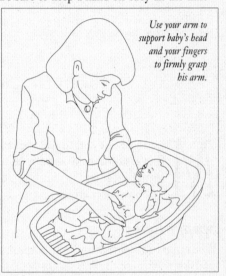

Use your arm to support baby's head and your fingers to firmly grasp his arm.

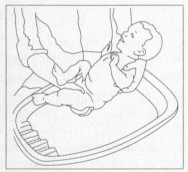

Tub Baths

Here again you can bathe him either sitting down or standing up. If the sitting down technique appeals to you, you will need a plastic bathtub (or basin) on a low table that is large enough to hold his towels, soap, etc. A small clotheshorse or another table for his clean clothes is also handy. If you prefer to stand up, the so-called bath/change table, which includes a bath with a padded cover on which you can undress, dress and change him, is ideal but expensive. A small bathtub on a firm table or a counter beside a sink can serve very well if you put a pad of some kind on the counter or table. A canvas change or dressing table is excellent as it gives a little when you put baby on it.

If you are using a hard bathtub, you may feel easier using one to two inches (5 centimetres) of water, with a mat or hand towel spread on the bottom to make it less slippery. Later on when your baby is older, fill the tub about half full and omit the towel liner. Use water at about body temperature 38 C (98-1OO F), which feels neither hot nor cold when you dip your elbow into it. Undress baby on your lap or on the change table.

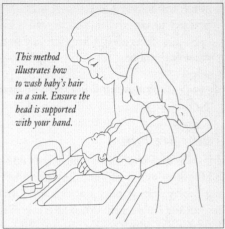

This method illustrates how to wash baby's hair in a sink. Ensure the head is supported with your hand.

Wash his face with water only – don't ever put soap on it. In fact, little soap is needed on his skin. Holding him in the tub with your left arm behind his neck and upper back and your left fingers gently but firmly grasping his left arm just below his shoulder, apply a small amount of soap on the washcloth to his scalp, body, arms and legs. Discard the soapy washcloth and rinse his skin free of soap with another washcloth. Tilt his head well back, as you support it with your left arm, when you wash the soap from his scalp. You do not want any soap to get into his eyes. If this does happen, he may become quite terrified of hair washing and then it becomes a major ordeal for everyone!

Rinse Thoroughly

When you are rinsing him, pay particular attention to the folds and creases in his skin – around his neck, in his armpits and his groin (where his legs join his body) and behind his ears. These are the places where secretions and powder are apt to collect;

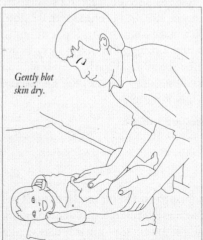

Gently blot skin dry.

and if you don't remove them they may irritate his skin, particularly in hot weather. You may find a little oil on a piece of absorbent cotton handy for cleaning behind his ears, but remove the oil afterwards with dry absorbent cotton. The genitals should be carefully rinsed with water.

Gentle Drying

After his bath, fold baby in a bath towel and blot – not rub – his skin dry. A baby's skin is very thin and rubbing may cause an abrasion. The folds of his skin will again need special care. A light amount of powder will help to protect these areas, but don't use too much as it may cake. Cornstarch makes excellent powder; and as it dissolves in water, it is easy to wash off.

Some parents apply petroleum jelly to the genital area to protect the skin and prevent diaper rash.

 Never mix petroleum jelly with cornstarch or powder.

Baths Are Fun

Bath time for a young baby is quite brief although unhurried. As baby grows he enjoys his freedom from clothes and the pleasant feel of the water. It is one of the times during the day when you can play with him, even when he is small; and he soon responds to your voice and touch. When he is able to sit in the bath have special toys available for water play. Plan it so that you can both enjoy bath time.

When Not To Bathe

If you can't get the house warm enough, if you are tired or if baby is suffering from a cold or other upset, omit his bath. Washing his face and his diaper area will be enough. Watch for any signs of irritation in his creases as well.

Washing Hair

For the first several months baby's scalp is washed daily. Sometimes it needs quite a firm rub to remove any scales or cradle cap. Many babies have a little cradle cap, but it usually clears up with daily washing and thorough rinsing. If the scales become marked, put some baby oil on them at night and wash it off when you bathe him. This will probably clear it up but you may need to repeat this treatment a second night. If the scales are thick and crusted, petroleum jelly (Vaseline), put on at night, will often soften the crusts sufficiently that you will be able to remove them in the morning bath. If you are unable to get rid of the scales, your doctor may prescribe an ointment for you to apply. In five to six months, washing his hair twice a week is often enough. When he is a year old, you don't need to give him a shampoo more often than once a week. At this age you can soap his hair and then rinse it off while he lies back in the tub.

 Shampoos, especially made for babies, are available that are less irritating to the eyes.

Ear, Nose, Eyes and Mouth

Nature provides its own cleansing means for these parts. The ear canal is cleansed and protected by the secretion of wax, that is sometimes light in color and sometimes dark brown. Any wax that reaches the opening – which you can see – you may remove with an absorbent cotton roll or a small corner of a washcloth. The ear canal is very sensitive and needs no cleaning. Never put anything into the canal itself. Babies are so wriggly, it is not safe to use cotton swabs, even at the opening. Wax may be accidentally pushed further into the ear canal.

The eyes are constantly being cleansed by tears, making them shiny. Occasionally some white mucus may gather at the inner corners of baby's eyes. You can easily remove this with a clean, wet washcloth or a moistened piece of absorbent cotton.

A tiny tube (near the corner of each eye) drains tears into the nose. (see diagram, page 109) Tears are useful because they continually wash the eyes. When we cry, so many tears are produced that the tube can't drain them away quickly enough and so they overflow down our cheeks. In some small babies one of these tubes may be blocked. Therefore his tears run down his cheek (this is called tearing) and in addition a good deal of white matter collects in the corner of that eye and along the edge of his eyelid. If this should happen with your baby, gently wipe away the matter with a piece of damp absorbent cotton. This condition is quite common and not serious. It often clears up of its own accord, but contact your doctor so that she can tell you how to look after it.

The mucus produced by baby's nose is plentiful when he has a cold but some babies have a little mucus at the openings of their nostrils every day. You can remove what you can see at the opening with a little roll of moistened absorbent cotton but don't put it or anything else further into his nose. Sneezing also helps to clear his nose.

The mouth cleans itself too. If you can see some small white patches (plaques) that look like coagulated milk in baby's mouth, it is likely thrush. These white patches are not washed off when baby takes a drink of water and they cannot be wiped off easily. They need to be treated by your doctor as thrush usually causes discomfort. Thrush is most common in very small or sick babies.

No cleansing that you do should cause baby any pain. If some of the ear wax and nasal mucus is not easily removed, leave it for a while until nature has moved it a little closer to the opening concerned. Then it will probably come out quite easily.

Lip Blisters

Young babies often develop blisters, called sucking calluses, in the middle parts of their lips. One will peel to be replaced by another. This may persist for several weeks. Sucking calluses do not bother him and they will clear up on their own accord.

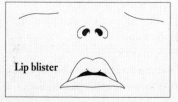

Blisters on the upper lip. *These are called "sucking blisters" and are due simply to the baby's sucking. They can occur at anytime while the baby is purely milk-fed. They may vanish between feedings. They are unimportant.*

Fingernails

Small babies and young infants often scratch their faces with their nails. Usually it is easier to cut their nails when they are asleep, preferably shortly before you expect them to wake up. Some parents prefer to use clippers rather than scissors.

DIAPER RASH

Prevention

Most babies have diaper scald or rash at some time. Often when baby comes home from hospital his seat is a little red because it is so sensitive that being wet or even the roughness of the diaper itself is enough to irritate it. Your main aim is to keep the skin in this area dry, cool and free from irritating substances. How can you do that? The following suggestions will help.

l) Change wet diapers every two or three hours, or more frequently if he is awake; but don't disturb him if he is sleeping. If his skin is red, wash him off with water, pat dry and powder lightly. Try to dress him comfortably cool.

2) If he has had a bowel movement, change him at once and wash his skin with water. If this happens when you are away from home, you can clean him with a non-perfumed diaper wipe or a little oil, which you then remove with a dry piece of absorbent cotton or soft toilet paper. However, water is the best.

3) If his buttocks (seat) become red, stop using plastic pants except on very special occasions. Plastic pants keep that area wet and warm, and you can easily see how this would increase the irritation caused by urine and stool.

4) If you are using cloth diapers, take extra care in washing them. Of course, scrape the stool and rinse the dirty ones before washing them. Then, after the day's lot has been washed in the hottest water possible, with a pure laundry detergent, see that they are thoroughly rinsed. Use the hottest setting and the longest cycle on your machine to get thorough washing and rinsing. Soap left on diapers will irritate baby's skin. The diapers provided by a diaper service are thoroughly washed and rinsed. Disposable diapers are a great help when you are away from home.

Treatment

1) Ask your doctor for an ointment to put on baby's skin. Most are thick ointments containing zinc, which has a drying effect. Apply the ointment when you know you will be unable to change him for several hours, for example, before he goes to sleep. A good deal of the ointment will remain on his skin to protect it.

2) If he develops some raw spots on his skin, keep them as clean as you can. Clean with lukewarm water and pat dry. Do not rub his bottom.

3) Lay baby down on his stomach with one or two cloth diapers underneath him, and leave his buttocks exposed to the air for 10-15 minutes several times each day. The heat from a gooseneck lamp is often enough to keep him warm while his diaper is

off. Of course, you will also take all the other precautions we have just mentioned above in prevention.

4) If you smell ammonia, give him more water to drink. Ammonia, produced from urea which is always present in urine, will burn baby's skin. Machine drying, sun drying or ironing baby's clothes and cloth diapers will kill germs which contribute to the production of ammonia.

Diaper rash can be a dreadful nuisance, and preventing it or catching it in its early stages is worthwhile.

Prickly Heat

Baby's sensitive skin often develops the red blotches or tiny red pimples of prickly heat when he becomes too hot. This rash is often in the creases, where the air can't keep the skin dry and cool. Prickly heat is first noticed in the folds of his neck, especially at the back, and in the armpits and groins. If you take care not to overdress him either in the summer or winter, you will probably avoid it. Blotting his skin dry and putting a thin layer of powder on the skin helps to relieve prickly heat.

6

The Benefits of Breast-Feeding

onsider breast-feeding your baby and discuss it with your doctor. If you have a health concern, and wish to nurse, do get expert advice. The vast majority of maternal health problems do not affect breast milk or its production. The hospital where your baby is going to be born may have rooming-in accommodation which is important for breast-feeding mothers.

Nearly every baby will thrive on breast milk. If you want to breast-feed your baby, we certainly hope you will do so. It is a rare opportunity, giving both you and your baby a pleasant feeling of satisfaction and togetherness.

Breast milk has some bonuses for baby: it is always sterile (free of germs), available and warm. Breast milk is utilized very efficiently by a baby, and it actually contains considerably more vitamin A and C and a little more iron than even undiluted cow's milk. Surveys have shown that breast-fed babies develop fewer and milder infections of all kinds (including colds) than very well-managed bottle-fed infants. This relative immunity lasts for some time because breast milk contains antibodies that act against certain dangerous viruses and bacteria. Breast-fed babies rarely have problems with the digestion of breast milk and far fewer of them develop allergic disease, in particular eczema.

The bowel movements of nursing infants are non-offensive, as the types of bacteria they contain do not produce foul odors. In addition, babies fed at the breast do not get constipated.

For a few days after birth, a dark green almost black, sticky stool is passed, called meconium. Once the baby starts nursing the stool changes in colour and consistency, until by the end of the first week there is a breast milk stool. The normal breast milk stool is pasty to watery, and of varying shades of yellow. The color may range from green to orange. The consistency may vary also, with curds or mucous being evident or the presence of air producing a frothy stool.

The frequency and the quantity of the bowel movement reflects the consumption of breast milk. During the first week, there may be four or five small movements a day. Towards the end of the first week, there may be 2-3 definite stools, with possibly some staining at each feed, daily. This is reassuring that the milk supply is more than adequate.

After a month or so, the pasty, yellow stool of a breast fed baby, may be passed every three to seven days without any apparent discomfort. The movement is much larger than usual but perfectly normal. Your baby may strain a bit to pass it, but that does him no harm.

Once you have become accustomed to breast-feeding, it actually takes less of your day than bottle-feeding. The total time needed to pick your baby up, change him, nurse him, burp him, possibly change him again and put him down, takes approximately 30 minutes. Warming a bottle to the right temperature, giving it and doing all the necessary changing and burping will take you just as long and on top of this, you may have to make up the feedings. In addition, breast-feeding is more convenient when you are visiting, travelling or night feeding.

One of the perceived problems with breast-feeding for some mothers is that they are concerned about their baby's milk intake. As baby nurses or suckles well, be assured that your milk supply will increase with his requirements. As you become accustomed to the rhythm of breast feeding, you will know that your child is getting enough. Throughout the day you will find it necessary to change soiled and wet diapers and this will also be reassuring to you. The actual amount baby obtains at different feedings during the day does vary a good deal. Remember that babies cry for many other reasons besides hunger.

Breast-Feeding Myths

The argument that breast-feeding causes your breasts to droop or remain large is not true. Breasts usually become bigger during pregnancy but they decrease in size to the same degree after weaning, whether this occurs during your stay in hospital or after months of breast-feeding.

Milk production is not related to the size of the breasts. Even if your breasts are small, you can be assured that you are producing enough milk by the number of wet diapers.

Breast-feeding helps you control your weight unless you eat more food than you need for your muscular activity and for all the internal processes that are going on constantly inside you. Some of your food goes towards milk production, so breast-feeding mothers actually require and use a few more calories and drink more fluid daily than those women who bottle-feed. It will cost much less to breast-feed than to bottle feed.

Will breast-feeding limit your activities? Breast-feeding mothers will have an advantage, as mother and baby are mobile together, regardless of place or time of day as far as feeds are concerned.

If you do go back to your former employment while you are still nursing, you will need to work out a routine for yourself that will best suit your new responsibilities. So much depends on the type of employment. Will flex-time be available? Is there a daycare close to your work so that you can nurse? Can you pump breast milk to be used during the day or will you require formula? The longer you nurse at home the better your milk supply will be established, and the more likely your child will be on solid foods when you return to work. This will make it easier all-round.

As for evening feedings, it is true that your partner can give baby his evening feeding if he is on bottles, but that is a very small fraction of his daily meals. Both of you will no doubt appreciate the ease of breast-feeding baby at night.

Will breast-feeding be hard on you physically? It is a unique additional function of your body; but if you are well, keen on nursing and willing to modify your routine, it will be a good experience. In fact, you may feel so pleased with yourself and so relieved that you don't have to bother with bottles and formula that it will be exactly right for you.

Prepare Yourself

Besides talking it over with your doctor during your pregnancy, discuss breast-feeding with your partner as well. He can help you carry it through; just as he may have encouraged you during the prenatal period. Another helpful idea is to find a friend or acquaintance who has successfully breast-fed her baby.

Learning about this "womanly art" is possible through contacting La Leche League in your area, a voluntary organization devoted to the encouragement of breast-feeding. The branches arrange series of informal meetings on how to nurse your baby successfully, including simple tested ways of avoiding or minimizing minor difficulties. The trained mothers who give these courses, usually in someone's home, have all successfully breast-fed their own babies. Local members will provide help – by telephone, letter or personal visit – to any mother who wants advice on breast-feeding. As well, you might find La Leche League International's book, *The Womanly Art of Breast-feeding*, useful – over two-million copies have been sold to date.

In The Hospital

The nurses in hospital can help you and your baby learn how to be a nursing couple. Choose a comfortable position to nurse. How to help your baby connect or latch onto your breast for easy nursing is the most important skill.

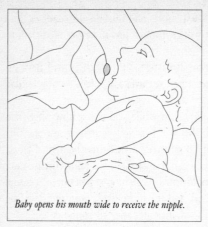

Baby opens his mouth wide to receive the nipple.

Nursing Positions
Mother
Many mothers can nurse their babies very comfortably lying down. This position gives you a little rest as well. If you are about to feed him from your left breast, prop up your head, left shoulder and upper back with a couple of pillows (the nurse will help you with this at first). Your baby is then laid on his right side on the crook of your left arm.

Other mothers prefer to sit up to nurse their babies. If you want to do so on your bed, prop up your back with a couple of pillows against the head of the bed and draw up your legs a little. A pillow on your lap may be handy for partially supporting him.

The baby will be turned towards you, almost in a horizontal position.

At home you will likely use a favorite chair; it is important to have a comfortable position.

Baby
Two important points you need to understand are; first, your baby's "rooting instinct" and second, the fact that in order to feed efficiently your baby needs to have considerably more of your breast in his mouth than just the nipple. This is referred to as latching.

Rooting is a search for nourishment. Run the nipple along the baby's lower lip, very lightly, from one corner of the mouth to the other – until the baby opens his mouth wide.

On bringing the baby closer to you, the baby will latch to the breast with the nipple and a considerable amount of the areola (the dark area) of the breast in his mouth. Support the breast with your other hand.

He will get milk by compressing between his gums, tongue and palate, the middle and outer parts of the dark areola under which the milk ducts and sacs are located. He cannot get the milk with only the nipple in his mouth.

In the first few days your breasts produce only small amounts of colostrum, or first milk – the forerunner of mature breast milk. Breast milk varies in amount and consistency, at a feeding, daily and as the child grows. This is not completely understood but in some way reflects your child's need.

The hours of nursing are now less well defined because of this recognized special relationship between you and your child. However you will come to know your child's "pattern".

Mother is lying on her side, stomach to stomach with baby. Mother can cradle the baby with her arm, resting on the side supporting her breast properly with the other hand. Using the arm holding the baby, she moves her/him close enough to guide the breast to the mouth.

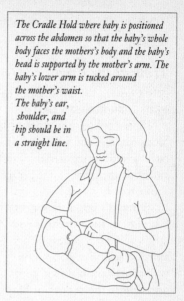

The Cradle Hold where baby is positioned across the abdomen so that the baby's whole body faces the mothers's body and the baby's head is supported by the mother's arm. The baby's lower arm is tucked around the mother's waist.
The baby's ear, shoulder, and hip should be in a straight line.

If you are concerned about the indefinite nature of demand feeding, talk it over with your doctor.

At Home

Many healthy, energetic women do not realize how many changes and demands, physical and emotional, will be made of them, when they first come home from hospital. As previously mentioned, the best plan is to have someone help you – a family member, or friend, neighbour or concerned person, for the first four weeks at least. Some partners may have programs at their place of work that allow them "parental leave" and this is worth investigating. If you have little or only part-time help, simplify your life. Use well-balanced convenient foods; let the housework go and take advantage of assistance, such as diaper and cleaning services. Try to relax and nap during the day while baby is still on night feedings. Eat well, drink plenty of fluids and enjoy moderate exercise. Discourage visitors for a few weeks until you and baby are into a routine.

During the first few days after you get home, your baby will likely want his feeds more often than you expected. There is no need to restrict him.

Washing nipples with clear water only, when you bathe, is all that is necessary.

Almost all drugs are secreted to some degree in breast milk. Avoiding unnecessary medicines would seem reasonable during this nursing period. Very few medications require the mother to stop breastfeeding. When a medication is truly not allowed for the breastfeeding mother, an alternative, acceptable medication is almost always available. Check with your doctor if you have a concern.

If baby is nursing well at the breast, having substantial yellow stools, and wet diapers, feeding on one breast alternately, may make it easier for mother and child.

Incidentally, at least three well-fitting nursing brassieres that support your breasts and open at the front are needed. Two-piece outfits and clothing with front openings are convenient.

Time at the Breast

Baby's time at the breast varies considerably. As demand feeding has become more common the frequency and time at the breast has been left to the mother and baby.

Breastfeeding should not be hurried. Many factors affect the time necessary to breast-feed and care for a baby. Since this is a 24-hour caring day, to state the time to do so at a particular feeding is difficult. As the mother has other responsibilities to look after, these will fit into her daily life as the child's appetite and demands become known to her.

How do you disconnect him after he has nursed? If you jerk your nipple out of his mouth it will hurt. If, however, you gently push down your breast near the corner of his mouth, you release the suction and you can comfortably remove your nipple. Some women slip a finger in the corner of their baby's mouth to help break the suction (see illustration).

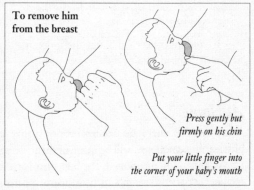

To remove him from the breast

Press gently but firmly on his chin

Put your little finger into the corner of your baby's mouth

Nursing Naturally

For nursing in a chair, an upholstered armchair with some kind of washable cover is favored by many mothers; others prefer a rocking chair. A footstool for your foot on the same side as baby and a small cushion on your lap may also be helpful. Listen to some restful music while you nurse.

Some women find it more relaxing to nurse in private. Of course this is not always possible if you have an active toddler to keep an eye on. Some babies are distracted by activities around them. The main idea is to be comfortable and minimize interruptions.

Let-Down Reflex

You may notice that soon after starting a feeding, your breasts become firmer and give you an odd tingling sensation. The breast that your baby is not using may leak a little. If he becomes "disconnected" from the nursing side, the milk may actually spray out of your nipple – the liquid looks rather thin and blue which is quite normal. You may notice that your baby must gulp to swallow it fast enough. This reaction is due to the "let-down" or draught reflex in which tiny muscles around the milk glands contract and force the milk out. It is a good sign that you have plenty of milk.

Some mothers are not aware of the let-down reflex, while others experience it throughout nursing.

Similarly your breasts may leak between feedings – sometimes when you think about your baby, sometimes when you are mildly excited and sometimes for no apparent reason. You can stop the leaking by pressing on the nipple when you feel that it is beginning to exude milk. The leaking usually becomes less common after a few weeks. You can save your clothes by putting nursing pads or a handkerchief inside the cups of your brassiere.

Avoid the plastic-coated bra pads as they can cause trouble, especially in hot weather, by keeping the moisture in and reducing the circulation of air.

Burping

Before switching to the other breast, or partly through a long feeding on one breast, you may find it helpful to burp baby to bring up what you can of any air he has swallowed.

One common way of doing this is to put a clean towel or cloth diaper on one of your shoulders and to hold your baby with his head on that shoulder. Then rub or gently pat his upper back. He will probably bring up some air and a little milk as well. Sometimes he will not oblige.

Try supporting him in a sitting position on your lap, rubbing his back as you do. Another way is to put him in an infant lounger for a few minutes.

When he is in an upright position any air in his stomach can come up. Burping

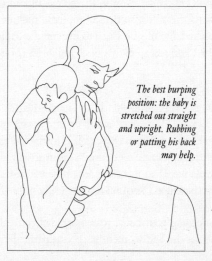

The best burping position: the baby is stretched out straight and upright. Rubbing or patting his back may help.

him for three minutes altogether is long enough. He is then more comfortable and willing to go to sleep when you put him back down. Lay him on his side when you put him to bed so that if he does bring up a little milk, it will run out of his mouth.

Quite a few babies, for no reason that their mothers can discover, cry for a short time before they fall asleep.

Bottles

Until your baby is six-eight weeks old, it is advisable to nurse at all feedings, except under most unusual circumstances. If all is going well, you can start giving him about one bottle a week after he is two months old if you wish, but it is not necessary to do so. A breast-fed baby will accept a bottle readily during his first two months. If a mother nurses beyond 6 months, a bottle may not be necessary as the child may drink from a cup.

To manually express breast milk (or use a breast pump) using only one breast for baby to nurse, will create a spare feeding. Pour the milk into a sterile feeding bottle or plastic bottle liner and store it in your refrigerator or freezer. You may need to express it after several feedings to collect enough for a bottle.

Expressing Milk

Although there are many different varieties of breast pumps on the market, many women choose to express milk by hand. To begin, wash your hands. Then cup your breast with one hand, and place the thumb and forefinger just at the outer edge of the dark area (the areola) above and below the nipple. Squeeze your thumb and finger together, pushing back towards the chest at the same time. Do not be surprised if nothing comes out the first few tries and do not move your thumb and finger towards the nipple. You will soon get the knack of it. Place your thumb and finger in several different positions around the areola so that all the little milk ducts that radiate out from the nipple are reached. Do this for three to five minutes, collecting the milk in a sterilized container. Most women express about 60 millilitres (2 ounces) at a time.

Vitamins

It is recommended that a baby receive 400 I.U. of vitamin D daily to promote growth and prevent rickets. Vitamin D is secreted in human and bovine milk in a form which provides between 25 to 80 I.U. per litre. Dairy milk is fortified with vitamin D.

Vitamin D requirements can be met entirely from solar radiation, but the diet must provide enough vitamin D to meet the requirements of those individuals who receive little or no direct sunlight. (Nutition recommendations of Health and Welfare Canada, 1989)

"If you are breastfeeding your baby, remember that some doctors recommend vitamin D supplements for the first six months. This is particularly important if your child will not be exposed to much sunlight, which helps the body synthesize vitamin D." (Nutrition Committee of the Canadian Pediatric Society).

Soreness

Some mothers may develop tender nipples. Taking care that baby grasps a good deal of the areola as well as the nipple helps to reduce this possibility.

If you can, change your baby's position with each feeding as this varies the pressure on your nipple.

Keeping your nipples dry and exposing them to the air after nursing also helps to relieve this trouble.

Inform your doctor if you experience sore nipples, especially if the condition worsens.

Biting Babies

This does not happen often even after babies have teeth. If you say "ouch" and stop the feeding right away, he will not likely bite again.

Weaning

By weaning we mean the process of transferring your baby from breast milk to cow's milk. Milk will be produced as long as a child continues to nurse at the breast. The age at which to wean your child is variable. It can range from months to years. The choice rests with the mother and depends upon the need of the child, and the mother's priority and desire to nurse.

As solid foods are added, the weaning process is simplified as the child is already accepting food other than breast milk.

Babies vary a great deal in their fondness for sucking. Some enjoy it greatly and are not very keen on semi-solid food. It would be better to delay or lengthen the weaning process for them. Other babies seem to enjoy their semi-solid food thoroughly and are not as interested in nursing at the breast.

Bottles rather than a cup will provide more sucking opportunity. The older the baby the more likely you will be able to wean to a cup.

You would be wise to postpone weaning if the weather is very hot or if your baby is not entirely well.

Gradual Weaning

This method is most comfortable both for mother and child. On the first day you give him one bottle or cup, instead of nursing him. Naturally you give him his cereal or other semi-solid foods with this feeding as well. Choose the feeding time that suits you best.

After an interval of several days or a week, replace two nursing sessions and carry on in this way until the switch has been completed. You might leave the 10 p.m. changeover until the last, and find that your baby will sleep through the night without it.

The tapering off of your baby's demands on your milk will lessen your supply gradually. Your breasts may continue to produce some milk for a few weeks but it is harmless.

Sudden Weaning

Before weaning your baby suddenly, seek advice for facilities to continue nursing. With changes in attitudes towards breast-feeding some concessions may be available.

If it is necessary to wean a baby suddenly, what do you do if he refuses point-blank to take milk from the bottle that you offer him? He may take it from his father or someone else, so try that first. If he refuses, feed him his cereal very well diluted with milk. A feeding cup may be helpful. Usually he will accept a bottle after a day or so, but you would be wise to talk with your doctor.

Abrupt weaning is hard on your baby and he needs extra attention and comforting during it. Sudden weaning is hard on you too. Reducing your intake of fluids and wearing a snug brassiere both day and night will help to cut down milk formation. Applying ice packs may help to lessen the discomfort.

Bottle-Feeding

7

Your doctor or, in some areas, a public health nurse is the person to tell you what type of feeding (formula) and how much of it to give your baby. They also will suggest suitable intervals between feedings.

A commercially prepared formula is the frequently substituted feeding for breast milk in a young baby. There are many brands available, and most resemble breast milk in composition. Cow's milk contains more proteins of somewhat different kinds and less sugar than breast milk. Thus, to make a day's formula of cow's milk that is suitable for a young baby, the milk is processed, either commercially or in the home, and a certain amount of water and a small amount (often two tablespoons) of a sweetening substance, (commonly white sugar in the home), is added. Diluting the milk with water reduces its energy (calorie) value; adding sugar increases the calories and also makes the feeding more like breast milk. Sugar is not used for its sweetness.

Infant Formulas

Commercially prepared formulas, while more expensive are less trouble to make up. They are called "humanized" as they have been made to simulate breast milk as closely as possible, and they are a most acceptable substitute for the first six months. They are available as a powdered or liquid concentrate to which water must be added or a ready-to-feed preparation.

Most are made from evaporated milk with the milk fat removed and other fats substituted. Suitable amounts of various sugars and both vitamin C and D have been added to nearly all of them. Some contain other ingredients. Babies grow well on these feedings and no other supplement is necessary.

For the occasional baby who is allergic to cow's milk, one or another of a number of very special types of feedings is prescribed by a physician. In most of these preparations, soybean flour has replaced the milk, and suitable amounts of vitamins, calcium and other minerals have been added.

Common Forms of Milk

Evaporated Milk

Evaporated milk is made from cow's milk. During its manufacture, it is heated under a vacuum with the result that a good deal of the water is driven off at a relatively low temperature. Then it is placed in cans and sterilized by heat. As you pour it from the can it is double strength; that is, you have to add an equal amount of water to make it similar to milk in food value. For young babies, roughly twice as much water as evaporated milk is used for formula feeding. Daily feeding for a 11 pound (5 kilogram) baby includes:

10 fluid ounces (300 millilitres) of evaporated whole milk
20 fluid ounces (600 millilitres) of water
2 tablespoons (30 millilitres) of white sugar

Until the can is opened, it keeps perfectly without refrigeration. Once opened, refrigerate the milk. Evaporated milk's long storage life when unopened, its sterility, its cheapness and the processing which it has undergone, all make it a very suitable ingredient in baby's formula. It contains approximately eight percent fat and has about twice the calories of whole milk because 60 percent of the water has been removed. As you would expect, the calories of partly skimmed evaporated milk are about 35 percent lower per ounce than regular evaporated milk. (Incidentally, this kind of milk is handy if you want to cut your calories but like cream in coffee.)

 All the evaporated milks, as far as we know, are enriched by the addition of vitamin D and C. Check the label.

 Do not confuse evaporated milk with sweetened condensed milk. Condensed milk is also a canned concentrated milk, but it has a great deal of sugar added, which makes it quite unsuitable as an ingredient in baby's feedings.

Pasteurized Milk

Pasteurization destroys any harmful germs (such as those that cause bovine tuberculosis, undulant fever or streptococcal throat infections) that may have been in the milk before it reached the dairy. Fresh pasteurized milk is best for a child after a year of age. If you are using this type of milk for a baby's feedings (a much less desirable alternative), it needs to be boiled for two reasons. First, it may have become contaminated with germs when you were making the feeding, and many common germs that are harmless to adults can make a baby sick. Second, boiling the feeding makes it more easily digested by a young baby.

Homogenized Milk

Homogenization refers to the process of breaking down the fat of milk so that smaller particles are suspended evenly in the milk. The cream does not collect at the top.

Whole milk contains all the natural fat (3.25 percent) of cow's milk.

Two percent milk has had about half the cream removed. This type is lower in calories than whole milk, which may be an advantage for some babies.

Skimmed milk has, ounce for ounce, roughly half the calories of whole milk. All the vitamin A (which dissolves in fat) and all the fat have been removed.

Dairies both in Canada and the United States now add vitamin D to all the usual types of fluid milk. On the package it reads "Contains 36 I.U. of vitamin D per 100 ml." If your child is taking enough of this milk, he probably does not need more vitamin D, although some physicians think it best to add more in the form of vitamin drops. Milks contain practically no vitamin C and this must be given in some form every day.

 Pasteurized milk can be bought in most of the settled parts of the country. Raw milk, that is, milk directly from the cow, is not a safe drink for anyone.

Dried Milk

Only skim milk is produced in the powdered form in this country. A very high percentage of the water content has been removed in the processing of the milk. This processing also makes the milk more easily digested. All brands have added vitamins A and D, but not vitamin C. Check the label.

Do not use any type of skim milk feeding for your baby unless your doctor prescribes it for a particular reason, and tells you which vitamin drops to use.

Children over two years who are eating plenty of yellow vegetables and fruits, green vegetables, cheese and eggs plus margarine or butter will obtain in all these foods together an adequate amount of vitamin A. For them, two percent milk is quite suitable.

Making Feedings

1. Terminal Sterilization Method

Equipment needed:

Bottles – at least eight 8-ounce heat resistant bottles

Clear plastic bottles are suitable, if they will withstand boiling.

Nipples and nipple caps – at least one of each for each bottle.

Reversible nipples with plastic caps are most popular.

Kettle for sterilizing filled bottles – a sterilizer containing a bottle rack is best, but a deep kettle with rack will do.

Bottle brush – long handle, stiff bristles and may have small nipple brush attached.

Large graduate (measuring cup) with spout – and utensils – measuring spoon, long-handled spoon, a knife and a can opener that punches holes (if using canned milk).

Method of making and sterilizing feedings:

When ready to make feedings, wash bottles, nipples and caps with hot soapy water, using the bottle brush. Rinse.

If using canned milk, wash can top with hot soapy water and pour boiling water over it and the opener.

Pour required amount of boiling water into graduate.

Level sugar in spoon with knife and add to water.

Open can and add required amount of milk.

Stir milk, sugar and water in graduate.

Pour the required amount of feeding into each bottle.

Fix nipples in inverted position in plastic screw-on caps. Screw up caps, then turn cap back one quarter turn. (If you leave caps tight, they may blow off during heating.)

Place filled bottles in rack in kettle. Put a bottle full of water only in rack also. Add water, preferably hot, to kettle.

If the bottles contain small feedings, add water to level of feeding.

If the feedings are large, water should reach two-thirds of height of bottle.

Put lid on and bring water in kettle to boil; boil for 30 minutes.

Remove rack of bottles and put in large pan or sink of cold water. Swish rack around so bottles cool rapidly.

When lukewarm, screw caps tight and put in refrigerator.

While feedings are cooling wash the other equipment using hot soapy water. Rinse well with clear water.

Cover equipment, preferably on a tray, with clean towel.

Note: The quick cooling helps to prevent formation of a scum which may block the holes in the nipples.

After baby has taken a feeding, rinse bottles out thoroughly with cold water (hot water coagulates milk and makes subsequent cleaning more difficult) and leave it full of water. Rinse the nipple and cap with water also, squeezing water through nipple hole. A toothpick or nipple brush to clean the hole is useful. Leave used nipples and caps in water in a small clean jar.

Nipples and bottles must always be sterilized before using them again. Sterilizing the feedings in them is no more trouble and makes the feedings safer.

Feedings are best made up daily.

2. Aseptic Sterilization

In this method, the formula, the bottles and other equipment, and the nipples and caps are all boiled separately, and then carefully put together.

Equipment needed:

Large preserving kettle with lid.

Bottle rack.

All the articles used in method one and also a pair of tongs, a funnel, a large and a small saucepan.

Method:

The cleaned bottles, funnel and tongs are boiled in the kettle for five minutes, with the handles of the tongs projecting above the water level so that you can grasp them easily.

Remove bottles with the tongs and place them in the rack.

If you are using a liquid formula food that needs only water added, you may pour through a sterilized funnel the required amount from the can into each sterilized bottle. Be sure to wash the can top with hot soapy water and pour boiling water over it and the opener. Then add the required amount of cooled boiled water to each bottle.

or

If you are making your own formula, while the bottles are boiling, measure out the ingredients of the feeding with the addition of a few extra ounces of water (as some of it will boil off) and boil the feeding for five minutes. Then pour the boiled feeding through the sterilized funnel into each bottle. A spare bottle could be filled with boiling water (especially useful in hot weather). Place rack of bottles in a large pan or sink of cold water, cool rapidly, moving rack around at intervals.

The nipples and caps need only three minutes boiling. When this time is up, put nipples and caps on bottles, taking care not to touch any parts of the nipples that go into baby's mouth.

Refrigerate.

Disposable Bottles

If the sterilization and cleaning of bottles seems to overwhelm you, there is an alternative – the sterile plastic disposable liners which replace the bottles. The nipples, the graduate and the device for putting the thin plastic liners into the firm liner holder do need to be sterilized, but when facilities are limited you are sure the bottle will be sterile.

You save the time it takes to clean glass bottles and there is no loss through breakage.

FORMULA GUIDELINES
Formula Requirements

A baby up to 15 pounds (7 kilograms) in weight needs between two to three ounces per pound (130-190 millilitres per kilogram) of body weight daily of formula (or liquids) and may take more. Babies are fed approximately every four hours. If your baby weighs 10 pounds (4.5 kilograms), then he will require between 10-30 ounces (600-900 millilitres) of formula a day. The strength of his formulas will vary with his age, but no baby is fed milk that is stronger than homogenized milk. This 10-pound (4.5 kilogram) baby will probably require five to six ounces (150-180 millilitres) of feeding every four hours, five times a day. If he does not take all the feeding, do not urge him to finish it. His appetite can vary just as yours does. If he continues to refuse much of his feedings, talk to your doctor about it. Do not give him his unfinished bottle a second time.

Feeding Schedule

As a newborn, a baby is fed every four hours for six feedings daily. As soon as his stomach capacity is large enough, the late night feeding is dropped and baby, hopefully, will sleep for eight hours. This may occur when he weighs about 10 pounds (4.5 kilograms). If a baby is under six pounds (2.7 kilograms), then feedings are usually given every three hours, seven or eight times a day.

Babies often waken and cry when they are hungry. Sometimes you may have to feed yours before the four hours are up, but on other occasions he will sleep longer than four hours. Let baby have some flexibility in his schedule.

Feeding Tips

Most mothers warm the bottles in warm water or a bottle warmer, and test the temperature of the feeding by letting a few drops fall on the inside of their wrists. The formula should feel warm – not hot. You can give baby his feedings cold if you like, but be consistent. Do not give some cold and some warm.

Test out the size of the hole in the nipple by holding the bottle upside down without shaking it. The feeding should not come out in a continuous stream. One drop every

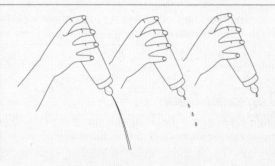

Checking the flow of milk
Invert the feeding bottle. If the milk comes out in a gush, the hole is too big. If the drops of milk come out in a steady stream, the hole is correct. If it takes a few seconds for a drop to form, the hole is too small.

second or so is about right. If baby can't finish his feeding in about fifteen minutes, you would be wise to enlarge the hole in the nipple. The handiest way to do this is to straighten out a big safety pin and heat its tip red hot in the flame of a candle or a burning match. Immediately push it through the hole in the nipple. It will melt enough of the rubber to enlarge the hole.

Unevenly warmed feeding might be hot in some areas, resulting in a burn. As this can happen in seconds in the microwave, it is not recommended for warming bottles.

When feeding baby, hold him cuddled in your arm in a semi-sitting position. He needs to feel close to you just as a breast-fed baby does. Hold the bottle so that the neck of it is always filled with milk. This keeps him from sucking in air which could make him feel that his stomach is full before he has taken enough milk. Also, in burping up swallowed air, your baby may spit up some milk along with it, and if you do not get rid of this air, he may feel uncomfortable and cry. At least once during a feeding and again after it, help baby bring up any air that he has swallowed (see Chapter 6). Never prop up his bottle and leave him to feed himself. If he takes too much food quickly or coughs he may choke on it. Also, the bottle can easily tilt over so that he sucks in a considerable amount of air. Besides, holding him is a pleasant experience for both baby and parent.

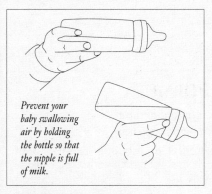

Prevent your baby swallowing air by holding the bottle so that the nipple is full of milk.

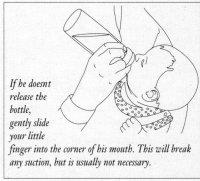

If he doesn't release the bottle, gently slide your little finger into the corner of his mouth. This will break any suction, but is usually not necessary.

Switching to Milk

Doctors will advise parents to switch to milk when their babies are six to eight months old. Whole milk is recommended for most babies. In some circumstances 2 percent milk will be advised by physicians. Sometimes they recommend leaving half the sugar out of his feedings for a few days before changing him over.

When you switch your baby to milk the doctor will probably tell you that you can stop sterilizing his bottles. Washing a bottle and possibly rinsing it with boiling water just before pouring in the milk is sufficient. If baby is given such a bottle right away, very few, if any, germs will be in it.

Stools

The bowel movements of a bottle-fed baby are yellow or brown in color. The shade depends on the kind of feedings your baby is getting. The stools are smooth, much like a thick brownish ointment. The number passed each day varies from one to three, usually the former.

If your baby is being given iron by your doctor, either in his feedings or in drops, his stools will be almost black in color. When vegetables are added to his diet, the color may vary somewhat from day to day. A little green on the stool need not worry you if your baby is doing well otherwise. If you notice anything really unusual in your baby's stools – for instance, if they are very pale in color, if they are foul smelling or if they contain mucus or blood – tell your doctor about it.

FOULING FORMULA

* Always wash your hands thoroughly before making formula.
* Don't use a drying rack or tea towel to dry sterile equipment.
* Don't take bottles out of the sterilized solution until you need them. (Air can contaminate the bottle.) Left in the solution, bottles will remain sterile for 24 hours.
* After 24 hours, discard any made-up formula.
* If you don't use warmed milk immediately, don't feed it to baby. (Heating milk facilitates bacterial growth.)
* Do not give a baby the same bottle twice if he doesn't finish it when it was offered the first time.
* When there is no refrigeration, feed formula immediately after making it.
* Always sterilize bottles and equipment – even if they're new!
* When travelling do not store formula in a thermos. Ultra-heat treated (UHT) formulas are ideal when you are away from home because they can be stored in a cool place safely and are convenient.

THE FIRST YEAR

Growth and development from birth to 12 months: here are a few guidelines to standard development — don't panic if your baby does not follow the pattern exactly. Every baby is unique and develops at his own pace.

ONE MONTH
○ Stiffens when picked up
○ Turns his head but cannot lift or hold it
○ Stares at human faces and moving objects
○ Enjoys being cuddled

TWO MONTHS
○ Able to lift his head when lying on his stomach
○ Follows moving light
○ Discovers his hands
○ Smiles and enjoys company

THREE MONTHS
○ Begins to drool
○ Follows moving objects
○ Blows bubbles and enjoys his own noises
○ Reacts to noise, laughs out loud

FOUR MONTHS
○ Sits when propped; holds his head
○ Opens his hands to grasp, but unable to grasp on his own
○ Follows a moving light up and down and from left to right
○ Laughs, recognizes familiar faces, enjoys attention

FIVE MONTHS
○ Puts his feet in his mouth when lying on his back
○ Holds his head straight
○ Looks for the source of noises
○ Babbles
○ Smiles at his reflection in a mirror; gets used to strangers
○ Cries when he wants something.

1A

6-7 MONTHS
○ First teeth appear (lower two front teeth)
○ Turns over on his own
○ Sits alone
○ Uses both hands
○ Listens quietly to a ticking watch or clock
○ Differentiates two objects

8-9 MONTHS
○ Upper front teeth appear
○ Turns over easily
○ Sits without help
○ Begins to crawl
○ Says 'mamma' and 'papa'
○ Recognizes faces
○ Pays attention to what goes on
○ Eats with his fingers
○ Claps his hands

10-11 MONTHS
○ Crawls on all fours, begins to haul himself on his feet by hanging on to furniture
○ Talks to his toys
○ Mimics people
○ Understands simple words and commands
○ Picks up crumbs between thumb and second finger
○ Understands his name
○ Reacts to music
○ Begins to explore his surroundings

12 MONTHS
○ Has tripled his birthweight
○ The first molars are appearing
○ Walks
○ Turns pages of books, enjoys tearing them up
○ Tries to put on his shoes
○ Babbles
○ Can identify objects and knows to whom they belong
○ Points to things he wants
○ Enjoys music
○ Feeds himself
○ Pretends to blow his nose
○ Understands the meaning of 'no'

Text supplied by Ross Laboratories

Homemade goodness from Heinz.

Up at dawn, pick at peak, prepare at once -
without salt, additives or preservatives. Naturally good nutrition.
Naturally good taste.

Heinz Baby Foods. Helping you do the best for your baby.

LEARNING TO EAT

0–3 MONTHS

When stimulated, will turn head and mouth and will search for nipple. Start to put hand in mouth. Drools a lot when nursing.

3–4 MONTHS

Does not drool as much when nursing. May reach out for objects and mouth them. Can hold a spoon if placed in hand.

5 MONTHS

May indicate fullness by turning head away from food. Can grab pieces of food. May splash liquids with hand.

6 MONTHS

Begins finger foods. May want to manipulate spoon alone. Starts chewing food with gums. Starts to drink from cup. May prefer certain foods over others. Enjoys variety and colorful foods.

7 MONTHS

Enjoys foods of different textures. May be able to remove food effectively from a spoon and sips competently from a cup.

8–10 MONTHS

May bite objects and get excited by foods he favors.

10–12 MONTHS

Improves ability to chew and feed.

12–15 MONTHS

Due to a reduced growth rate, appetite may decrease. Starts to manipulate bits of food on a spoon. Starts to use cup on his own. Often throws or spits foods. May point to what he wants.

18–24 MONTHS

Gains some control over spoon but is still a messy eater. When thirsty, can pick up and put down cup. Enjoys drinking from a straw. Continues to play with food more than eat it. May prolong feedings.

With Heinz Cereals your baby gets what she naturally needs.

NO SALT OR SUGAR ADDED.
Heinz Cereals contain absolutely no added salt or sugar.
Other cereals may. Check the label to be sure.

A GOOD START FOR BABY.
All Heinz Cereals are specially fortified for infants, with iron,
calcium, vitamins and minerals.
Nutrition experts recommend a "single grain" infant cereal as baby's first solid food.
Heinz offers a wide range; including Rice, Barley and Oatmeal.

CEREALS TO GROW ON.
Once your baby is used to single grain cereals, introduce mixed grains
and cereals with fruit. Infant cereals are recommended as part of baby's diet
until 24 months, because they remain the best source of iron for your baby.

Heinz Baby Foods. Helping you do the best for your baby.

SPEECH & COMPREHENSION

MONTHS	B	2	4	6	8	10	12	14	16	18	20	22	28	32	34	36	48	60
EXPRESSION																		
COOS		✔																
LAUGHS		✔																
BABBLES				✔														
MAMA/DADA					✔													
1ST WORD						✔												
4–6 SINGLE WORDS								✔										
TELLS NEEDS									✔									
2–WORD SENTENCES											✔							
50+ SINGLE WORDS												✔						
USES NOUNS & VERBS														✔				
TALKS IN SENTENCES																✔		
USES ALL SPEECH SOUNDS																		✔
COMPREHENSION																		
RESPONDS TO VOICE	✔																	
DIFFERS SOUNDS	✔																	
RESPONDS TO 'NO'				✔														
1–STEP COMMAND						✔												
POINTS TO BODY PARTS									✔									
2–STEP COMMAND											✔							
POINTS TO OBJECTS																		
DESCRIBED BY USE													✔					
COMPLEX COMMANDS														✔				
WHAT? WHO?															✔			
HOW? YESTERDAY?																	✔	
GENERAL																		
SMILES	✔																	
RECOGNIZES PARENTS	✔																	
RECOGNIZES OBJECTS		✔																
RESPONDS TO FACIAL		✔																
EXPRESSIONS																		
INITIATES GAMES				✔														
INITIATES CONVERSATION															✔			

Adapted from the Elm Scale & OSLA Speech Hearing Checklist

1D

Nutrios.
For your teeny weeny in-betweeny.

If your baby won't eat infant cereal anymore, try Heinz Nutrios.
Unlike adult breakfast cereals, Nutrios are specifically fortified to meet the
nutritional requirements of toddlers, and are an excellent source of
iron, riboflavin, niacin, thiamin, and calcium. They're naturally flavoured with
apple juice, and contain no added salt. Plus their shape and texture are
perfect for babies who are learning to feed themselves.
Look for Nutrios in the baby food section of your grocery store.

New from Heinz

A CLUB SO POPULAR IT'S GOT A 9 MONTH WAITING LIST.

If you've just had a baby, join the Heinz Baby Club. You'll receive 4 booklets timed to coincide with the feeding stages of your little one, jam-packed with answers to your questions regarding nutrition, as well as special offers and coupons. All 4 booklets are incorporated into a beautiful keep sake poster by renowned Canadian artist Heather Cooper. Best of all, it's absolutely free!

Just fill out the coupon on the adjoining page and send it in, and we'll send your poster and first booklet.

DEVELOPMENT RECORD

Holds head up for
a few seconds   ....

Smiles   ....

Laughs   ....

Sleeps through night   ....

Rolls over   ....

Sits unsupported   ....

Crawls/Shuffles   ....

Waddles about   ....

Walks   ....

First tooth   ....

Starts solids   ....

Is weaned   ....

Feeds 'self   ....

First words   ....

Points to parts of the body   ....

Makes simple statements   ....

Pedals tricycle   ....

Stays dry throughout nap   ....

Can do up buttons   ....

Draws a circle   ....

Gains bladder control   ....

Gains bowel control   ....

Starts playschool/
nursery school   ....

First visit to the dentist   ....

Mail to: *c/o Baby Club*
H.J. Heinz Company of Canada Limited
P.O. Box 5720, Leamington, Ontario
N8H 9Z9

BABY'S NAME

BIRTHDATE (D/M/Y)

YOUR NAME

ADDRESS

APT. NO.

CITY   PROVINCE

POSTAL CODE   TELEPHONE

LANGUAGE PREFERENCE (E/FR)

1E

FIRST AID

Call 911 or Emergency Ambulance for any severely injured child.

BURNS AND SCALDS
MINOR BURNS WITHOUT BLISTERS
Place burned extremity into cold water or cover burned part with a towel soaked in cold water until the pain stops (at least 15 minutes).
BURNS WITH BLISTERS
Same as above. Do NOT break the blisters. Call your doctor for advice on how to cover the burn. ANY burn on the face, hands, feet, or genitals and any large burn should be seen by a physician.
DEEP BURNS
CALL 911 or an emergency ambulance. Do NOT apply cold water or any medication. Keep child warm with a clean sheet and then a blanket until help arrives. Remove smoldering, wet or chemically contaminated clothing.
ELECTRICAL BURNS
Disconnect electrical power. Do NOT touch victim with bare hands. Pull victim away from power source with wood or a thick, dry cloth. ALL electrical burns need to be seen by a physician.

CONVULSIONS
Protect the child from injury. Lay on side with head lower than hips. Put nothing in the mouth. Call 911.

EYE INJURIES
Do NOT press on an injured eye. Do NOT apply medication. Any injured or painful eye should be seen by a physician. Consult a physician before removing a foreign body from the eye. Gently bandage the painful eye shut until you can get medical help. If a chemical is splashed in the eye, gently flush with water; continue this for at least 15 minutes.

FAINTING
Keep in flat position and raise legs. Turn head to the side. Do NOT give anything by mouth. Call your doctor.

FRACTURES
If an injured part is very painful, swollen, deformed, or if motion causes pain, suspect a fracture. A fractured part should not be moved until it has been splinted. Call a physician or ambulance. Do NOT move a child who may have a neck or back injury, as this may cause paralysis. Wait for help to arrive.

SPRAINS
Apply a cold compress and elevate the injured arm or leg. If you suspect a fracture (see above), call your doctor.

Information from the American Academy of Pediatrics.

What the happiest babies are wearing this season...

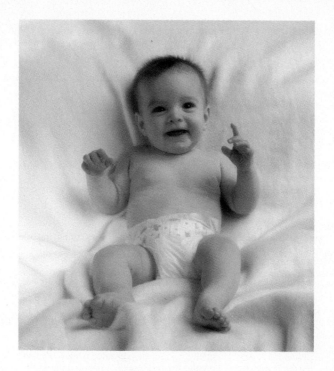

Huggies®!

LEAK
SHIELDS

H uggies babies are also wearing a happy smile! Keep your baby happy. Start off right – with the leakage protection of Huggies Supertrim diapers.

Huggies have a gently gathered waistband, and leak shields, soft inner cuffs that keep whatever's inside the diaper <u>inside</u> the diaper. Even messy bowel movements.

It's Huggies' best leakage protection ever. And Huggies babies are happier than ever!

<u>Only</u> Huggies offers blue and pink diapers for boys and girls as well as white non-gender specific diapers.

Call 911 or Emergency Ambulance for any severely injured child.

HEAD INJURIES
Seek immediate medical assistance for any of the following:
• Unconsciousness or drowsiness
• Convulsions
• Inability to move any body part
• Oozing of blood or watery fluid from the ears or nose
• Severe or persistent headache
• Head injury in any child less than 1 year old.
If there are no symptoms, you may let your child sleep, but awaken every one to two hours and make sure the child can recognize you.

POISONS
If a child is unconscious, becoming drowsy, having convulsions, or having trouble breathing, call 911 or emergency ambulance.
SWALLOWED POISONS
Any non-food substance is a potential poison. Call the Poison Centre immediately. Do not induce vomiting except on professional advice. The Poison Centre will give you instructions for use of Syrup of Ipecac.
FUMES, GASES OR SMOKE
Protect yourself first. Get the victim into fresh air. Call 911 or fire department. If the child is not breathing, start CPR and continue until help arrives.
SKIN EXPOSURE
If acids, lye, pesticides or any potentially poisonous substance comes in contact with a child's skin, brush off dry material gently. Wash skin with large quantities of soap and water. Remove contaminated clothing. Wear rubber gloves if possible. Call Poison Centre for further advice.
EYE EXPOSURE
If any substance is splashed in the eye, flush with water for at least 15 minutes. Call the Poison Centre for further advice.

SKIN WOUNDS
BRUISES
Apply cold compresses for half an hour. For extensive bruises, crushing injuries or bicycle spoke injuries, consult your doctor or emergency department.
CUTS
Apply pressure with a clean cloth to stop the bleeding. If the cut is large and deep, call for help and maintain pressure until help arrives. For minor cuts, wash with soap and water and cover with dressing.
SCRAPES
Wash scrape with soap and water. Cover with a non-stick dressing.
SPLINTERS
Wash with soap and water. Remove small splinters with tweezers. If not easily removed, call your doctor.
PUNCTURE WOUNDS
Do NOT remove large objects such as knives or sticks. Call your doctor. For minor puncture wounds, wash with soap and water and call your doctor. Your child may need a tetanus booster.

Call 911 or Emergency Ambulance for any severely injured child.

NOSE BLEEDS
With child sitting, squeeze nostrils together between your thumb and index finger for at least 5 minutes. If bleeding persists, call the doctor.

BITES AND STINGS
SNAKE BITES
Call the Poison Centre. Do not apply ice. Take the child to the emergency department. For a snake bite on the arm or leg, if you cannot get medical advice within the hour, LOOSELY apply a WIDE band of cloth between the bite and the child's heart. Do not make it too tight.
STINGING INSECTS
Remove the stinger with the scraping motion of a fingernail. Do NOT pull the stinger out. Put a cold compress on the bite to relieve pain. If hives, pallor, weakness, nausea, vomiting, tightness in the chest, breathing difficulty, or collapse occur, call 911.
For spider bites, call your doctor.
TICKS
Place tweezers close to the head of the tick and pull tick away from point of attachment. Call your doctor if head remains attached.
ANIMAL BITES
Wash wound thoroughly with soap and water. Call your doctor. If the animal is a bat, racoon, skunk, or fox, or an unprovoked cat or dog, it may have rabies. Call your doctor.
MARINE ANIMALS
For sting ray, lionfish, catfish, and stonefish stings, submerge sting area in warm water to inactivate the toxin. For other marine stings, flush with clean water and call your doctor.

TEETH
BABY (PRIMARY) TEETH
If knocked out or broken, apply clean gauze to control bleeding and call a dentist.
PERMANENT TEETH
If knocked out, find the tooth and rinse it gently without touching the root. Insert and gently hold the tooth in its socket or transport the tooth in cow's milk. Go directly to the dentist.
If broken, gently clean the injured area with warm water. Place a cold compress to reduce swelling. Go to the dentist immediately.

BE PREPARED
KEEP EMERGENCY NUMBERS BY YOUR TELEPHONE

IN CASE OF ACCIDENTAL POISONING

If an accidental poisoning occurs or is suspected,
think clearly and take the following steps:

1

Identify the suspected poison and the amount taken.

2

Immediately contact your Poison Information Centre (hospital
emergency department) or your family physician.

Hospital: .... Physican: ....

Address: .... Address:..

Telephone: .... Telephone:..

3

If necessary, quickly take the child to the nearest
hospital emergency department.

This does not necessarily mean you need an ambulance. If there is a family
car or immediate source of door-to-door transportation available, this will
often be faster.

Ambulance: .... Telephone:..

4

Bring the package or container of suspected poison with you.

PLACE THIS NOTICE IN PROMINENT POSITION

Information Supplied by Ontario Ministry of Health

POISON CONTROL CENTRES

If there is no listing below for your town/city, check the front of the telephone book white pages. There should be a Poison Information Centre listed with the other emergency numbers.

BRITISH COLUMBIA
Vancouver ....(604) 682-5050
Victoria ....(604) 595-9211
ALBERTA ....(800) 332-1414
SASKATCHEWAN
Regina ....(306) 359-4545
Saskatoon ....(306) 966-1010
MANITOBA ....(204) 787-2591
Winnipeg ....(204) 787-2444
ONTARIO ....(800) 268-9017
807 Area Code Call Collect
Toronto ....(416) 598-5900
Ottawa ....(613) 737-1100
....(800) 267-1373
QUEBEC ....(800) 463-5060
Quebec City ....(418) 654-2254
Montreal ....(514) 934-4456
NEW BRUNSWICK
Saint John ....(506) 648-7111
Moncton ....(506) 388-3005
Fredericton ....(506) 452-5400
Campbellton ....(506) 753-5212
Edmundston ....(506) 735-7384
Bathurst ....(506) 546-4666
NOVA SCOTIA
Halifax ....(902) 428-8161
PRINCE EDWARD ISLAND
Charlottetown ....(902) 566-6250
Summerside ....(902) 436-9131
NEWFOUNDLAND
St. John's ....(709) 722-1110
Corner Brook ....(709) 634-7121
Gander ....(709) 651-2500
Grand Falls ....(709) 292-2900
Labrador City ....(709) 944-2632
St. Anthony ....(709) 454-3333
NORTHWEST TERRITORIES/THE YUKON
Yellowknife ....(403) 920-4111
Fort Smith ....(403) 872-2713
Hay River ....(403) 874-6512
Inuvik ....(403) 979-2955
Whitehorse ....(403) 668-9444
Frobisher Bay ....(819) 979-5231

THE
FIRST AID KIT

The kit shown here is recommended for all households. Other items, not illustrated, may be added for special purposes, but for basic First Aid requirements this kit should be adequate. Keep it well stocked and replace the disposable items as they are used. Keep a separate kit in your car or boat and for hiking and camping.

BASIC KIT
1   Absorbent cotton wool.
2. Band-aids.
3. Adhesive tape (various widths).
4. Calamine lotion
5. Cotton tipped swabs.
6. Children's aspirin/acetaminophen — according to doctor's advice.
7. Calamine.
8. Antiseptic.
9. Triangular bandages — for tying splints.
10. Safety pins.
11. Sharp needles — to remove splinters: sterilize first.
12. Sharp scissors with rounded ends.
13. Sterile gauze bandages.
14. Sterile gauze pads.
15. Thermometer.
16. Tweezers.
17. Elastic support bandages.
18. Sun screen with the highest protection factor.
19. Insect-repellant spray.

NEW BLOCK ON THE KID

Effective sun protection is especially important for kids. That's why mom's got into the new habit of using JOHNSON'S* Baby Sunblock every day.

Waterproof, and specially formulated to block harmful sunrays, Baby Sunblock provides kids with the protection their sensitive skin needs.

The only ones, from day one.

CARDIO PULMONARY RESUSCITATION (CPR)

To be used in situations such as drowning, electric shock and smoke inhalation or when breathing or heartbeat stops.

TECHNIQUE OF PULMONARY SUPPORT (D)
Begin the following if the child is not breathing:
• Place victim on back.
• Straighten neck (unless neck injury suspected) and lift jaw.
• Give slow steady breaths into infant's nose and mouth and into larger child's mouth with nostrils pinched closed.
• Breathe at 20 breaths per minute for infants and 15 breaths per minute for children, using only enough air to move chest up and down.

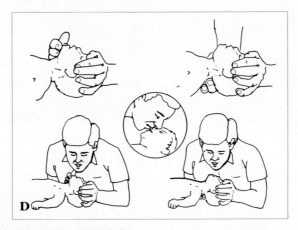

TECHNIQUE OF CARDIAC SUPPORT
Begin the following if the child has no heart beat:
• Place victim on firm surface.
• In the infant, using two fingers, depress breastbone 1/2" to 1" at level of one finger's breadth below nipples (E). Compress at 100 times/minute.
• In the child, depress lower one third of breastbone with heel of hand at 80 compressions/minute. There should be five compressions to one respiration (F).

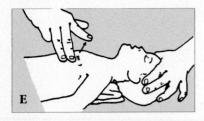

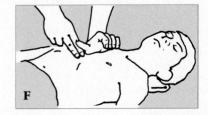

Supplied by the American Academy of Pediatrics

CHILDRENS' HEALTH HISTORY

CHILD	ILLNESSES/OPERATIONS	DATES	INJURIES

CHILD	DRUG SENSITIVITIES	ALLERGIES

NAME _____ BLOOD TYPE _____

NAME _____ BLOOD TYPE _____

Pure soap can damage pure skin.

You see, pure soap is alkaline and can damage the protective top layer of baby's skin, leaving it dry, irritated and red.

Dove® leaves it looking soft, healthy and smooth. That's because Dove is not a soap, and is non-alkaline.

It's a gentle cleansing bar made with ¼ moisturizing cream that leaves baby's skin just the way nature intended it — soft, smooth and pure.

IMMUNIZATION SCHEDULE

	(DPT)				(MMR)			
	DIPTHERIA TOXOID	PERTUSSIS VACCINE	TETANUS TOXOID	ORAL POLIOVIRUS VACCINE (OPV)	MEASLES VACCINE	MUMPS VACCINE	RUBELLA VACCINE	H. INFLUENZAE B VACCINE (HIB)
2 MONTHS	✔	✔	✔	✔				
4 MONTHS	✔	✔	✔	✔				
6 MONTHS	✔	✔	✔	✔				
12 MONTHS					✔	✔	✔	
16–18 MONTHS	✔	✔	✔	✔				
AFTER 18 MONTHS								✔
4–6 YEARS	✔	✔	✔	✔				
14–16 YEARS	✔		✔	✔				
EVERY 10 YEARS THEREAFTER	✔		✔	✔				
RECORD KEEPER: DATE (Y/M/D)								

Just what the doctor ordered

Children's TYLENOL Drops to bring the fever down.*

We understand what you, as a parent, can go through when your baby has a fever. Your child feels hot and cranky. You feel frustrated and helpless.

It's for those times that doctors recommend *Children's TYLENOL* Drops. In fact, Children's TYLENOL* is the medication doctors recommend most often to relieve fever and pain in babies and older children.*

Ask your doctor. *Children's TYLENOL* is a safe, effective way to reduce fever fast. It makes kids – and parents – feel a whole lot better!*

*Trademark

Recommended by doctors. Trusted by parents.

WEIGHT AND HEIGHT CHART

Name...

Birthdate................................Weight at birth......................Length at birth.................

Name...

Birthdate................................Weight at birth......................Length at birth.................

CHILD 1/DATE	WEIGHT	HEIGHT

CHILD 2/DATE	WEIGHT	HEIGHT

FAMILY HEALTH HISTORY

	DISEASES	HIGH BLOOD PRESSURE, HEART OR CIRCULATORY	GLAUCOMA	DIABETES	CANCER	TUBERCULOSIS	ASTHMA	SEIZURES	OTHER	CAUSE OF DEATH
FATHER										
MOTHER										
BROTHER (SIBLING)										
SISTER										
BROTHER										
SISTER										
GRANDFATHER										
GRANDMOTHER										
GRANDFATHER										
GRANDMOTHER										

INSURANCE RECORDS

MEDICAL PLAN: .... POLICY #: ....

COMPANY: .... ADDRESS: ....

DENTAL PLAN: .... POLICY #: ....

COMPANY: .... ADDRESS: ....

GIRLS–BIRTH TO 24 MONTHS
AVERAGE PHYSICAL GROWTH
HEIGHT

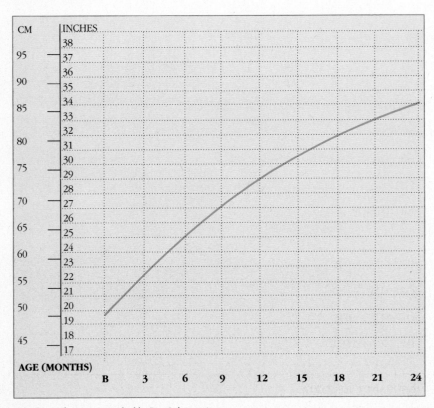

Based on information supplied by Ross Laboratories.

GIRLS–BIRTH TO 24 MONTHS
AVERAGE PHYSICAL GROWTH
WEIGHT

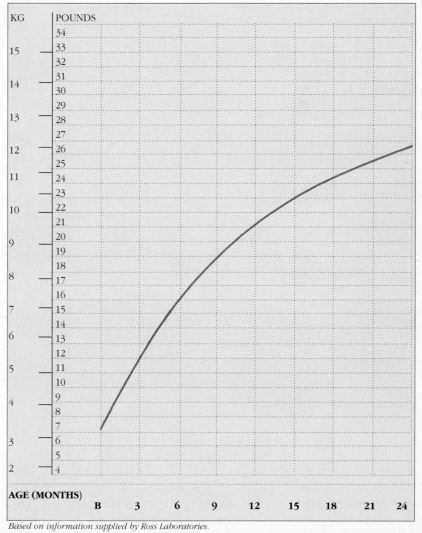

Based on information supplied by Ross Laboratories.

BOYS–BIRTH TO 24 MONTHS
AVERAGE PHYSICAL GROWTH
HEIGHT

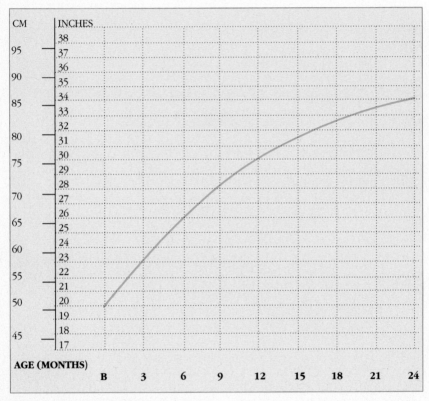

Based on information supplied by Ross Laboratories.

BOYS–BIRTH TO 24 MONTHS
AVERAGE PHYSICAL GROWTH
WEIGHT

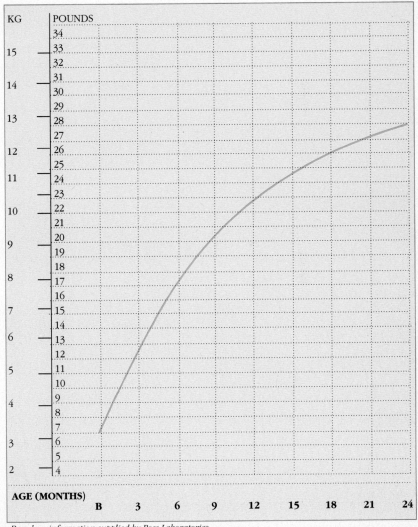

Based on information supplied by Ross Laboratories.

GIRLS–AGED 2–10
AVERAGE PHYSICAL GROWTH
HEIGHT

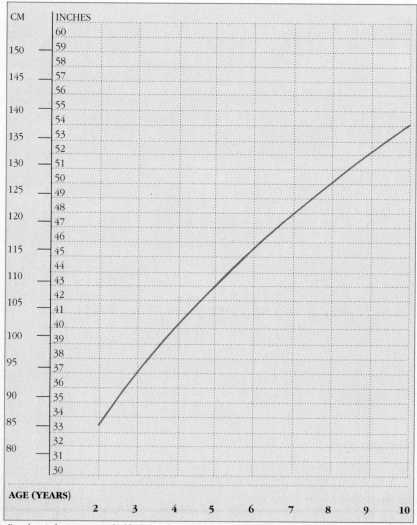

Based on information supplied by Ross Laboratories.

BOYS–AGED 2–10
AVERAGE PHYSICAL GROWTH
HEIGHT

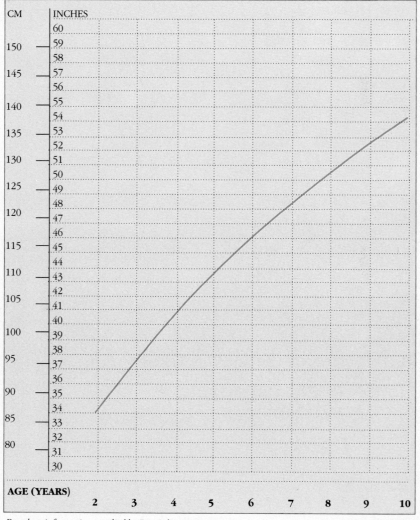

AGE (YEARS)

Based on information supplied by Ross Laboratories. 1V

BOYS AND GIRLS–AGED 2-10
AVERAGE PHYSICAL GROWTH
WEIGHT

AVERAGE WEIGHT KEY—BOYS: BLUE/GIRLS: PINK

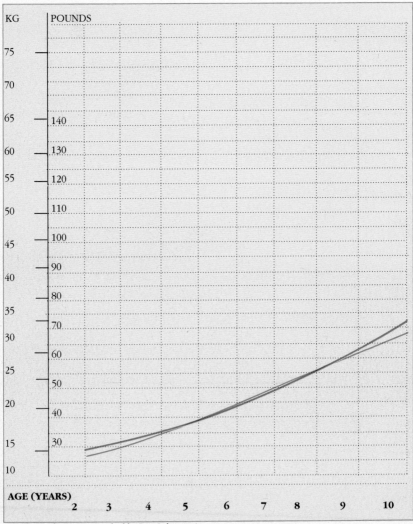

Based on information supplied by Ross Laboratories.

8

Common Health Concerns in Babies

Blood in the Stool

If baby passes a hard constipated stool, he may break a little blood vessel near the opening and you will see a streak of blood on his bowel movement. A small amount of vaseline, placed around his anus, will ease the passage of the stool. This is not at all serious and giving him more laxative food will relieve the situation.

Blood here and there throughout his stool, usually with white mucus as well, would likely mean that he is suffering from a bowel infection. A child may pass blood in his stool with a cry, as though in pain, possibly abdominal pain. When blood appears in a baby's stool, consult you doctor at once.

Colic

A colicky baby is one who feeds well and gains weight but is uncomfortable for many hours during the day and night. He will cry and fuss and draw his legs up. Although it is unclear what causes colic, motion sometimes helps – rocking, a snuggle, a ride in his carriage, a walk in his infant carrier or a drive in the car. Some boiled, tepid water may also relieve his discomfort. Occasionally medication is prescribed and given to the baby before feedings to help him relax and fall asleep quickly.

After three months of age, spells of colic are less prolonged, and there seems to be less discomfort after feeding. In fact, many mothers speak of "the three-month colic" and seem to yearn for the magical age of four months. However, most babies get over this trouble gradually.

Common Cold

Whenever possible it is best for babies to avoid anyone with a cold. Babies have little resistance to the cold viruses and may develop one following brief contact. Cool air does not give a baby a cold. He should be kept comfortably dressed; if he is dressed too warmly, skin rashes may occur.

If your baby does develop a cold, he will be miserable for several days. He will also have to work quite hard to feed if his nose is blocked. Try to keep his nose clear. A vaporizer will help to keep his nasal secretions loose. Nose drops will help to clear the passages in his nose. Sometimes oral medications are recommended by your doctor to achieve this. Follow the advice of your doctor.

If baby sleeps on his side or is held upright, the secretions will drain out of his nose more readily. If he sleeps on his back, the mucus secretions accumulate at the back of his throat and make him cough. Your doctor may want to prescribe medicine to relieve the coughing. If he swallows a lot of mucus, it may make him vomit.

If your baby has no fever and is not vomiting, then he may want his feedings. However, sugar and water or diluted sweet drinks such as apple juice, orange juice or ginger ale will help to clear the secretions from his throat and stomach and will also help to prevent vomiting. Baby may need sweetened drinks for 24 to 48 hours and then he will be able to tolerate his feedings.

If baby has a fever, acetaminophen will help but follow the advice of your doctor when administering any medication.

Acetylsalicylic acid has been linked to Reye's Syndrome – a rare but serious illness. It is not given to children suspected of having chicken pox or flu. Generally, it is avoided altogether.

Constipation

Constipation in small babies is uncommon. If baby's feedings provide sufficient liquid, then nature will see that his bowels are moved regularly. Some breast-fed babies may miss three, four or even five days, but when the stool does come it is large and soft, not constipated.

After cereal has been added to the diet, some babies may pass hard, infrequent, constipated movements. Switching to oat baby cereal or giving baby strained prunes or prune juice will make his stools softer and more frequent and alleviate this problem. Laxatives, such as milk of magnesia, are rarely given to young babies.

Diarrhea

Diarrhea means frequent, loose bowel movements, often with an offensive or different odor from the usual. If a baby develops diarrhea he must be treated more cautiously than an older child as he will require a larger amount of liquid for his size. If the liquid which he is losing is not replaced he will become dehydrated. If he is unable to take sufficient liquid by mouth for his needs, because of vomiting and/or nausea, he may have to be admitted to hospital where he can be given liquids intravenously (by vein).

When it is an infection which is causing the diarrhea, an older child may not be hungry and usually loses his appetite for regular foods. Similarly this may occur in a baby and feedings must be replaced by clear liquids recommended by your doctor. This will lessen the risk of vomiting occurring.

Consult your doctor if you baby develops diarrhea. She may recommend that feedings be replaced by clear liquids depending upon the severity and/or cause of the diarrhea.

Projectile Vomiting

Pyloric stenosis causes a blockage of the lower end (pylorus) of the stomach. It is a relatively rare condition and occurs in babies several weeks old, more commonly in boys. It causes such forceful (projectile) vomiting that the stomach contents are thrown out for a distance of one or two feet. A baby who is vomiting like this needs to be carefully examined by a doctor, who may even want to admit him to hospital to observe him more closely. If the trouble is due to pyloric stenosis, a simple operation will correct it.

Spitting Up

Most babies do some spitting. To minimize this, allow 15-20 minutes to feed your baby, burping him when he is about halfway through. The speed with which he gets his feeding depends on his vigour, the size of the hole in the nipple and the strength of the rubber. Small babies with a weak suck need soft nipples and a comparatively large hole. Vigorous babies require firm nipples with a relatively small hole.

After you have fed your baby, keep him in an upright position for a few minutes – this will assist bubbles of swallowed air to escape and allow some of his meal to pass out of his stomach. Either hold him on your lap or let him sit in his infant seat. When holding a very small baby on your lap, you will, of course, support his head. If you wish, you can put a cloth diaper over your shoulder and let him rest there well supported. Keeping baby relaxed and quiet after his feeding is important.

Vomiting

A baby that vomits repeatedly needs to be examined by a doctor. In spitting, the milk merely runs out of baby's mouth, but vomiting is a forceful emptying of the stomach. If baby is gaining normally, vomiting may mean that he is eating too much too quickly. However, some babies who cry a lot and become colicky may vomit. Another cause of vomiting in babies can be the onset of an acute infection such as a cold. It would be wise to contact your doctor.

When a baby vomits, stop all his feedings with the exception of breast milk. Offer a small amount of water with sugar (eight ounces of water with one tablespoon of sugar) to settle his stomach and to give him extra liquids. The amount varies with his size: for a small baby half an ounce would be suitable; for a larger one, two ounces would probably be about right. If baby retains the sugar and water for an hour, you may safely give him more. Do not force him to drink. From then on you will be guided by what your doctor advises.

9

Adding Semi-Solids and Other Foods

Breast milk or cow's milk formulas are essential foods for normal babies, but both of them contain very little iron, especially cow's milk. Remember too, that babies need additional vitamin C and D, which the manufacturer may have added to the formula ingredients. If baby's formula does not contain these vitamins, you must give them to him, usually in the form of vitamin drops, most of which contain vitamin A.

If a young baby is taking only small amounts of a vitamin-enriched formula, he may need vitamin drops as well. The drops are gently squirted into the corner of his mouth at the beginning of a feeding. The amount that gives him 400 I.U. of vitamin D and 20 milligrams or more of vitamin C daily is sufficient. It's best to start the drops when baby is two to three weeks of age.

Some doctors start apple juice or orange juice around four weeks of age. A small amount is used. Most babies like these juices and digest them without any trouble. The occasional young baby spits it up, is made uncomfortable by it or develops a rash. For him, vitamin drops are needed.

Begin with only one teaspoon (5 millilitres) each of juice and water, but increase them both by one teaspoon (5 millilitres) every day until you reach one ounce (30 millilitres) of juice. Then, gradually increase the juice and decrease the water until your baby is getting two to three ounces (60-90 millilitres) of "straight" juice.

When your baby is five or six months old, you can begin to teach him to take his

juice from a trainer cup. It is a good idea to give
it to him shortly before his bath, an hour or so
before his next feeding.

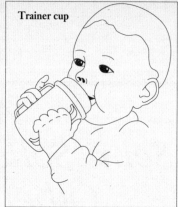

Trainer cup

A healthy baby, born after a normal nine-
month pregnancy, starts off with a very generous supply of iron in his body. As he grows the
iron is used for making blood and other body
cells. By the time he is three months old, his
original supply has dwindled, but he has also
developed the ability to use the iron supplied by
his food.

Special Baby Cereals

The first special baby cereal (Pablum) was devised almost 60 years ago by two
Canadian pediatricians who were experts in nutrition. Now there are other similar
products on the market. All these special cereals are heavily enriched with iron and
three of the B vitamins. They are often started when baby is four to six months old,
partly to give him extra calories and partly because he needs more iron. Some physicians introduce cereal at an earlier age if the child is not satisfied on his recommended
feeding. Often this is a child whose size is above average.

Ordinarily cereals are not thought of as being unusually good foods, but special
baby cereals are just that. A good helping, about three heaping tablespoons (45 millilitres), of the moistened cereal, will give your baby five to 10 times as much iron as half
a jar of strained meat, liver or egg yolk. This is partly because the strained meats and
egg yolks have been diluted with broth (as the label states) to make them easier for
baby to swallow. Special baby cereals are also much cheaper sources of iron than meat
or egg yolk.

The cereal is pre-cooked – all you have to do is pour a small amount of a liquid
(baby's formula or boiled milk) into a bowl or porringer and then stir in the desired
amount of the cereal. Make the mixture fairly thin at first – thin enough that it will
drop off the spoon slowly – as most babies prefer that consistency. After he has
learned to accept it, you can make the cereal a little thicker and increase the amount
up to two to four tablespoons (30-60 millilitres) or more according to his appetite.
Your doctor may suggest that you start with rice cereal. Usually baby is given it with
his mid-morning feeding. Probably he will take less of his formula or milk at this
feeding. Soon he will be ready for cereal twice a day – usually at his mid-morning and
evening feedings.

When baby is taking the rice cereal nicely, introduce him to the other special
baby cereals, such as those made of oats, barley, soybean flour or mixed grains (oats,
wheat and corn). Their textures and flavors vary – the rice and tasty soybean ones are

the smoothest in consistency. Several types contain dried fruit, which makes them general favorites. Thus baby has a choice and if he does not fancy one of them, put it away and buy another kind. You might try the rejected one again after a month or so; by then he may have forgotten his prejudice against it. If he has not, the rest of the family can eat it in some way. If your youngster continues to enjoy any or all of these cereals, keep on giving them to him, as babies and young children need plenty of iron in their meals. The oatmeal cereal has a slightly laxative effect which is helpful to some babies.

The first taste of cereal is a surprising experience for a baby. It feels and tastes quite different from his feedings, and he doesn't know how to manage it. Even the spoon feels odd. Ordinary-sized teaspoons are rather large for a small baby. A small shallow-bowled coffee or feeding spoon usually works better.

When he pushes his tongue up against his palate, as he does when he sucks on a nipple, some of the cereal runs out of his mouth. That does not mean that he dislikes it. He just does not know how to push it back in his mouth so that he can swallow it. Give him a small teaspoonful once a day until he learns the way to swallow it, which usually takes a week or more.

As he loves his milk feeding, you will probably have less trouble if you offer the cereal after the milk. Later on, as he becomes more expert and interested in the cereal, try it in the middle of his feeding and eventually at the beginning.

The occasional baby will not like cereals even though you have patiently tried to feed him. In which case, try him on strained fruit, which he will probably take. After he has accepted food from a spoon, try him again on cereals.

Fruits

Strained fruits are often added at about four months of age. As they are sweet, babies nearly always like them. Some physicians prefer to start strained vegetables first, especially if the baby is a hungry one, because he will probably accept them more readily if he has not previously tasted the pleasantly sweet fruits. Introducing vegetables first may help some children to prefer vegetables over fruits and hence avoid picky vegetable eaters.

A variety of factory-made strained fruits for babies are available, including apple sauce, blueberry, peach, pear, apricot, pineapple, prune and mixtures of several fruits. Initially, choose the ones made of a single fruit, as this will teach your baby to accept each distinctive flavor. Also, if one of the single fruits does not suit his digestive system (which is rare except for the laxative effect of prunes), you will know which one it is.

These strained or junior fruits contain very little vitamin C and many of them are thickened with tapioca.

If you are using the jarred baby foods, don't feed your baby directly out of the jar as the saliva and mouth bacteria on the spoon can cause food to spoil quickly even if it is put back in the refrigerator promptly. Instead, scoop what you need into a small dish and put the rest of the jar back in the refrigerator. If you treat it in this way, the same jar of fruit can be used safely for three days.

When baby has learned to take one fruit nicely, switch to another. Thus there will be an interval of some three days between each new fruit. Eventually baby will probably take one-third or half of a jar, most often after his cereal at his supper meal.

Vegetables

Strained vegetables are often introduced at midday around five months of age. Here again the darker yellow types like carrots, squash and sweet potatoes have the most vitamin A. Green beans and peas are quite good in this regard also, but none of the vegetables add more than a trace of vitamin C. Start with individual vegetables in preference to mixtures of several. Give your baby just a little the first day. If he takes it happily, increase the portion next day. If the jar is not finished by then, add it to a soup, stew or casserole, as strained vegetables don't keep as well as fruits.

What if your baby seems to dislike his first taste? Try him again with a little nibble the next day. If he still objects or feels even more strongly against it, forget about that vegetable for a month or so. Then try it again. He may have forgotten about his dislike by then. If he has not, you have other alternatives. As we mentioned earlier, vegetables are less attractive to a baby than fruits and there are advantages in starting vegetables first.

Nearly all babies dislike the vegetables belonging to the cabbage family (cabbage, cauliflower, Brussel sprouts, broccoli and kohlrabi), onions, parsnips, turnips and asparagus. Therefore they are not recommended, although you may try them (sieved at first) if you wish. Don't feed corn, unless you buy the strained baby food type. Many babies do not like potatoes, even when you make them smooth with added milk. They particularly dislike them when they are sticky. You might try a few nibbles of them at intervals. If baby is not interested, they are no great loss.

If you keep on using strained vegetables or junior chopped vegetables (which are almost smooth) for too long, your baby may object vigorously to lumpy food for months. Around eight months of age, gradually switch to mashed or sieved home-cooked vegetables, leaving more small lumps in them. Let him pick them up in his fingers if he so desires.

 Do not feed baby hard foods such as nuts. He cannot chew them and he may inhale them into his lungs which will make him very sick.

You may notice some undigested vegetable in baby's bowel movement; this is of no consequence. If, however, his movement is loose and contains mucus, stop giving him that vegetable temporarily.

If you have fed him beets, his movements will be red and his urine may also show a little of this color. Both of these changes are harmless.

Meat

Strained beef is usually introduced at the midday feeding at about six months of age. Occasionally meat is introduced at an earlier age, but if your baby is taking the special baby cereals twice a day, he will be receiving plenty of iron, B vitamins and protein. After he has become accustomed to meat, baby is usually offered half a small jar at his midday meal.

Most babies like it, but again, start gradually and if there is some left in the jar after two days, use it up in some other way. Introduce the other "baby" meats – lamb, veal, ham, pork (which is extremely lean), turkey, chicken, fish, liver and bacon – one after another. The last two – the most nutritionally valuable – often are unpopular with babies.

Egg

A small amount of soft-boiled yolk, a little hard-boiled yolk mashed smooth with milk or a nibble of bottled strained egg yolk is introduced at about eight months. If this is accepted, the amount is increased over the next few days, and then the white may be added too. Soft boiling the egg is usually the best way of preparing it, but you may prefer the bottled strained egg yolks.

If anyone in your family suffers from an allergic disease such as hay fever or asthma, delay introducing egg to baby's diet for a few months as it is a common cause of allergy.

Combination Dinners

Meat dinners cost considerably more than strained or junior "baby" vegetables or fruits. You know you are buying a meat dinner if the word "meat" comes before vegetable in the product name. However, if vegetable is first, then there is much less meat. Meat dinners are about one-third meat and two-thirds vegetables. If you use them, you have only to open one jar to give baby both his meat and vegetables. They have the disadvantage that your baby is not learning to accept a variety of different tasting foods. However, these products are very handy when you take baby away for the day because you have only one jar to carry.

A large variety of meat, poultry, egg and vegetable combinations – all of which are sometimes described as meat soups – are sold at the same price as straight vegetables. They contain little meat, poultry or egg. These products should be classed as alternatives for vegetables.

Puddings

Puddings may be added to baby's meals when he is about six months old, but they are the least important of his foods in his first year. If you are serving smooth puddings, such as yogurt or milk pudding (cornstarch), to the rest of the family, baby can have some instead of his usual fruit. Most of the packaged pudding mixes are very sweet but you may be able to find some to which you have to add your own sugar. Avoid over-sweetening.

If baby is already having eggs, he can have homemade custards. Jelly desserts made from gelatine are really just sweetened, colored sugar and water and have no nutritional value. Gelatine is the only poor type of animal protein. Such jellies are useful when baby is feeling sick and has lost his appetite as they are easily digested. Thus, you would be wise to serve them occasionally when he is well so that he becomes used to them. When he becomes older, jelly containing cut-up fruit served with custard sauce is a good dessert.

Making Baby Food

Mothers sometimes wonder if it would be cheaper and just as satisfactory to buy an electric blender and to purée home-cooked fruits, vegetables and meats for their babies. Making foods that are attractive to baby is quite a lot of trouble. You will need to freeze the individual servings promptly and keep them frozen until needed. In addition, each baby is fed puréed foods for only a short time.

Gradually, around four months, when baby is still on strained baby foods, you can start giving him small amounts of homemade puréed foods. They may include any food that can be easily puréed such as apple sauce, very ripe bananas, butternut squash, also strained and sieved canned fruits, such as peaches or pears.

At eight months, when baby is ready for "junior" foods – those that have a slightly lumpy texture – you can start mashing cooked vegetables.

Finger Foods

As soon as your baby has some teeth, he is ready to gnaw and suck a dry crust, zwieback or an arrowroot. Some brands of biscuits are especially rich in the B vitamins and were devised for baby feedings. Even though baby has no grinding teeth (molars), he can mash and swallow such foods. True, they are messy, but these and other finger foods stimulate his interest in feeding himself.

Sliced banana is another finger food. When he is about a year old you can give him small pieces of mild cheese that is neither hard nor crumbly. Keep an eye on him when he is working on these solid foods.

Drinking from a Cup

At six months or whenever he can hold a cup, try introducing baby to a plastic feeding cup (trainer cup) with a lid. Just put water in it at first, until he learns to raise it to his mouth. Later give him vitaminized apple juice, orange juice or milk in it. When he is a little older, a small plastic glass that his small hands can encircle will help him learn to feed himself.

Using a Spoon

Let baby have a spoon as soon as he shows interest. A short, straight-handled, small spoon with a shallow bowl is a good type, as he will grasp it from above at first. An unbreakable dish with a broad base and raised sides will make it easier for him to scoop up food such as thick cereal, but expect him to spill a great deal. A big plastic bib, possibly with sleeves as well, will lessen the mess. When he becomes tired he will usually let you help with another spoon.

When baby can sit up steadily – often at seven to eight months – a high chair is handy. Ensure that it meets safety standards. It should have a wide base to make it as steady as possible, a catch and a harness to prevent him from raising the tray. Hook-on chairs are the economical alternative to the high chair. However there have been accidents reported with these devices and they generally occur with larger babies – any child weighing more that nine kilograms (20 pounds) should not use a hook-on chair and may be ready for a booster seat.

Menus

Your child's appetite will vary from day to day and from meal to meal. Although one meal is eaten well, he may play with the next. Do not try to force a child to eat. His appetite will come when he is hungry, and this may well be after he has eaten very little at the preceding meal. Fresh air and sunshine help to stimulate your child's appetite. If he is overtired, he may prefer to sleep and then eat.

Sample Menus*

From 9 to 12 months

*Please note that the times and amounts cited below may vary greatly from child to child and are meant to be general guidelines only.

7 - 8 a.m. Special baby cereals made up with milk
Toast, zwieback or a plain muffin
Milk

10 a.m. Two to four ounces (60-120 millilitres) of orange juice or
Vitaminized apple juice
Vitamins if prescribed by your doctor

12 - 1 p.m. 1/2 jar of strained or junior meat (beef, chicken, turkey,
lamb, pork, fish, etc.)
1/3 to 1/2 jar of junior or mashed vegetable
(such as carrots, green peas or beans, squash, sweet potatoes)
1/3 to 1/2 jar of junior fruit (apple sauce, peach, pear, apricot) or a
portion of mashed ripe banana or a milk dessert such as yogurt, rice,
milk pudding (cornstarch) or custard
Milk

3 - 4 p.m.	Orange or vitaminized apple juice (if not given at 10 a.m.)
	A plain cookie (arrowroot)
5 - 7 p.m.	Special baby cereal made up with milk
	1/3 to 1/2 jar of junior or mashed fruit
	Milk
10 - 11 p.m.	Some children require milk at this time; others will sleep
	through the night after their evening meal

From 12 Months to 2 Years

7 - 8 a.m.	Special baby cereal or a dark whole grain cereal
	Toast, zwieback or muffin
	Milk
10 a.m.	Orange juice or vitaminized apple juice, with possibly a plain
	cookie, provided he is hungry again by lunch time
	Vitamins if prescribed by your doctor
12 - 1 p.m.	One to two tablespoons (15-30 millilitres) of minced beef or chicken
	or lamb or other lean meat or boned fish
	Small servings of mashed potatoes and vegetables
	A small serving of a milk or rice pudding or custard
	Milk, water or fruit juice
3 - 4 p.m.	Fruit juice or cut-up peeled apple or plain cookie
5 - 6 p.m.	A scrambled or poached egg with toast, bread and cheese or a
	soup, preferably creamed or thickened with baby cereal
	Cut-up or mashed fruit
	Milk

If the mid-morning snack takes away his appetite for his noon meal, stop giving it. His afternoons are usually longer, and a snack when he wakes from his nap often helps him to get through the rest of the day happily.

Around two years of age your child should be able to join the family and have small servings of the food served. His foods should be plain, not fried and preferably not too highly seasoned or spiced. They should be finely cut-up for him. Any food that cannot be cut easily, such as nuts, should not be given to a young child. If the child wishes to try your adult foods, give him very small helpings until he is older. In this way he becomes part of the family and his experience with different tastes is widened, yet he himself has a simple diet.

Be Flexible

Babies vary greatly in their reactions to new foods. Some, after this first learning process is over, will accept any new food readily. Others have to be gradually introduced to practically every new taste and texture. Although such a baby may seem averse to the food at first, he may later become very fond of it. Do not hurry him or try to coax or force him to take it. This does not help at all and often makes him more cautious and suspicious. Even if your baby is not getting a variety of foods, he is still eating well. Follow your doctor's directions and, within reason, play along with your baby's whims.

Allow some leeway in baby's feeding schedule and let him decide how much of a food he wants from day to day. His appetite will vary just as yours does. His food habits are developing, so guide him to a wide variety of the more nutritious foods. If he refuses his meal, offer him water and wait until he is hungry. He may be developing a cold or some other upset or he may just not want to eat. If his lack of appetite is due to some real cause, it will soon become evident and if it is at all serious, consult with your doctor.

HOW TO INTRODUCE NEW FOODS**

As food habits develop, guide your baby to a wide variety of nutritious foods.

- Introduce new foods, one at a time, about a week apart, so if your baby develops an intolerance, it will be easy to identify the food responsible.
- Foods should be offered by spoon. Begin with small amounts (about a teaspoon) and gradually increase the amount.
- New foods should be served unmixed as a way of teaching your baby to recognize and enjoy basic food flavors.
- Offer new foods when your baby is in good spirits.
- Your baby's taste buds are sensitive enough to enjoy the subtle flavors in food. Adding butter, margarine, salt, sugar or other sweeteners is unnecessary.
- Coaxing or forcing a baby to eat a particular food may increase your baby's dislike for it. If your baby refuses a new food, offer it again in a few days.

** These suggestions were provided by the Ontario Ministry of Health.

10

The Well-Dressed Tot

When your baby becomes more mobile he may move surprisingly quickly. For a while, you can safely leave him in his cot or playpen or, under suitable conditions, on the floor. As long as he will play happily and later practise walking in his playpen (often watching or "talking" to you as well), you would be wise to keep on using it. Once he is on the loose, it will be a constant job for someone to protect him from hazards even though your home is baby-proof. Until he is an accomplished walker, he will often fall, but he is close to the floor and usually lands on his well-padded behind.

With the move to the floor, which is cooler and dirtier, and when he begins to play outside, you will want heavier and sturdier clothing. Corduroy and cotton jeans both wear and wash well. Many of the stretch synthetic suits, although not as warm as the heavier fabrics, are easier to launder. As he grows older and shows an interest in dressing himself (between two and three years of age) buy garments that pull on and off easily or that have a strong zipper at the front that he can manage. Later he will gradually learn how to button garments.

Rain Wear

It is wise to have waterproof clothing for a walking child. When the weather is a little wet, he will still enjoy being outside. However, he will fall in the mud. Rain wear that will go over heavy clothing is necessary. As rain gear will get roughed up, become badly soiled or even permanently stained and will likely be outgrown in a year, it is not worth spending a lot of money on it.

Rubber boots are an essential, as every puddle, regardless of size, is a temptation.

Foot Wear

Once baby starts to stand, have him fitted for soft shoes. As his shoes need to be changed every three to six months at first, do not buy more than one pair at a time. Boots are probably best because they give more support to his ankles and he cannot pull them off. When he begins to run outside, a firmer sole will be needed. Most children's shoe stores are co-operative in checking the fit of shoes, even when the child does not need new ones. Until he is about two years old, the pliability of his foot bones and the presence of a pad of fat on his soles make his feet look flat, but they are not really flat. Boots or shoes give ample support.

Training Pants

Some time between one and two years of age when you notice that every now and then he is dry for two hours at a stretch, you will need training pants for your youngster, as they encourage him to stay dry. They are made of terry cloth or multiple layers of cotton. You may have some on hand that you used as soakers during your baby's first month. Training pants have the advantage of being relatively easy to push down when an urgent call for "potty" comes.

Sleep Wear

The choice of sleep wear is based on preference more than anything else. Your child will eventually sleep in a conventionally made bed, so it is wise to move in that direction as soon as he is able to sleep soundly.

Many children are so restless at night that they will not keep any covers on. For them, sleepers with arms, legs and feet are ideal. They allow a child to move about but keep baby warm on cool nights. Heavy, cotton knit, two-piece sleepers are fine for most babies. They are warm and so absorbent that they usually save bedding from becoming soaked. Most have feet in them – a good idea as children won't bother with slippers until they are much older. Nightwear should be flame-resistant.

Daytime Clothes

The choice of clothes for a boy or girl is almost endless. Children love bright colors. They also want to be dressed like their playmates. Your child may prefer one garment to another, often because an older brother or sister or one of his parents has a similar outfit.

You will be cautious about exposing your toddler's bare skin to the summer sun. All children need protection from the sun. During the summer months choose some light, cool clothing that will cover much of his skin. Close to the water, the sun's rays may feel cool but they can cause sunburn or possibly even sunstroke if a small child is exposed to them for too long. The water reflects the ultraviolet rays that are responsible for the burning and skin changes that may cause trouble later in life. In winter, the reflection of the sun off the snow will cause a burn unless protection of the skin is provided. Sun screen lotions with a high sun protection factor (SPF) may be used. Light-weight clothing which covers the arms and legs will be necessary during the summer months.

During the middle of the day or during prolonged exposure to sunlight, a sun hat is advisable for both boys and girls.

11

Feeding Preschool Children

Most babies are quite plump, but healthy preschool youngsters are much slimmer, and many mothers worry about this normal change in shape. These youngsters are not becoming thin – they are just growing more slowly in weight and, as you know, they are very active. Do not over-feed them, which is easy to do with docile youngsters. At the end of this chapter we will give you some advice regarding the diet of an overweight preschool child.

Daily Menu

During the day some food from each of the following groups is recommended. In most cases we have not specified the amounts, as many preschoolers have relatively small appetites because their rate of growth is rather slow. It is a good idea to give your child less than you think he could eat and let him ask for more. Also, there is no special time in the day for these foods, although frequent snacking is a disadvantage, especially if the snacks are sweet or starchy.

Milk – 20 ounces (600 millilitres) – 2-1/2 measuring cups
Fruits or juices – two servings, one high in vitamin C
Vegetables – two or more servings, one green or yellow if possible
Cereals and bread – a whole grain or enriched porridge or cereal; bread, rolls or
    muffins
Meat, poultry, fish, eggs or cheese – two servings or more

Vitamin D (400 I.U.) – either in milk, drops or chewable tablets

You will notice that sugar, jam, marmalade, jelly, honey, syrup, candy, cake, cookies and pie are not mentioned. They are all non-essential foods – they add little but calories, which is the least you can say about any food. They are sometimes called empty calories. All the other foods give your child calories (energy) and something else as well. Another objection to sweets is that they satisfy the appetite quickly. Thus, if sweets are eaten early in a meal or shortly before it, your child is likely to have a poor appetite.

Broadening Food Choices

1. Fresh Fruits Galore

If he has a sturdy digestion, you can start giving your child ripe raw fruits such as apples, bananas, oranges, apricots, plums and seedless grapes during his second year. Always wash them and preferably peel them until he is three to four years old.

The child will know the taste from the cooked puréed fruits which he has been receiving for several months. The consistency is right for babies: the fibre has been softened in cooking. They are nearly always tolerated well.

As the child becomes older he must learn to chew. Fresh fruit gives him this opportunity. The increased fibre in fresh fruits (and vegetables) will keep his stool soft and his bowel movements regular.

As the food has not been cooked, vitamins have not been destroyed. However, parents of children with allergies or sensitive bowels will need to introduce fresh fruits and vegetables more cautiously. The cooking process will tend to lessen problems for them.

Apples are usually enjoyed, and they are very well tolerated. You could try him on some well-washed pitted cherries and some mashed blueberries. Fresh strawberries and melons may be tried but tend to be less acceptable to young children. If the rest of the family is having one of these foods and he wants to try it, let him have a little taste.

2. Cereals and Bread

If your youngster still likes one or more of the baby cereals, keep on using them for breakfast or even as a supper dish. Home-cooked rolled oats, either quick or regular, have the highest food value and are much cheaper than all the ordinary porridges. The quick type takes little time to cook and many children like it, believe it or not. The other dark (whole grain) home-cooked cereals are also excellent. The white cereals, such as semolina, farina and white wheatlets, are not as nutritious because a high percentage of their food valuable has been removed in the milling.

The various shredded wheat products are good and are the cheapest of the ready-to-eat cereals, but the vigorous processing that they undergo robs them of half their vitamin Bl (thiamine). Their ingredients are listed on the packaging. If sugar is mentioned first, you know that cereal contains more sugar than any other ingredient.

The better types are enriched with two or three of the major B vitamins and some have had iron added as well. Bran flakes have the most laxative effect and they are useful if your child tends to be constipated. Those with raisins added are usually popular.

Enriched white bread, whole wheat, oatmeal or other dark breads can replace the cereals. Macaroni or other pasta products that contain added vitamins (see label) are far higher in the B vitamins, sometimes also in iron, than the ordinary types.

3. Meat, Poultry, Fish and Cheese

All of these foods are rich in excellent proteins and B vitamins and, with the exception of cheese, they all add valuable amounts of iron to your child's meals. Tests have shown that children who eat generous amounts of these foods are more likely to have better growth, to suffer from fewer infections and to have richer blood. These foods also help to keep them from getting very hungry between meals, which reduces their tendency to snack. For older children, peanut butter, which is high in both fat and protein, is a good alternative.

Most young children have difficulty in chewing firm meat such as roasts or steaks. Mincing or chopping makes them more manageable, and stewing ground meat or cooking it in the top of the double boiler makes it softer. Although wieners (hot dogs or frankfurters) contain little more than half as much protein and three times the amount of fat as lean beef hamburgers, most children eat them with great relish. They are highly spiced and salted but this adds no nutritional value. If your youngster likes them, let him have them.

4. High Fat Foods

Many children enjoy high fat foods, such as fried potatoes, commercial hamburger, pie or peanut butter but you would be wise to limit them.

As diets with a high fat content have been associated with an increased incidence of heart disease later in life, there have been efforts to reduce the level of fat consumed in Canadian diets.

5. Variety in Vegetables

Preschool youngsters can be offered a large variety in vegetables but usually do not like the gas-forming vegetables such as cabbage, turnips, onions and baked beans.

Do not give them ordinary canned or boiled corn until they are at least two years old, as they may choke on the kernels. After that age you can try them on a little canned corn or some kernels cut off boiled corn. If at three or four years you give them corn on the cob, cut down the centres of the kernels with a sharp knife. Then when they chew on the cob, they obtain most of the soft contents of the kernels.

If your youngster has good digestion, you can give him small salads towards the end of his second year. Lettuce, celery (preferably green), grated carrots, peeled tomatoes, cottage cheese, raw apple or banana and cut-up oranges are possible ingredients. He probably will not want any dressing. Mayonnaise or the usual salad dressings that contain oil are unsuitable, as they are high in fat. Try some boiled or low calorie dressings.

Encouraging Good Eating

Keeping your child's helpings small is tremendously important as large helpings discourage him. Your toddler depends on you to judge his capacity. If he does not eat as much as you had hoped, do not try to coax, scold or wheedle him. He soon realizes that refusing some of his food disturbs you, and without any conscious thought on his part, he may find that spurning some of his food is more fun than eating it. Dawdling usually means he is not hungry – ignore it. After half an hour remove the remains of his meal without comment. All this advice is easier to talk about than to follow, but it is worthwhile to consider.

It is also wise to have him play quietly, look at a book or television or listen to records for half an hour or so before his meal is due. He will eat better if he is not tired. Announcing a few minutes in advance that his meal will be served is also helpful.

When you take your child shopping, could he help choose some of his own food? If he says he wants a certain item, especially if he can help prepare it, he will usually enjoy eating it. Giving him little tastes of adult foods encourages him to accept new flavors. For many people, eating habits developed in childhood persist for years.

Children who learn to enjoy a wide variety of different foods are more socially acceptable and are better off in terms of health as well. Besides, varied meals are more fun. Teach your child patiently and with ingenuity to eat all kinds of foods, although he will no doubt like some more than others. Inviting your child's friends in for meals and having him visit them, often encourages him to try new foods.

As a general rule, preschoolers do not like casseroles or creamed dishes that contain several different foods. Possibly they suspect you are trying to hide something they do not like. They often dislike stringy foods like spinach, green and wax beans or celery.

By the age of two, most youngsters are ready for a fork. In his fifth year, if you give him a blunt knife for spreads, it will probably increase his interest in his meals.

If his appetite is regularly small, try gradually switching to two percent milk or even skim milk instead of whole, and cut down the butter or margarine on his bread.

Snacking

Many preschool youngsters get through the day more happily if they have a small glass of fruit or tomato juice in the middle of the morning and a piece of banana or apple, a plain cookie or some similar food when they get up after their midday nap. Without a snack they often become too tired and hungry in the latter part of the afternoon.

When your child is thirsty between meals, encourage him to drink water. Today, many children are given or help themselves to bought or home-prepared sweet drinks. They practically never use water as a thirst quencher. This is a pity for several reasons. Not surprisingly, such sweet drinks often take the edge off their appetite. In addition, such amounts may cause diarrhea in a young child.

Other small youngsters frequently munch candy, popcorn, corn chips, potato chips and even peanuts between meals. It is best to keep such attractive foods out of sight or reach. Candy or sweets between meals has been proved to increase tooth decay. Give treats only after meals and preferably not too frequently. With your first child this will not be too difficult; if he has not tasted candy he will not cry for it.

Psychologists feel that sweet foods such as candies, desserts, cakes and cookies should not be used as rewards, as this makes them appear very desirable, which they are not. Thus, they say, the time-honored practice of giving a child his dessert only if he has eaten his first course is a bad one.

Potential Problems

Meeting Milk Requirements

Do not give a small youngster too much milk. If he takes 20 ounces (600 millilitres) of milk in any form each day, that is plenty. If he takes too much, he may not be hungry for his other good foods. On the other hand, some children turn against milk, which may be worrisome. You can conceal a good deal of milk by serving it in other ways – in milk puddings, yogurt, cheese, cottage cheese, ice cream and ice milk. You can use it instead of water for making home-cooked porridge or for mixing up "baby" cereals. Often a child will drink more if he can pour his own from a small pitcher or teapot or if he can take it through a straw. Try putting a sticker under the bottom of his glass which he is unable to see until it is empty.

Two Food Child

How do you handle the child who will eat only hamburg and bananas or some other combination of two or three foods? The following plan has been thoroughly tested and it works. Give the youngster the full meal you had planned, including a small amount of hamburg and banana. If he eats only the last two items, he will feel mildly hungry after it. Do not give him anything to eat until the next meal, which again features small amounts of his two favorites but with other suitable foods as well. If you keep up this routine regularly for three days, he will usually begin to sample some of the other foods. By the fifth day of this regime he will be eating all the foods in his meals and enjoying them.

Your major challenge will be to refuse him any other food or snack between meals. Do not think that such partial starvation will hurt him. Similarly, if he wants only peanut butter and jelly sandwiches for lunch, after five days of them he will be ready for a change.

Vegetable Hater

Other young children turn completely against vegetables. For the time being replace them with more fruits, which have similar food value. As time goes on, try introducing small amounts of the vegetables that they previously found most appetizing.

Overweight Preschoolers

Fat children are handicapped both socially and physically, and they very often become fat adults. During the preschool period you are better able to control their meals than you will be later on. If your child is too heavy, and after consulting with your doctor, you will help him a great deal if you gradually substitute lower calorie foods for the higher calorie ones.

The idea is to decrease his gain in weight but not his gain in height, so that he becomes more suitably proportioned. Give him raw vegetables instead of cooked ones because they are more filling and he will eat less of them. Use raw fruits which are largely water, instead of sweetened canned, frozen or cooked ones. You might omit bananas, as they are the highest in calories. Gradually switch from whole milk to two per cent and eventually to skim milk. Cut back on his sweet foods and bread. Give him very little margarine or butter. Choose the leanest meats you can buy, cutting off any fat you can see. Avoid cooking meat or any other food in fat.

Encourage the youngster to exercise, especially some sport that he seems to enjoy. This may mean coaching him or enroling him in classes where he can be taught a sport such as skating or swimming.

12

Sleep
and
Exercise

In healthy children, much growth occurs and in sick children, considerable healing takes place during sleep. The amount of daily sleep required by individuals varies widely. A sound sleep often follows a routine of quiet relaxation, and may be affected by the emotional and physical surroundings of the child.

Psychologists have recognized two kinds of alternating sleep – REM (rapid eye movement), and non-REM. The deepest, most sound sleep, occurs in the latter. It can be a problem to waken someone in this stage of sleep. REM sleep is a restless form of sleep, with body movements, dreaming, groaning or vocalizing, less regular breathing and heart rate, and, of course, rapid eye movement. Monitors show a different pattern during these normal sleep rhythms.

Babies

A young baby sleeps a great deal. However, it is not possible for him to sleep 22 hours a day, as is sometimes stated, because his routine care alone (feeding, changing and bathing) takes at least four hours of the 24. Babies usually go to sleep after their meals. If they are handled much after a feeding, they are likely to bring up some food. Therefore, change baby's diaper and get him ready for sleep as much as possible before you feed him. After he has eaten what he wants, hold him on your lap or against your shoulder and rub his back gently to help him bring up any gas. Do not hurry him too much during this "bubbling" process. Chat to him or sing lullabies to him; they are worth relearning. Then change him again, if necessary, put him into bed, cover him up, open the window (if weather permits), turn out the light and leave him to go to sleep.

In the newborn period, about 50 per cent of baby's sleep is REM. When he is first put to bed his initial sleep is of the REM variety. (In an adult the REM sleep totals 20-25 per cent of sleep and the first sleep is non-REM.)

After one month of age, the temperature of his room at night in the wintertime can be gradually reduced to 65 Fahrenheit (18 Celsius), if you wish.

It is not necessary to walk about on tiptoes or to keep the rest of the household quiet after you put baby to sleep. Training him to sleep through noise will be to his advantage, both now and later.

As for baby's bed, his mattress should be firm and his bed clothes warm but not too heavy. He should not have a pillow. Tuck the covers in loosely so that he can exercise himself by squirming and kicking. As we have mentioned, many older babies are so restless at night that you will need to put them into infant sleeping bags or sleepers to keep them warm enough.

After the first few months, when baby begins to stay awake longer, encourage him to have his waking period between 4 p.m. and 6 p.m. If he sleeps past 4 p.m. he will be less likely to fall asleep after his evening feeding.

It is normal for some breast-fed babies to continue waking at night for feedings. In the last half of the first year, most babies sleep at least 14 hours each day – this includes both a morning and afternoon nap. When your baby is a one year-old, you can start gradually training him to have only one nap after his noon meal. When there is a change in baby's routine, you can run into a few difficulties, so it is best to do so gradually. For instance, baby may not be able to stay awake all morning if he has his breakfast at 7:30 a.m. or he may be so sleepy that he cannot eat his noon meal properly. In this case you would be wise to give him his noon meal earlier for a week or so and then gradually lengthen out the morning until he is on the usual three meals a day schedule. His afternoon nap follows his noon meal promptly, so that he is awake in the latter part of the afternoon.

Try to accommodate yourself to your baby's routine as much as you can. If you do not introduce changes too suddenly, you can usually rearrange his program so that it suits both of you. Routines, as long as they are not too rigid, make everyone happier.

Crying

As mentioned earlier, if you hold your baby, or put him in his infant lounger for five minutes or so after his feeding, he will often go to sleep faster than if you put him to bed right away. However, it is not unusual for him to cry a little after you tuck him in. If he keeps it up for some time, you will go to see what, if anything, is bothering him. He may have some more bubbles in his stomach, which you will help him bring up if you can. If he is wet or dirty, you will change him, of course.

Sometimes, nothing seems to settle baby. If he is not getting enough food, he may cry more and not sleep as much as usual, but on the other hand, he may be equally restless and noisy if he is eating too much and gaining very quickly.

Crying, especially by a young baby, is very apt to bother a mother who is breast-feeding him. Her first thought is that she is not producing enough milk, but she can usually be reassured if baby is gaining weight and there are lots of wet diapers.

A healthy baby usually cries loudly. Some mothers and nurses feel that they can tell from his cry whether he is hungry, uncomfortable or just unhappy. Others similarly experienced admit that they usually cannot be sure why he is crying.

A sick baby often cries weakly and whimpers. A hurt cry has the sound of someone in pain and you will react quickly. Occasionally baby's sleep is disturbed when he is cutting teeth. It helps to remember that crying may be due to many different causes, including baby's dislike of being alone.

If your baby's crying is a problem, talk to your doctor about it. She may want you to come to her office, where she can weigh your baby, and examine him.

Preschool Children (two to five years of age)

Most preschool youngsters sleep at least 11 hours at night, and until their fifth birthday, they will usually sleep in the early afternoon if they are given a chance to do so. A regular bed time at night, with perhaps 20 minutes' leeway, is best.

Warn him of his approaching bed time so that he can finish what he is doing. Noisy games, romps, exciting stories or television just before bed time are unwise. If he goes to bed in an excited frame of mind he is likely to have a disturbed night. On the contrary, a quiet story or game calms him down and helps him to drop off quickly.

See that your child's preparations for bed are complete – that he goes to the toilet, washes or has a bath, cleans his teeth and has a drink (if he has learned not to wet the bed) before you tuck him in. Unless all this routine is followed, he will no doubt hop out of bed to finish it himself, or will demand further attention, which may be annoying.

Plenty of vigorous play outdoors will help your child both to sleep and to eat well. Indigestion or some minor physical defect occasionally may prevent him from sleeping soundly. Healthy children sleep well, although most of them twist and turn a great deal.

If your child does not sleep well, have him checked by your doctor to ensure that there is no physical reason for it.

Fear of the Dark

Many youngsters are afraid of the dark, and this fear can originate in different ways. Often it is due to their dislike of being alone and inability to see familiar objects about them.

Fear may be caused by a casual remark by some adult, such as, "It's getting dark, I must hurry home." Lying in bed, a child may brood on this statement.

Occasionally, though rarely now, a child is put in a dark room as punishment and is frightened as a result.

What can you do to help your child get over this fear? Leaving a light on in the hall or a nearby room is quite helpful. Staying in the room for a while, perhaps telling a story or chatting with him, after you turn out the light will help to reassure him. Imaginative children may be worried by creaking beds, flapping blinds or flickering shadows. Reassure them by showing them what is making these noises or shadows. If you yourself are afraid of staying alone in the house at night, you will likely pass this fear on to your child. Talk about burglars, fires at night or other such terrifying possibilities can very seriously disturb a child and should be avoided. Often he hears and understands much more than you suspect. If he seems unusually upset, try to get him to tell you what is troubling him.

Show him the stars and the moon; if in the country let him listen to the sounds of the night; he will then feel the beauty of the night.

Naps for Preschoolers

An afternoon nap helps these energetic youngsters to get through the day happily. During his third and fourth year a child will likely go to sleep regularly if you put him to bed in a darkened room. If he lies still he is more apt to drop off. It is a good idea to give him his noon meal relatively early so he will be awake and out to play by 3 p.m.

In his fifth year he will probably sleep on some days but not on others. Nevertheless, you would be wise to have him lie down quietly for at least half an hour with a picture book or a cuddly toy. Some preschool youngsters who do not take naps are often very tired and cross by supper time.

School Children

The amount of sleep needed by these children varies from child to child. If you have to wake him up in the morning, or if he gets tired or irritable in the late afternoon and evening, he is probably not getting enough sleep. Most of these youngsters need from 10-11 hours of sleep. Exciting television programs or games are best avoided shortly before bedtime. Children who break these rules may shout out at night and sleep restlessly.

It is a good plan to talk over the day's activities with your child at bedtime. If he has had any trouble this is an ideal time to discuss it. This practice will help him to settle down peacefully.

Having a child lie down occasionally, possibly with a book, for half an hour after lunch may be necessary.

Routines can be made to suit the needs of the individual child.

Exercise

Babies and children seem to take the exercise which they need if given the opportunity. Try to arrange play times and defined areas – both indoor and outdoor – in which these activities can be carried out daily.

One to Five Months

The only way a young baby can exercise himself is by crying, kicking and waving his arms about. It is not surprising that he wriggles and kicks when you carry him. He needs to have a reasonable amount of such exercise in order to expand his lungs and develop his muscles.

A good way to give him more exercise is to lay him in the middle of a wide, firm bed every day. Take off all his clothes except his shirt and diaper. Most babies quite obviously enjoy this chance to kick their legs and wave their arms about, but keep your eye on him so that he will not roll to the edge and fall off.

Over Five Months

It is helpful to give baby some exercises every day from the time he reaches five months of age until he learns to crawl or stand. Here are two simple exercises. Lay baby on his back on a blanket or a table with his legs towards you. Grasp his hands with your own and pull him gently up into a sitting position. He will help all he can, and this will exercise his arm, shoulder, neck and abdominal muscles. Repeat this exercise two or three times a day.

The second exercise is even simpler. Baby is placed in the same position as described above. Then you simply grasp both his feet and gently prevent him from moving them. This usually stimulates him to kick. Hold his legs for one to two minutes – this exercise strengthens his leg muscles.

It is quite all right to prop up babies of this age in a semi-sitting position providing they enjoy it.

Physical Growth
13

T he changes that take place at birth are immense. From a protected, constant environment in the womb, the infant is born into new and more variable surroundings. The newborn period is a critical one in a child's life.

If your baby is born at home, his room should be very warm, approximately 75 Fahrenheit (24 Celsius), for the first week or so. Watch him carefully for any blueness or difficulty in breathing. If anything else abnormal is noticed, consult your doctor immediately. No person with a cold, sore throat or infection of any kind should look after or come near a newborn baby.

As it takes two or three days for the breast milk to become established, a baby loses weight during this period. Bottle-fed babies lose weight also. This weight loss is of no consequence. Babies are often back to their birth weight by 10 to 14 days; some do not achieve this until three weeks of age.

Weight Gain in the First Year

During the remainder of their first three months, normal babies gain in weight rapidly – usually at the rate of six to seven ounces (168-198 grams) per week. In the next three months they add approximately four to six ounces (112-168 grams) of weight each week, so that by the age of five months they have commonly doubled their birth weight. During the second six months, the rate of gain usually drops to three ounces (84 grams) per week, which is still considerable. Consequently, by one year of age your baby will likely have tripled his birth weight. Babies that are heavier than the average at birth usually remain heavier than average all through the first year. Similarly, those that are lighter often remain lighter than the average during their first 12 months. A normal baby's rate of gain is more important than his total weight.

If you like, although it is not necessary, you can weigh your baby once a week from the age of two weeks to six months but this will not take the place of regular visits to your doctor's office. Use a beam type of scale that reads in grams, or half ounces. It is best to weigh your baby without his clothes, just before you bathe him.

Growth in Length

The weight of a baby is a more accurate gauge of his progress than his increase in length or height. However, it is interesting to know that most babies are about 20 inches (50 centimetres) long at birth and that they grow 10 inches (25 centimetres) in height in their first year. At two years of age they usually are close to 35 inches (88 centimetres) tall.

Changing Proportions

At birth, a baby's head is large compared to the size of his whole body. His head is about 13 1/2 inches (34 centimetres) in circumference at birth. It grows a good deal during the first year to keep pace with the rapid increase in size of his brain. By one year of age his head is about 18 inches (45 centimetres) around.

His chest is a little smaller in circumference than his head at birth, but by the age of one year, they are about the same size. From then on his chest becomes the larger of the two.

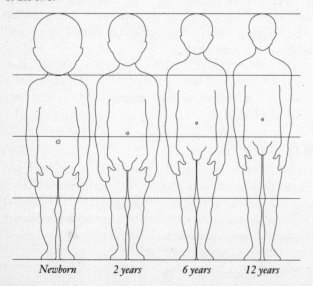

As your child grows his proportions will change as the graph illustrates.

Newborn   2 years   6 years   12 years

Soft Spots or Fontanelles of the Head

A newborn has two definite soft spots or fontanelles on the top of his head. The larger anterior fontanelle, near the front of his head, is roughly diamond-shaped, and its size varies greatly in different babies. The actual size is of no consequence. These soft spots are areas where the bones of the skull have not grown together; instead of bone, a very tough membrane is present. This membrane is very strong and you need not think that you can do any damage to your baby's brain by washing that part of his head vigorously. Some people are afraid to do this, and this may be one reason why babies sometimes develop cradle cap. As your baby gets older the bones gradually grow into the membrane of the fontanelles and finally these areas are completely closed by bone and are no longer soft. The larger anterior fontanelle is normally closed some time between the ninth and sixteenth month. If it stays open after the age of two years, it is abnormal.

There are two soft spots, called fontanelles, on the top of his head

The posterior fontanelle is much smaller and is roughly triangular in shape. As you would expect, it is towards the back of the head. It normally closes between six and eight weeks.

Head Shape

Not infrequently, a baby's head is somewhat misshapen when he is born due to pressure in the relatively narrow birth canal. During the first month or so, this odd shape disappears spontaneously.

The bones of a baby's head are relatively thin. If he lies on one side continuously, his head will become flattened on that side. This does not cause any injury to him and it will disappear later on. To prevent this change, lay him on his right and left sides alternately.

Bowed Legs

Normal babies have a slight outward curve in their legs. This is often more apparent than real, as many babies lie with their knees wide apart and with the soles of their feet opposite each other.

Preschoolers

By the time your child is two years old he usually weighs nearly four times his birth weight. When he is four years old he will weigh roughly five times his birth weight. During this preschool period, which extends from two to five years of age, he is therefore growing rather slowly. In fact, it is his slowest period of growth. His girth seems not to change. Also, his extreme activity at this age works against his weight gain. As a result, many parents notice that their chubby baby has become a relatively slight preschool child. However, provided your child is growing continuously in height and weight and your physician finds no sign of physical defects when he is examined every six months you do not need to worry.

Because of their slow rate of growth, these youngsters usually do not eat large meals. Forcing or urging them to eat more than they want is often the cause of eating problems. As these youngsters are so energetic, provide them with as much free play space as possible and appropriate toys.

School Children

From five to 10 years of age children gain approximately two inches (five centimetres) in height and six pounds (2.7 kilograms) in weight each year. Boys are a little larger than girls. During the first year or two of this period there is a considerable increase in their muscular development. Many communities have centres for physical activity. If it is difficult to find safe play areas in your community it might be wise to make inquiries about the location of such centres. Plenty of vigorous play is needed by these youngsters as well as sound sleeps at night.

14

Learning Skills

To direct a child to adulthood by daily guidance is a long winding road. At times, the anticipated goal of a happy, self-reliant, intelligent and industrious adult seems to be forgotten in the numerous crises that develop.

Do all you can to keep yourself in good health. If you are not feeling well and not pleased with life in general, it will reflect in your handling of the child. Discuss problems of discipline with your partner, so that you will be in agreement. This way your child cannot play one parent against the other.

Protecting a young child from physical hazards seems an almost endless job. Until a toddler understands the meaning of hurt, cut and burn, often through minor experiences, it is a big chore for someone to guide him. Often a small injury will teach him to be more cautious.

Your protectiveness must be lessened as the child learns safety rules and becomes ready to go on to new experiences. This is one of the reasons why constant care from a concerned person contributes to a child's growth. There is so much to be learned! How he handles the multitude of new experiences in infancy and early childhood may set a pattern that can last a lifetime. If he seems fearful of new situations, he should be given many pleasant surprises so that he will perhaps approach the next novel experience with enthusiasm.

Random Thought

The thoughts of a young child are, for the most part, poorly expressed. You may suspect a bit of what he is thinking, or you may have a particularly communicative child who gives you more than the usual number of clues. If you listen to a child playing imaginatively with his toys, at the preschool level and a little older, you will occasionally be able to enjoy his play activity as he assigns roles to different playthings and objects. A simple drama may unfold about your child's thoughts.

He forms many accurate ideas, but others must be corrected at the time so that he can widen his understanding. Thoughts about life, growth and death are expressed by a youngster between five and 10 years and they are factual to him. Help him to understand the world around him. Try to put yourself in his place – it will help you to understand his ideas and needs.

Discipline

A child has to learn self-discipline. Often this can be encouraged by his play activities. Providing toys with which he can build or shape an object to his satisfaction is the beginning of a productive life. They do not have to be expensive; they may be homemade. As well, common household objects often are used by him in an imaginative and constructive fashion.

It does help in training a child to give him his own play areas inside and outside that are safe for his age and development. Here he has greater scope to express himself.

A child learns slowly, and there are often slip-ups in his performance that are best ignored. Avoid allowing him to do something one day and not the next, confusing him and putting him under an unnecessary strain. Be sure that he obeys you when you have concerns for his safety. Consistency and firmness are essential, especially the former.

Corporal punishment is rarely, if indeed ever, needed. It should not be used to express the adult's anger or frustration with the problem relating to the child's behavior. Also, later on he may use aggression and anger when he is not able to achieve what he wishes through more acceptable means such as give and take, sharing and being a considerate friend to his playmate. You can usually discipline him quite effectively without spankings or slaps. If he cannot play with other children peaceably, removing him from the group to play in another area will help him to adjust more slowly to group activities.

Temper Tantrums

Nearly all children have temper tantrums in the preschool period. In your child's training he will frequently have to do things he does not want to do and sometimes, too, he cannot do things he wants to do. Consequently, he will be frustrated and angry. He may show his anger by crying, kicking and shouting. By throwing a temper tantrum, he hopes to have his way. You will set a precedent if you give in to him, so be firm. Remember that he is a child and that this is the juvenile way of expressing anger. After the tantrum is over, he may be quite co-operative and do what was originally asked of him. He may also be tired and want to sleep. In fact, fatigue is often a major factor in causing tantrums. Don't discuss the difficulty that set off the tantrum at this time; take time to explain the situation to him later in the day. If the same situation crops up again, be consistent. He will gradually accept his frustrations better and become more co-operative and understanding.

There are several precautions that will minimize the number of tantrums. You can often divert him if you see trouble brewing. Remove from sight things that he would like to have but cannot. Put requests in such a way that he will do what you ask agreeably. Try to say "yes" to his requests if they are not unreasonable. At times you will have to follow some line of action that seems senseless to you but which is important to your child. However, if there is danger in a particular type of play, then be consistent with a firm "no." Try to keep the "no's" to a minimum. He will learn to be co-operative and agreeable from your behavior.

Fantasy

Children are full of make-believe and fantasy play. For the most part adults are not part of this play. In his famous book Winnie-the-Pooh, A. A. Milne gives some wonderful samples of make-believe. Reading it might help you to enjoy this stage of your child's development.

Young children often confuse fact with fancy – it is universal in early childhood. You can help him understand the difference by showing interest in his stories of imaginary doings and by remarking in a non-critical way that although it was a good story, he and you both know that it really did not happen.

Skill Development

Your baby learns how to do a great many different things during his first two years of life. However, some youngsters are much slower learning these skills than others. These youngsters will learn when they are ready, provided suitable opportunities are available. For instance, they may not be able to grasp a rattle if you don't give them one; they will not pull themselves up unless they have a playpen or some other firm object on which they can pull; they will be slow learning to talk unless you talk with them in plain simple words.

In the following table, we have listed the times at which most babies do various things. Don't take these age levels too seriously because there are differences amongst children. Also, it is well to remember that any prolonged illness temporarily slows a baby's development.

Behavioral Milestones

Newborn

Sucks objects placed between his lips. If you touch his cheek, turns his head and reaches with his mouth. Is frightened if he feels he is about to be dropped. After a few days is frightened by loud sounds nearby but will sleep through ordinary household noises. Can sneeze and cough.

Four-Six Weeks

Opens his eyes widely. Once in a while looks at your face briefly. Usually keeps his hands clenched. Often makes small throaty noises. By six weeks you will be able to exchange greetings with a glowing smile from you baby.

Four Months

Reaches out towards objects and watches them as they are moved about one foot away. Holds head up steadily when lying on his abdomen. Turns his head in the direction of a voice. Can roll over. Coos, chuckles and laughs. He will be most awake and sociable after his feeding.

Six Months

Picks up things with a paw-like grasp. Bangs a rattle. Will transfer an object from one hand to the other. Puts his toes in his mouth.

Seven to Eight Months

Usually can sit up unsupported. Often "makes shy" with strangers.

Nine to 10 Months

Says monosyllables – da-da, ma-ma. First attempts to pull himself to standing position and to respond to bye-bye or pat-a-cake. Grasps small objects with thumb and forefinger. Responds to "no, no". May begin to creep. May have feelings of anxiety when separated from care giver. May express this concern by objecting to sleeping alone. Comfort or security blankets or favorite dolls or stuffed animals may become a means of comfort.

One Year

Stands with support. Tries to walk when held. May creep freely. Says two or three words besides da-da and ma-ma. Is often upset by strangers. Tries to help feed himself.

18 Months

Walks well, seldom falling. Associates words with objects. His favorite word is "no". Needs regular protection against dangers. Understands simple statements – for example coat, hat, out. Repeats words or short sentences just spoken by another person.

Two Years

Uses three-word sentences. Runs well, pulls on simple garments. Often likes to please others and is pleased by them.

Three Years

Should be able to communicate simple thoughts and ideas. Enjoys playmates. Rides a tricycle and enjoys nursery rhymes.

Toys

Providing toys, games, books, music, pictures and equipment suited to your child's growing abilities, will encourage interests and skills. Early in baby's life, parents often show more interest in their child's food and clothing and less in play and equipment.

When your baby is about two months old, it is a good idea to buy a bright-colored balloon or a baby mobile to tie at the foot of his crib. Soon he will amuse himself by watching it bobbing about.

At about four months of age, he spends a good deal of time playing with his own hands and batting himself with them. He can now hold a toy in his hand.

 Hand-held toys should not be tied to the crib, playpen, carriage or stroller as some children have become entangled in the cord.

Choose approved washable toys that are too large to fit into his mouth. A rattle is the traditional first hand-held toy. Rubber or soft cotton dolls of a size that he can hold and wave about will interest your child when he is about six months old. All his toys should be washable, as they all are well drooled on and sucked. Be wary of parts of a toy that could come loose, for example, buttons. At this stage he picks up his toys with his whole hand rather than his fingers. He is interested in playing peek-a-boo or pat-a-cake with you. He will soon become more skilful at grasping objects.

By eight or nine months he can usually sit up steadily, which he greatly enjoys. Now he is certainly ready for a playpen – in fact you can use one any time after five months. The fine mesh are very handy because they are so light. A raised floor is warmer and as baby will sometimes sleep in the playpen, this is important. Wooden playpens are also popular. The slats must be well secured and close enough to protect the baby from being caught between the slats (no more than 2 3/8 inches or six centimetres apart). Both types should be of firm structure with baby-proof locking mechanism of the sides and in good repair. Your baby can get a lot of exercise creeping about and hauling himself up in his pen. With constant supervision, he will play happily while you are close by to meet his needs. It trains him also to amuse himself. After he is about a year old, he can play in his pen both in the morning and in the afternoon.

Some parents feel that playpens are too confining for a baby, especially after he has learned to stand up. On the other hand, he is free to do what he likes in his pen, which he isn't if he is running unconfined in most rooms. No one has ever shown that the use of a playpen has slowed a child's progress. Some babies rebel against playpens earlier than others, but if you give your child plenty of playthings and set the pen up where he can see and "talk" with you, he will probably accept it for some time.

Toddler's Toys

Around 10-12 months, a plastic cup, a little saucepan, a spoon, empty spools, small brightly colored blocks, and soft balls (securely made, not of foam) will help baby to learn how to use his fingers and keep him happy. He likes turning the pages in an untearable cotton book. His interests change, of course, as he develops. If he takes to a toy and plays with it, that's fine. If he doesn't the toy may be either too simple or too advanced for him. You can probably decide which of the two is the more likely from his other interests.

At about 10 months he usually starts pulling himself up to the standing position in his pen or by a chair. He is so pleased with this that he can think of nothing nicer than doing it over and over again.

At a year he can usually walk if someone holds his hand, and six months later he is quite nimble on his feet. Once he is walking, he is ready for toys that he can either push or pull, such as the bell on wheels that is pushed with a stick, slinky toys, little trucks, wagons, wheelbarrows with two wheels, wooden trains, and animals on wheels. A simple wagon can be made out of a small wooden box by screwing four casters into it. A cardboard or light wooden box, even without any wheels, can be dragged about with a great deal of pleasure. Unbreakable doll's dishes, shovel and pail, or brooms help the child to play pretend and develop his imagination, as well as providing him with exercise.

In the preschool period choose toys that are strong, that have no sharp edges, and that the child can do something with creatively. Mechanical toys are usually poor because they are broken easily and provide practically nothing for the child to do.

Sometimes a youngster uses a toy in quite an unusual way, but as it is his toy he should be at liberty to play with it as he likes. For example, he likely will not use blocks for building until he is about four years old.

He will grow to enjoy large blocks and peg boards, sturdy picture books, blunt scissors, colored paper, plasticine, poster paints, good-sized paint brushes and large sheets of paper on which to paint. If he wears an apron and you spread newspaper on the floor, little harm can be done.

Outside he will soon be ready for a low swing, slide, and/or sandbox with lid. Coach him on how to use them and watch him until he learns how to play safely on them.

The Toy Report, by the Canadian Toy Testing Council (950 Gladstone Ave, Ste. 110, Ottawa, Ont. K1Y 3E6, 613-729-7101), is an annual guide to toys that you will find quite useful when selecting appropriate toys for your child.

Playmates

A child under two is not ready to play interactively with other youngsters. He will, of course, play with siblings and neighborhood children, but more on the other child's direction than on his own. It will help with his development, particularly in the area of language. To encourage him to be self-reliant, teach him to play by himself for at least an hour, morning and afternoon. A room of his own, where he is safe and free to play at will, is best. If not a room, then a corner somewhere is desirable. The end of the afternoon, when he is beginning to tire, is a good time for some quiet play with his parents or his older brothers and sisters.

At 24-30 months, he needs playmates of his own age. It is worthwhile finding them, even though you have to mind your neighbour's youngsters as well as your own. At first, young children don't know how to play with each other agreeably, and constant but unobtrusive supervision is necessary.

All along, children need to be encouraged to do all they can on their own, such as washing, dressing and feeding themselves.

Sibling Rivalry

The arrival of a second baby is almost sure to upset your firstborn to some extent, especially if he is under five. A certain amount of jealousy is inevitable and understandable. You can make this new role easier for him in several ways. Be sure to tell him months beforehand that he is going to have a new baby brother or sister who, at the moment is growing inside your body. If you plan to use his room for the new baby, move him to his new quarters several months before the baby is expected, telling him that he is more grown-up. If he feels he is being shoved out to make room for the new arrival, that certainly won't help.

If possible, be sure that he knows the person who is going to look after him while you are in hospital (if it is not your partner), and explain that you will be away for a few days and will be bringing the new baby back with you. If your child is under two-and- a-half years, much of this may not register, but some of it may. Plan a visit to the hospital for him to see the new baby.

Fortunately during the first couple of months your new baby will be sleeping a good part of the time so you can spend extra time with your older child.

Whenever you can, have your toddler busy somewhere else while you are feeding or caring for the new baby. If you have someone helping you, this is a good time for that person to play with the toddler. Of course, if your older child is in the room where you are working with the new baby, let him stay. Try not to talk about the new baby too much. Talk with your older child about activities planned for him and let him know that he is still very much part of your family and activities. Praise his skills in talking, feeding himself and dressing himself so that he will perhaps begin to understand how important he is in the family group.

When guests arrive with a gift for the new baby have a surprise wrapped and ready for your toddler and/or let him help to open the gift for baby.

Often the older child, when he see what attention his new baby brother or sister is getting, will slip back into baby ways such as wetting himself or wanting a bottle. Cheerfully fix a bottle for him – he probably won't enjoy it much. These temporary regressions rarely last more than a week or so.

It's worthwhile playing up the things your toddler can do and have that the new baby can't, so that he feels he has many advantages on his side. In addition, he can occasionally be quite helpful, fetching diapers or other things.

Older preschoolers often like playing the role of a third parent and enjoy being thanked for their help, but don't expect too much. If you talk about how little the new baby can do, it will make your toddler feel more competent and grown-up.

Your older child may be rather mixed-up in his feelings about his new sibling. Sometimes his jealousy is so great that he wants to hurt the new baby. Watch that he treats the baby kindly and you should express more love and attention towards the older child. You might tell him that you understand how he feels and that you still love him too. Your partner can help a great deal by spending more time with your toddler until he becomes used to his new role in the family.

Children over five are less jealous, as they have far more interests outside the home.

The arrival of a third child is also easier for the first two to accept.

Rivalry Among Older Siblings

Living with siblings helps children learn how to get along with other people, but it is certainly not a peaceful process. Much of the quarrelling between them is based on jealousy, which is said to be greatest between adjacent members of the same sex.

Each child (except for identical twins) differs considerably from any other in the family. A parent may find that one child is more attractive or easily managed than the others. You probably can't avoid a certain amount of favoritism entirely, but if you realize what is happening, you can make a real effort to curb it. Treat each child according to his needs.

One sibling may envy the looks, athletic skills or talents of another. You increase this envy if you talk about the "special" one too much. Rather, encourage each child's achievements and certainly never compare one unfavorably to another.

If an older child constantly dominates a younger, the latter may become so discouraged that he stops trying to compete. Plan so that each child has playmates of his own age – this helps the younger to develop his skills. Naturally you will expect less from the younger. Giving them equal privileges, duties and presents will please neither of them and is unfair. Spoiling the eldest or the youngest is resented by the others.

Avoid judging quarrels unless one child is evidently and grossly to blame. Within reason, let children settle their own differences.

Musical Interest

Soon after a child is born he is able to hear many sounds. He will listen to music on records, or radio, but of course one cannot be certain how well he distinguishes one sound from another. At about four months, a child is usually soothed by lullabies and by his parent's comforting voice. If a child is able to carry a tune by three years of age, he is doing well. Playing music in your home is a good quiet pastime for both of you. Formal musical training is normally begun when the child is learning to read. Choose a teacher who will stimulate his interest; skills will then follow.

Talking, Reading and Play School

Talk with your child a great deal. He learns to speak from listening to you. Unless he hears words he cannot learn them. During the first three months he will make sounds that a mother can often interpret.

By six months he coos and babbles in response to a familiar voice. He may begin to understand "no", if said firmly. Around 9-10 months, mama or dada will be recognized, with other single words following in the next few months. His growing vocabulary will help him to express himself, but he makes most of his wants known by pointing and making expressive noises.

Between 1-2 years his vocabulary will develop quickly. Children vary considerably in the age at which they learn to talk, and girls, on the whole learn earlier than boys. Try to talk clearly and simply, (not baby talk) to help with his speech. He will have short 2-3 word sentences before the age of two.

By three years of age he should be able to communicate simple thoughts and ideas. He will begin to ask questions. Nursery rhymes teach him words, sounds and rhythm and are about the length of story that a young child can listen to with interest. Try to read or tell a story to him at bedtime. Trips to the library may start at about two years of age. He will be pleased to choose a book and have you read it to him. Often a favorite book must be re-read until he knows it by heart. He may correct you if you inadvertently change or skip a word or page. In many cities, story-telling hours at the library are available for children over three years of age. His interest in books and rhyming words aids in developing reading skills.

Speech development continues through the preschool age into the early school years. Word or phrase repetition occurs during the school period, but this hesitancy usually does not last longer than a few months. All the speech sounds should be clear and audible by seven years of age.

Your doctor and the teacher will be aware of how your child's speech is developing. If there appears to be a problem, a speech and language consultant will be recommended.

Your child will continue to visit the library and enjoy books after he starts going to school. His introduction to the world of education may be a nursery school. If your child can keep himself happily busy at home there is no great need to send him, but if he is not able to entertain himself and is often unhappy and bored, the stimulation of such a school may be very helpful. Children enjoy being with other children, and fairly soon they learn to play together and to share. Many children whose speech is slow are motivated to improve by playing with other youngsters. Even though all parents should be careful to keep their children home when they show signs of an illness, colds and other infections are more common in classrooms. However, these are minor objections.

Varied Experiences

It is thought that exposing a baby or child frequently to a great variety of suitable sensory stimuli such as sights, sounds, textures and odors helps his brain to develop, especially if these experiences are associated with the object or person producing them. Be sure your child has the chance to grow through happy family outings to new and different places. At home, share with him your own pleasure in the smell of a flower, or the feel of earth in a potted plant. Encourage him to discover the joy of self-expression by marching or dancing with brothers and sisters to the music of radio or record player, and by participating in the games and songs on suitable children's television.

PLAY IT SAFE**

To a child a toy can be a world of wonders. But danger can lurk in a seemingly innocent play thing when it's in the wrong hands. That's why toys must be chosen carefully.

The following are some important facts to keep in mind when shopping for toys.

• Choose a toy suited to the child's age.

• Look for sturdy toys.

• Mobiles have rods and strings that could easily endanger a child. Make sure you hang them out of reach of young children.

• Read any instructions with the toy.

• Keep all toys in good repair.

Selecting Toys

Take the time and trouble to choose your child's toys carefully. Here are some shopping tips.

• Keep in mind who else in the house might play with the toy.

• Check instructions and really look the toy over.

• Show the child how the toy should be used so that it brings joy, not harm.

• If a toy breaks and sharp edges are exposed, throw the toy out.

**These tips are provided by Consumer and Corporate Affairs Canada.

15

Toilet Training

Bowel Control

With toilet training, it is important for parents to maintain a friendly, encouraging, interested attitude. Don't be discouraged by "accidents" – they are bound to occur. During his first year, your baby empties his bowel and bladder automatically – he is not aware of what he is doing. In order to acquire bowel control, he has to realize when he is going to have a bowel movement and how to let you know in some way that this is about to happen.

In addition, he has to learn how to hold back, and even harder, how to let go in the right place. His brain and his nervous system are not sufficiently developed to do all this until he is more than one year of age. Your baby does a great deal of the training himself but he needs a lot of help and support from you.

Until a youngster is about two and a half years old, it is best to use a potty seat or chair for his training. These are free-standing devices that rest on the floor as opposed to the potty rings that sit on top of the toilet. (Some rings are outfitted with arm and foot rests!) The safety and smallness of the chair appeals to a tot. Using it, he can plant his feet firmly on the floor, which helps him to expel the movement completely. Also, the chair is portable – a great convenience.

After your youngster has become fairly well trained, if you take his potty when you travel, he will be more likely to co-operate. Children find it difficult to void away from home. Using the familiar potty in a strange bathroom may help overcome this problem.

During his first and second years, avoid flushing the bowel movement down the toilet while your child is around. Some children will mimic their parents by flushing toys away – while others may be upset that something belonging to them has disappeared with a noise and a rush of water.

WHEN TO START TRAINING**

Look for any of the following signs:
- The child remains dry for at least two hours at a time during the day or is dry after naps.
- The child's bowel movements become regular and predictable.
- The child lets you know through facial expression, posture, or words that a bowel movement or urination is about to occur.
- The child can follow simple, verbal instructions.
- The child can walk to and from the bathroom, pull down pants, and pull them up again.
- The child becomes uncomfortable with soiled diapers and wants to be changed.
- The child asks to use the toilet or potty chair.
- The child asks to wear grown-up underwear.

A child need not show all of these signs in order to be ready.

When to Wait
- The family has just moved or will do so in the near future.
- A brother or sister has just been born or is expected in the next few months.
- There is a major illness in the family

**These suggestions are from the American Academy of Paediatrics*

Some children habitually have a bowel movement five to 10 minutes after their breakfast. Such children, if placed on their potty when they are a year of age, may have a movement. However, many physicians feel that it is best to wait until two years of age when children will be aware of what is expected of them. Younger children are not able to cooperate knowingly, but after a few weeks' experience, contact with the seat may stimulate them to push out the movement. Psychologists feel that they become conditioned to the seat but that does not mean that they are actually toilet trained.

At this age he cannot hold his movement back or expel it when he wishes. When he has a movement, show him you are pleased. Conditioning him in this way will likely make it easier to train him later on but do this only once a day. He will probably soil himself at other times.

If your child does not usually have a movement after breakfast or at any other regular time, do not try to condition him.

Most youngsters are ready to be trained by 24 months. Watch closely for any signal that he is about to have or has had a movement. Often he looks uncomfortable afterwards and indicates to you that he wants to be tidied up. Even though he tells you too late, it is progress. He is more likely to tell you if you have explained earlier that you want him to do so. Praise him for telling you and suggest that he let you know earlier next time so that he can use his chair. After a few weeks of this training, he may get tired of it and want to stop; but stay calm and persist tactfully. Each day, make a few simple comments about use of the potty. He is learning the difference between the right and the wrong way of doing things. When he finally does master this skill, it will give both of you a great deal of satisfaction. His fondness of imitation and his desire to please both help.

Usually the training will take weeks or even months. Putting him in training pants when he is partly trained encourages him to stay clean and dry. After he has become quite reliable about signalling to you in time, he will still expect you to take him to his chair.

30 Months Plus

By the age of two and a half years, you can probably start using a potty ring that fits on your regular toilet. He will also need a firm footstool to support his feet and to help steady him. Being perched up on the regular toilet, even with a foot support, is usually frightening to a child younger than 30 months. If, by chance, your small youngster falls off or if an older child flushes the toilet while he is on it, he will get a long-lasting scare. By two and a half years or soon after, many children are able to go to the bathroom, pull down their pants, climb up on the small toilet seat (which you regularly leave attached) and have a movement. Now is a good time to suggest that he wipe himself, even though you will have to help as well. Teach boys and particularly girls to wipe from behind.

Boys are often a little slower in learning bowel control than girls.

"Accidents" are quite common until he is three or so. If he is very busy playing, (especially outside), if he catches cold or develops diarrhea or if your household routine is changed by the arrival of a new baby or a visitor, he is likely to backslide. Do not discourage him by nagging or giving him the impression that you are greatly disappointed in him. He won't forget what he has learned, and will soon be performing as usual.

When your child gets a little older, explain to him that we need to eat food in order to grow, work, and play and that most of the waste products of the body must be excreted through the bowel and the bladder. This normal process occurs in everyone.

Bladder Control

During his first year and in the initial few months of his second year, a baby's urinary bladder automatically empties itself; that is, he wets himself very frequently. For a person of any age it is easier to control a bowel movement than it is to control urination. Therefore, helping a young child to learn to keep dry is a slower process than teaching him bowel control. Boys are usually a little slower than girls in learning bladder control.

By 17 to 18 months, you may find him dry several times during the day. If it is two hours or so since he urinated, he will probably go soon after he gets to his potty. At this age he will rarely give you any signal. A little later (18-24 months) many youngsters will tell you, by saying the word or by some other signal, after they have become wet, because they are more aware of being wet than having a full bladder. Let him know that you are pleased but that next time you would like him to tell you beforehand. Change him whenever you find him wet so that he will prefer being dry. Putting him on his toilet chair every two hours is often enough. Say the word you have planned to use as you take him there and show him that you are pleased when he is successful. When you find him dry several times a day, put him in training pants. They are quite an incentive towards keeping dry and are easier to pull down. Even after he has let you know fairly regularly, when he needs to go, he may wet himself often until he is about two and a half years. He is most apt to forget when he is very busy doing something or playing outside. You will need to remind him when it is time to go and you can often see from his actions that his bladder is uncomfortably full. By three, many children can take themselves to the toilet.

As with bowel control, any unusual event may result in more frequent "accidents." However, after such interruptions he will likely continue with his former routine.

Many parents prefer to delay bladder training until after their child has learned to signal that he is about to have a bowel movement – a habit that he usually acquires around 24 months of age. A month or so after he has reached this stage, his parent encourages him to say the word that means he is ready to urinate. Often he will achieve both bowel and bladder control at about the same time. With this method he does even more of the training himself than with the first method.

Boys usually learn to urinate standing up at two to three years of age. Occasionally watching their brothers, playmates and their father encourages them to do so.

Fortunately, during the night the kidneys produce less urine and make it more concentrated. Late in their second year or early in their third, many youngsters stay dry at night even though they may be still wetting in the daytime. Girls are usually ahead of boys in learning this habit, and it is also easier for relaxed youngsters to achieve. Slowness in staying dry at night may be a familial trait.

All children train themselves for the most part, and praising them in moderation is wise. They certainly should never be scolded, punished or mocked when they wet their beds. They do so unconsciously, and such painful tactics hinder rather than help them.

If your youngster continues to wet his bed fairly frequently when he is over five years old, you would be wise to talk to your doctor about it.

16

Common Habits

School Years

Thumb Sucking

Many parents dislike seeing their babies suck their thumbs or pacifiers. Try to overcome this feeling because tension and irritability on your part make it harder for you to cope with the situation. Keep in mind that some babies seem to need a lot more sucking activity than others – in fact it sometimes seems to be a familial characteristic.

All young babies suck their thumbs or hands when they are hungry before their feedings, but if a baby under three months of age also sucks his hand after his feeding and whenever else he can get it into his mouth, he needs more sucking time. If you are breast-feeding him, let him nurse longer. If you are giving him bottles, screw the caps tighter and use firmer nipples with smaller holes, so that his feeding will last about twenty minutes. However, don't make the sucking so difficult that he has not the energy to take as much as he needs. Keep up his evening feeding as long as he will take it, and do not be in a hurry to teach him to drink from a cup.

Another help is to hold him in your arms for all his feedings, as that gives him additional comfort just as his thumb sucking does.

Pacifiers: Pros and Cons

The use of a pacifier is helpful for young babies who need a lot of sucking. Babies given pacifiers rarely become thumb suckers. By the age of three or four months, your infant may suck his pacifier for only a short time and then spit it out. Do not encourage him to use it more than he wants. When he becomes drowsy, remove the pacifier, if he does not object, or take it out after he falls asleep. A teething ring is also useful at this age – often he will chew and suck on it instead of his thumb or a pacifier.

 If you use a pacifier, use a sturdy one piece unit, with holes in the shield. Babies have choked on a poorly made pacifier. They can also become entangled in the cord attached to it.

Persistent Thumb Sucking

From about 12 months on, thumb sucking, if it persists, takes on a different significance. If your baby just sucks his thumb when he is dropping off to sleep and occasionally during the day, you can ignore it. But if he does a good deal of it, you would be wise to review his daily program. When he feels ill at ease, shy, unhappy, bored, tired or hungry, he is likely to seek comfort from his thumb because it eases his tension.

Is he wearing himself out by playing too hard with older children? Here your plan would be to have him play quietly, preferably by himself, for part of the day. This will lessen the fatigue. Has he enough interesting toys and later, after two-and-a-half years or so, at least one playmate his own age? Try to prevent boredom. Of course, none of these reasons may apply to your child, and it is a fact that contented youngsters with good daily routines still unaccountably suck their thumbs. Some of them probably have inherited the tendency from parents or relatives who were thumb suckers themselves.

Most dentists believe the teeth, made crooked by the habit, will come back to their proper positions if thumb sucking is given up before the permanent teeth come through. Remember that a good many cases of malocclusion, or badly placed teeth, are due to heredity.

Restraints produce anger and are annoying and frustrating to him. He cannot play as easily with his toys nor as easily with his playmates. Scolding, shaming or slapping are not effective deterrents either. Going off by himself to suck unobserved is even worse, for he becomes sneaky and feels guilty as well.

By three years or more, you can probably appeal to his pride. He does not want to be criticized for this habit. Stars to stick on a calendar to mark "good" days help. Thumb suckers eventually do less of it and finally stop – most often between three and six years of age. The need for the comfort of his thumb has passed.

Other Comforting Habits (Transitional Objects)

An older child comforts himself with a "security" blanket or a cuddly toy, just as in his earlier days he may have stroked his mother's clothing while being fed. This favored comfort helps to reduce the anxiety when he is separated from a care giver. Unfortunately, a blanket becomes increasingly ragged and dirty. Wash and dry it when he is asleep and it may last until he grows out of the habit, between three and six years. These "supports" do not hurt him, and you cannot foretell what will be his favorite.

Rhythmic Habits

Some babies develop the habit of rocking against the back of a chair or couch and then bouncing forward. Others jounce their cots by rocking on their hands and knees. The cot moves as they do and can cause a dreadful racket when it repeatedly hits the wall. Eventually it may even damage the wall. Anchoring the cot or padding the outer end of it is about all you can do. Any wheels on the bed should be removed.

Other small youngsters bang their heads on the ends of their cribs or roll their heads from side to side. Using crib bumper pads with extra padding will at least prevent such a child from bruising his head. Maybe these rhythmic movements comfort him in the same way as rocking did when he was younger. These habits are all harmless and quite common. They are usually carried out when the youngster is tired, bored or ill at ease.

Masturbation

A young child naturally explores all parts of his body, especially when in his bath. No one part has any greater significance to him than another. The fact that he happens to touch the sex organs has no sexual significance. Do not scold if he does such exploring. This habit will do the child no physical or psychological harm. If a child has developed the habit – and it is quite common between the ages of two and five years – ignore it. Calling his attention to it only makes it stand out in his mind; try to direct the child's attention elsewhere.

Be aware that tight underclothes can cause irritation. Cotton will be less irritating for some youngsters than cotton-polyester. Sensitivities to soaps or creams may cause a problem as well as unclean genitalia.

Halting Habits

You can't stop habits directly, but you would be wise to try to arrange your child's day so that he has more enjoyable things to do, more playmates after the age of about two-and-a-half years, perhaps more play-time with you and possibly more sleep. In other words, do your best to make his life more interesting and less tiring and frustrating.

Habits may last weeks or months, or sometimes a year or more. A child will get over them in time without active interference from you, and without harm to himself.

PREPARING FOR SCHOOL
Dressing and Grooming

To a toddler, learning to undress and dress, to brush his teeth, to hang up his clothes is an exciting and grown-up process. It is best to start teaching him to do these and other jobs for himself as soon as he shows any interest in learning them. Of course, he is awkward and slow at first, but try to sit back and let him try. You can come to the rescue when he hits a snag or gets tired.

A small child enjoys helping to do such things as putting away the cutlery, setting the table or washing the vegetables. He is happily busy and learning, as many curious questions are often asked. Soon he can learn to do even more interesting things, such as running errands, clearing the table and helping to tidy his own room. These are important jobs to him and he likes to please his parents. Naturally, you will praise him for his help, even though the results are not perfect.

You can help him to make choices. This most important discipline comes by letting him choose which of two sweaters he will wear, what he will buy for Daddy's birthday, how he wants his own room arranged and so on. Some youngsters find it difficult to make choices, mostly because they have had so little practice.

He needs to learn to get along without you, so arrange playtime with other children in the neighborhood. Plan a short visit for him to a friend's house or a few days stay with his grandparents, when you feel that your child will enjoy it.

Street-Proofing

When you take him out, teach him the safety rules and also the reasons behind them. Begin as soon as he can understand. Walk with him to the parks for play and stop at the curb before crossing the road. Let your child decide when the road is clear and when you should cross together.

BIKE HELMETS MAKE SENSE**

Wearing a bicycle helmet can reduce you child's risk of serious head injury by 73 percent!
- Head injuries can have serious effects.
- "Flying over the handlebars" can leave your child disabled for life.
- Bicycle helmet use is the best way for you to protect your child's head.

When to Wear Helmets
- Every ride! Falls and crashes can happen in parks, paths and driveways; not just on streets.
- Every ride, every time! Develop the "helmet habit."
- Every ride for everyone! Wear a helmet to set a good example for your children.

Where to Buy a Helmet
- Lock bike shops; some retail, department, catalogue and toy stores.
- Make sure the helmet you buy meets safety standards.

** This advice is from Washington Children's Bicycle Helmet Coalition

---

By the time a child is six years old he should have learned always to walk on the sidewalk, how to use the crosswalks, to walk straight across the street and to obey the traffic lights or crossing guards. If he rides a bicycle, he should wear a protective helmet and stay on the bike paths or areas that you have designated safe.

Children should be taught to take the route to school that you have planned for them, and to come directly home from school. In this way you are aware of your child's whereabouts. Some children are not as aware of a potentially dangerous situation as others. They all should be told of Neighborhood Watch signs on the streets (if such exist) where they travel, and to think of the policeman as a friend. Be sure that he knows his home address, phone number and parents' name.

These and other safety rules have to be dinned into him, and, of course, adults must invariably set a good example.

Playmates

A child who has played by himself almost exclusively is at a disadvantage when he starts school. Young children have to learn how to play with other youngsters. This requires unobtrusive supervision for some time until they know the rules of give and take, and following and leading. Nursery schools are a help, but mothers can do just as good a job themselves if they are willing to put the time into it. It's a mistake to think that youngsters naturally know how to play together. Many things are learned from example, such as social behavior and personal care.

Unpopularity

Older children develop fears of being different or of not being liked. Girls and boys feel it very important at certain stages to dress, speak and act just like their gang. Within reason, do your best to provide clothes that are like those worn by their pals. This will help your child feel more comfortable with his peers.

Shyness

Self-consciousness is another form of fear – a fear of disapproval. Unnecessary fault finding, criticism, and urging your child to do better than he can, tend to develop self-consciousness. Commending the child for his good efforts and helping him to prepare by practicing his skills in a game or hobby will make him a valued team member. Other pursuits,such as drama, may help overcome feelings of shyness.

Fears

Fear is not always harmful – in fact it is often very valuable. You want your child to be cautious in dangerous situations, and a reasonable degree of fear is an aid towards this end. But in spite of this, you don't want him to be too timid.

Some children are naturally courageous and daring, others are just as naturally fearful. They seem to be born with these characteristics, just as they vary in so many other respects. For some it is easy to be courageous and take a chance or risk. For others it is difficult to summon the courage to move or act.

Many childish fears are due to ignorance and inexperience – by explaining the whys and wherefores of many of the common occurrences, you help your child to learn what to expect. Sudden events that are new are the most likely to frighten children.

Young babies are afraid of loud noises, loss of balance or falling – a feeling of insecurity. You naturally try to comfort infants by cuddling or talking to them. If there is pain, there may be fright as well, and here again you try to reassure and relieve him of his fear. The bonding which begins in the newborn period between parent and infant will prevent or lessen some of the fears of childhood.

A three to five year old is most often frightened by the unreal or imaginative situation or relationship. It may be a misinterpretation of the circumstance. Older children are more aware of the reality of the situation and are concerned about their relationship to family and friends. Broken homes, illnesses, death or prolonged absence of a family member may produce fears and concerns.

Occasionally children are afraid of getting lost. Children who are not too happy in their homes, because of fighting or friction within the family, may feel insecure. A threat by a thoughtless adult may frighten a child.

Sometimes overcautious parents have not given a child enough opportunity to find his own way in play or controlled learning situations. Providing children with safe toys and equipment and letting them play on their own or with other children, with little adult involvement, will lead to creative play.

Naturally we want our children to develop necessary caution, but not to the point of frightening them or making them timid. Keep in touch with what your child is thinking and feeling.

Anxiety

Some children are frightened by violent or supernatural presentations, on radio and television, in movies, stories in books, or newspapers. Avoid this material. If it happens that your child comes across it, listen to how he feels about seeing a movie which disturbs him and acknowledge and accept his feeling. Try to give his feeling a name in recognizing it, so that he will know this reaction when he feels it again. Explain to him that the events are imaginary or/and don't involve him or in an older child the explanation may come from the child, which is better. Be ready to listen.

Other situations, which are not readily apparent, may produce anxiety, Nightmares, difficulty falling asleep, inattention, temper tantrums, or irritability may be signs of anxiety.

Stage fright is an unpleasant experience – hearts pound, knees tremble, palms sweat, faces pale and stomachs get "butterflies." Even a small child feels uncomfortable before a group of people. If your child is about to perform in public, see that he is well drilled in what he is to do and let him rehearse in front of the family. Encourage him by praising his performance at these rehearsals. When he sees that others are interested and appreciative, he will feel more confident.

SCHOOL YEARS
Learning Difficulties – an Overview.

With growth, development, and nurturing in the home and community, a child will become a responsible caring adult. The path is not always straight, nor smooth, and the time in which an individual reaches a defined level of learning varies. This continues through life and everyone should be accepted as he is at a particular moment.

In the school system, levels of achievement have been set as standards of learning. When a child has a problem in reaching this standard there is concern on the part of the parent and the teacher for the child's progress.

The child may be referred by the teacher to consultants in the education system. An assessment of the child's physical condition with visual and hearing tests is advisable. This may be done by your family doctor. If a physical problem is identified then further investigation and recommendations will be made. A physical concern may be visual, auditory, or physical signs suggesting other problems such as cerebral palsy or chronic illness. Many children with learning disorders will give no evidence of abnormalities on physical examination.

An assessment of the child's development and learning potential may be necessary. As no two children are alike, it is an individual assessment, which is very time consuming. An individual recommendation will be made in response to the child's particular need. A great deal of patience is necessary on the part of the teacher and the parent to help these children.

As there is a wide range in the temperament of children – from highly irritable to very placid – it is possible that the child is under undue stress because of the classroom situation. Is the class too large for a very placid child to respond well? Does the teacher appear too strict for an over-reactive anxious type of child? Is there too much distraction in the classroom? With a change of class, or even school, the learning situation for some children improves dramatically. Some children will be under emotional stress in their home, perhaps of a cultural or domestic nature; others are hyperactive or exhibit behavioral or attention difficulties.

It can be hard to decide whether the learning difficulties produce frustrations resulting in a child being difficult to teach or if the behavior of the child is not conducive to learning. Certainly each aggravates the other.

Many children in the school system have language skill problems. As these children listen or read, understanding may not be occurring. As they speak or write, a lack of comprehension and ability to communicate may be evident. Some children may exhibit difficulty with spelling or mathematics.

Social behavior may be learned or acquired in differing ways. Some children have difficulty understanding the results of what they say and do and how it affects their relationships with others. They do not seem to sense the reaction of peers to their behavior.

Special assistance in identifying and managing these children has helped to keep them up to the level of their peers. Of course, there is a range in the disability of the child, so that results cannot be accurately predicted. The skills which a child has and enjoys should be encouraged. This will help to improve the child's self-esteem, which is of the utmost importance. Encouraging a child to progress at his own rate, possibly by means of special tutors or classes does help.

The teacher, parent, school and family doctor will give support and assistance to such children. Siblings should be supportive also. They will come to realize that some youngsters, through no fault of their own, vary a great deal in their ability to learn. If you talk about this, you will probably help children to be more kind and tolerant to those who have problems in certain aspects of learning. The child with a handicap may benefit greatly from the help given by such a team.

Recommended reading:

Learning Disabilities – Your Child Can Win
J. Noyes and N. MacNeil, MacMillan Press, 1982
How To Talk So Kids Will Listen and Listen So Kids Will Talk
A. Faber and E. Mazlish, Avon Books, N.Y. 1980.

17

Development and Care of the Eyes

Very soon after a baby is born, drops or ointment are put in his eyes to kill any harmful germs (especially those that cause gonorrhea) which he might have acquired during his passage through the birth canal. Years ago, before this precaution was made compulsory, many babies were blinded by gonorrheal infections. Both medications work well, but they may irritate some babies' eyes slightly for a few days after birth.

If your baby has relatively fair hair and skin, his eyes will probably be blue when he is born, but you can't tell for sure what their permanent color will be until a few months later.

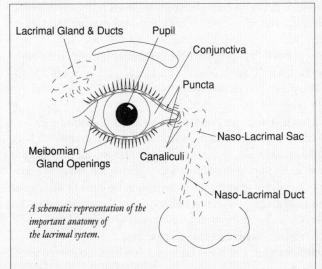

Lacrimal Gland & Ducts
Pupil
Conjunctiva
Puncta
Naso-Lacrimal Sac
Meibomian Gland Openings
Canaliculi
Naso-Lacrimal Duct

A schematic representation of the important anatomy of the lacrimal system.

Cross-Eye, Squint or Strabismus

During his first two or three months, baby's two eyes do not act together (remain parallel) all the time – they wander a bit. By four or five months of age, they usually coordinate well together, and by six months his eyes are normally "straight."

If you notice from the start that one of your baby's eyes regularly turns in or does so most of the time, tell your doctor about it. (Sometimes, because the bridge of his nose is usually so wide, you may think one of his eyes is turning in when it really isn't.) You can test whether this is so or not. While standing in front of him, looking directly at the child, hold a small flashlight about 15 inches (38 centimetres) in front of his nose. If he looks at the light, as he usually does, you will see that the two bright spots of light (the reflexes) are in the same position on each of his pupils (the central black spots). If his eyes are crossed, the reflexes will be seen in different parts of the two black spots.

If your physician confirms your suspicions, he will have your baby examined by a medical eye specialist (ophthalmologist). Sometimes the strabismus only occurs when the baby is tired or not feeling well, and the eye specialist may have to examine him several times before he can be sure whether or not he is cross-eyed. Usually one of his eyes turns in too far – much less frequently one of them turns out too much (divergent strabismus, also known as walleye).

A squint may be first noticed between 18 months and three years. Usually these youngsters are very far-sighted, that is, their eyeballs are relatively too short for their optical system. Often this type of strabismus can be relieved by testing the baby's eyesight and correcting his defective vision with suitable shatterproof lenses in a pair of glasses. A little harness behind his head holds them on. As the child grows older his eyes grow longer, which decreases his far-sightedness, and then he may not need to wear the glasses. However, sometimes glasses do not prevent the crossing fully, and an operation is necessary as well.

Strabismus occurs in two to four percent of the population and runs in the family. It used to be thought that it would cure itself. This idea is quite false, and if nothing is done about it until the child is six or seven years old, the sight in his crossed eye will have become quite poor.

How can squints result in defective vision in one eye? When a person with normally straight eyes looks at any object he sees practically the same image with both eyes, and in his brain he fuses the two. A cross-eyed person sees two different images, in other words, he sees double (diplopia), which is both annoying and tiring. As a consequence, he develops the habit of ignoring the image sent to his brain by his crossed eye. In fact, if he stops using this eye for seeing, and does so for the first four years, he probably will never be able to see clearly with his eye again. The unused eye may be called a "lazy" eye. The aim is to prevent this from happening.

A small child with a divergent squint (eye turns out) may have it corrected surgically at any time.

The eye specialists use a variety of methods in treating strabismus, including patching the good eye so that the youngster has to use his lazy eye for seeing, glasses to correct the vision and straighten the eye and an operation to further straighten the crossed eye. These operations are highly successful. Occasionally, a second operation is required. Surgery is often performed when the baby is 10-12 months old, but occasionally at as early an age as six months.

Long-Sight

Babies' eyes are always quite small at birth and as a result they are very far-sighted (hyperopic). Their eyes grow rapidly during the first year, and continue growing more slowly until three years. Little change occurs after puberty. If the eyes don't grow enough, the child remains far-sighted. This occurs frequently, and glasses can be pre-scribed that will compensate for it. Some far-sighted youngsters don't like reading possibly because their eyes tire more quickly than normal eyes, but suitable glasses can remedy this trouble.

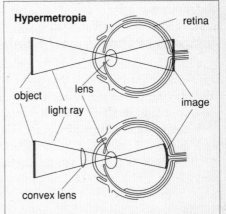

In hypermetropia, or long-sightedness, distant images cannot be focused clearly on the retina. The natural point of focus would be behind the retina, but glasses with a convex lens correct this problem.

Short-Sight and Astigmatism

Sometimes a child's eyes grow too much. The result of this is myopia or short-sightedness. These youngsters can see things close at hand clearly but not those at a distance. Short-sight runs in families – it is definitely inherited, although some of the children may not show it. If the eye grows somewhat more in one diameter than another, astigmatism is the result. Not infrequently, the child has both short or far sight and astigmatism. A short-sighted child that hasn't glasses may do quite poorly at school even though he seems to be bright otherwise.

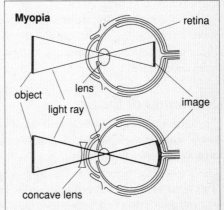

In myopia, or short-sightedness, glasses with a concave lens are prescribed so that the light rays are focused on the retina. Without glasses the natural point of focus would be in front of the retina, causing a blurred image.

Testing

Eyes may be tested at any age. By dilating pupils with appropriate solutions and the use of a retinoscope, the vision of small youngsters can be approximated and suitable glasses prescribed. A young child will wear glasses quite happily if he needs them. Wearing them is important for those requiring corrective lens. Most children accept glasses when they become aware of how much they help his vision. As children's eyes often change quite quickly, they need to be tested once a year and may require a change in lens.

Inflamed or Pink-Eyes (Conjunctivitis)

The layer on the outer surface of the eyeball and inside the lids (the conjunctiva) is very sensitive. Even a speck in the eye can irritated it. Sometimes this layer becomes red and inflamed. This may be due to many causes, such as exposure to wind and dust, eyestrain, allergy or germs. When it is caused by germs, it is often called pink-eye. Some forms of pink-eye are contagious. Teach your child to use only his own wash-cloth and towel. Consult your doctor if your child develops pink-eye.

If the eyelid or the tissue surrounding the eye becomes more swollen it is suggestive of a more serious problem. Consult your physician.

Styes

A stye is a small infection in the hair bulb or root of one of the eyelashes. One of the common bacteria found on the skin is usually the culprit. The stye comes to a head, and then the pus escapes. If the eyelid is rubbed or touched, the germs are apt to cause a stye in another eyelash.

Your doctor may prescribe an anti-bacterial ointment to put on the eyelid, to speed up the healing of the stye and to reduce the spread of the germs. Applying clean, hot compresses to the eye of a co-operative child, will help to make the eye more comfortable.

Substances in the Eye

The surface of the eyeball is easily irritated. Even a tiny particle of grit on it will cause considerable pain and redness. As a consequence, extra tears are produced, which may wash out the offending material.

If it is not sufficient to do this, try pulling the upper lid down over the lower lid. This removes foreign bodies that are on the back of the lid. This may not do the trick, and you should then look at the eye to see where the particle is and if possible remove it. Get a clean, soft cotton handkerchief and wet the corner of it with water or roll some absorbent cotton into a point and dampen it. Seat the child in good light and examine his eye. If you can see the object, remove it gently with the handkerchief corner or the cotton.

If you cannot see any object, but the eye remains painful or if you can see something that you can't gently wipe away, take your child to a hospital or a doctor's office at once. Don't let your child rub his eye, as the foreign body may scratch the surface of the eyeball, which will make the trouble worse.

If irritating chemicals (particularly alkaline agents such as drain cleaners) get into his eye, this should be treated as an emergency and the child should be taken immediately to hospital. Multiple particles of sand in the eye should be flushed out with water by a doctor or at the hospital as quickly as possible.

Penetrating Injuries

Injuries to the surface of the eye are very dangerous and frequently lead to loss of the sight in that eye. Pellet or BB guns, darts, arrows, catapults, knives and scissors are all potentially dangerous. Blunt-ended scissors are the only kind for a young child, and you must keep pointed objects out of his reach. If he manages to pick up a sharp knife, take it away from him firmly and give him a "grown-up" spoon instead. Older children have to be taught not to run when they have sharp things in their hands. You need to caution them also on the danger, when they are walking through woods, of letting bent twigs fly back into the faces of those behind them. Walking some distance apart and warning those following are helpful precautions. Quite a number of people have been blinded in one eye by just such a simple accident. If your child does wound the surface of his eye, get medical help at once.

Good Lighting

Due to the fact that we use our eyes so much for close work, it is important to have good lighting. When you are reading or working, your book should be directly illuminated by a light shining down over your shoulder. On no account should the light be in front of you, so that it is reflected into your eyes. Indirect lighting avoids this problem. Ensure that your child has a good light by which to do his homework or reading.

CANADA'S FOOD GUIDE

ENERGY BALANCE

Needs vary with age, sex and activity. Balance energy intake from foods with energy output from physical activity to control weight. Foods selected according to the Guide can supply 4000-6000 kJ (kilojoules) (1000-1400 kilocalories). For additional energy, increase the number and size of servings from the various food groups and/or add other foods.

MILK AND MILK PRODUCTS

Skim, 2%, whole, buttermilk, reconstituted dry or evaporated milk may be used as a beverage or as the main ingredient in other foods. Cheese may also be chosen.

Some examples of one serving
250 ml (1 cup) milk
175 ml (3/4 cup) yoghurt
45 g (1 1/2 ounces) cheddar or process cheese

Children up to 11 years	2-3 servings
Pregnant and nursing women	3-4 servings
Adults	2 servings

In addition, a supplement of vitamin D is recommended when milk is consumed which does not contain added vitamin D.

BREAD AND CEREALS – 3-5 SERVINGS

Whole grain or enriched. Whole grain products are recommended.

Some examples of one serving
1 slice bread
125 ml (1/2 cup) cooked cereal
175 ml (3/4 cup) ready-to-eat cereal
1 roll or muffin
125 to 175 ml (1/2-3/4 cup cooked) rice, macaroni, spaghetti or noodles
1/2 hamburger or wiener bun

CANADA'S FOOD GUIDE

VARIETY

Choose different kinds of foods from within each group in appropriate numbers of servings and portion sizes.

MODERATION

Select and prepare foods with limited amounts of fat, sugar and salt. If alcohol is consumed, use limited amounts.

MEAT, FISH, POULTRY AND ALTERNATIVES— 2 SERVINGS

Some examples of one serving

60-90 g (2-3 ounces) cooked lean meat, fish, poultry or liver
60 ml (4 tablespoons) peanut butter
250 ml (1 cup) cooked dried peas, beans or lentils
125 ml (1/2 cup) nuts or seeds
60 g (2 ounces) cheddar cheese
125 ml (1/2 cup) cottage cheese
2 eggs

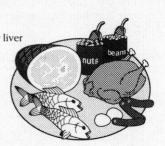

FRUIT AND VEGETABLES – 4-5 SERVINGS

Include at least two vegetables.
Choose a variety of both vegetables and fruits —cooked, raw or their juices. Include yellow, green or green leafy vegetables.

Some examples of one serving

125 ml (1/2 cup) vegetables or fruits—fresh, frozen or canned
125 ml (1/2 cup) juice — fresh, frozen or canned
1 medium-sized potato, carrot, tomato, peach, apple, orange or banana

Health and Welfare Canada, © *Ministry of Supply and Services*

Health and Welfare Canada

Santé et Bien-être social Canada

10 VALUABLE TIPS FOR SUCCESSFUL BREAST-FEEDING

Today, three times more women are breast-feeding their babies than 20 years ago. Here are 10 valuable tips for successful breast-feeding:

Canadä

1 AN EARLY START IS THE BEST START

Breast-feed your baby as soon as possible after birth. Babies are often more alert and interested in feeding in the first hour following birth than later that day. Use the help of experienced nursing staff. *Relax—you're both learning!* So feed often on request; perhaps every two to three hours during the day and when baby wakes at night. Have your baby room-in with you in the hospital.

• As soon as you are able to, sit to feed your baby, support your back and put a pillow on your knees for everybody's comfort. Bring your baby to your breast rather than your breast to your baby.

• Hold the baby close to your body, skin to skin, tummy to tummy, face to breast, mouth to nipple.

• Support your breast by holding four fingers underneath, away from the areola (dark area), with your thumb on top.

• Stimulate baby's lips gently with your nipple until his mouth opens as big as a yawn. Arouse your baby's sense of taste and smell by expressing a few drops of milk.

• When his mouth is open wide, pull baby towards you quickly; when the baby feels your nipple with his tongue, his lips will close over the areola and seal it; both lips should be rolled outwards. You should see the sucking motion along the jaw line.

• To release the baby's suction, gently place a finger into the corner of his mouth until you break the suction. *(See illustration at right.)*

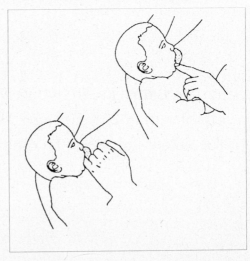

GETTING STARTED

What Happens?

At birth your first milk is colostrum, a yellowish fluid rich in vitamins, protein and immune factors. Breast-feeding often on request will help the milk come in gradually and the quantity to increase. As the colostrum decreases, mother's milk may look thinner and watery, but it is your baby's perfect miracle fast food.

Usually, the milk will be "let-down" and fill your breasts when the baby starts to suck. You may feel the tingling sensation of your milk letting down. But sometimes it happens earlier, spontaneously or in response to a baby's cry, and the breasts fill up and leak. If your breasts should leak, tuck breast pads into your bra to absorb the extra milk.

How to Hold Your Baby

There are many breast-feeding positions; discover the one that is most comfortable for you and your baby. Sit up as soon as possible. If you have had a caesarian birth, you may need help to position yourself and your baby comfortably. Get help from nurses, your doctor, midwife, or breast-feeding counsellors.

The football position

How Often?

Breast-fed babies prefer a span of two to three hours from the beginning of one feeding to the beginning of the next. Mother's milk is digested more easily than formula. You don't need to give any kind of supplement—not even water. With frequent nursing, your baby will get enough nourishment. The usual pattern is this: nurse the baby on one side; then, after time out for a burp or diaper change, switch to the other side. At the next feeding, reverse the order, offering her the last used side first. Some babies prefer several "short courses," others prefer one long feeding. Don't rush her—take your time.

How Much?

A breast-fed baby needs frequent feedings. Allowing your infant to nurse at need (ranging from eight to 12 times in a 24-hour period), will help establish your milk supply. Wake a sleepy baby during the daytime to feed him, especially if he sleeps for long stretches at night.

Your baby is likely getting enough when he has six or more wet diapers a day, has frequent bowel movements, and is gaining weight and growing longer.

REMEMBER, IT'S THE LAW OF SUPPLY AND DEMAND!

The more your baby nurses, the more milk you produce. As your baby gets older, she may nurse every three to four hours and be content. Your baby may have growth spurts in the first few months. Often they are around three weeks, six weeks, three months and six months. Frequent feedings perhaps every one to two hours, for a few days will help increase your milk supply and satisfy her increased appetite.

Remember that your baby's nutritional needs can be completely met by your milk supply without added supplementary feedings.

THE COMPLETE FOOD

Breast-milk is the most balanced food you can offer your infant! It has just the right level and quality of nutrients to suit your child's first food needs. It contains antibodies that reduce the likelihood of allergic reactions. Breast-feeding aids the return of the uterus to normal size, allows mom and baby to begin a special relationship, and is convenient and economical.

With breast-feeding, there is no need to sterilize or warm bottles, nor are there any bottles to take when you leave home with your child. The process is simple, natural, free and safer for the environment!

LOOKING AFTER MOM, TOO

In the early days, your nipples may be tender. Because this part of the body is not usually exposed, nipples need lots of air and light to toughen.

For the first few days, expose your nipples to air or light after each feeding. Allow some breast milk to dry on your nipples; it has lubricating and anti-infective properties.

Change nursing pads when they are wet.

Sometimes breasts get swollen and hurt because of increased blood supply and the accumulation of milk. This condition is called "engorged breasts." Wearing a well-fitting bra, applying warmth (warm towels or shower) to ease the milk flow, expressing some milk before feeding to relieve fullness, and nursing frequently to allow your breasts to empty will help.

Proper positioning of baby on the breast is also very important. Ask for help from the nurses to learn comfortable positions for you and your baby.

When your milk supply is established, you may learn to express or pump milk so that it can be left with a care-giver to give to the baby, and then you can get out occasionally or just have a well-deserved break.

WORKING AND BREAST-FEEDING

It is important to understand that the first weeks are the learning period for both of you, and that time, patience and humour will solve many problems.

During this time, your milk supply is becoming established, so it's difficult to have any one but you feed the baby. After that, you can express milk manually or mechanically, by using a breast pump before you go to work or at work, for feedings throughout the day. Your own breast milk can be stored in the refrigerator (for up to 48 hours) or frozen. Refrigerate or freeze breast milk in plastic bottles or bags and date them. Then warm it up in hot tap water before it is used. (Using a microwave oven is not recommended.)

BREAST-FEEDING AND PREGNANCY

Don't rely on the old myth that you won't get pregnant because you are nursing! It's not always true. It may postpone the return of ovulation and menstruation, but ovulation can occur, so you and your partner should use precautions! Discuss birth control alternatives with your doctor.

THOUGHTFUL REMINDERS

Get Lots of Rest

Be as good to yourself as you can. Try to nap when baby naps. Accept help with housework and meals from your partner, family, and friends. Do only what housekeeping *must* be done. Limit your visitors. Go to bed early.

Eat Well

The foods you choose are important when you are breast-feeding, to ensure good health for you and your baby. Follow Canada's Food Guide for basic nutrition and drink extra fluids to keep your milk supply adequate. The only foods you must avoid are those to which you might be allergic.

Nursing mothers are discouraged from going on weight loss diets as they may cause the milk supply to decrease. While nursing, you may gradually lose weight, and the extra weight gained during pregnancy is used to provide part of the energy needed to make breast milk.

Have Plenty to Drink

You'll find you are extra thirsty, so have a glass of juice, milk or water every time the baby nurses.

Remember if you smoke or drink alcohol: tobacco, alcohol and other drugs can pass into your breast milk and may harm your baby.

Be Comfortable

Relax in the bathtub. It's good therapy. Walk. Gradually resume some exercise. Plan an evening out regularly. Motherhood and fatherhood are new roles that need to be talked over and learned together. Keep the lines of communication open!

TALK TO OTHERS

Personal contact with other nursing mothers is important for confident breast-feeding. Don't keep concerns to yourself. Call a friend, La Leche League, the public health nurse, a lactation consultant, or your doctor or midwife. It helps to talk with someone.

ENJOY YOUR BABY!

10

Holding your baby close stimulates his senses of touch, smell, and taste. A baby who is smiled at, talked to, and cuddled develops a sense of security. Breast-feeding is more than simply providing nutrients and calories for physical growth–it contributes to a special closeness. So have confidence in nature and in yourself and give your little one the very best start in life!

Published by authority of the Minister of National Health and Welfare
For additional copies contact:
Health and Welfare Canada
Publications Department—5th Floor
Jeanne Mance Bldg.
Tunney's Pasture, Ottawa, Ont.
K1A 1B4

Également disponible en français sous le titre
"*10 précieux conseils pour allaiter avec succès*"

NUTRIENT FACTS

VITAMINS

VITAMIN A
Egg yolk, milk, butter, liver, yellow and dark green vegetables

Contributes to healthy skin, bones, and teeth and helps maintain good vision

VITAMIN D
Egg yolk, milk, liver; with sunlight the body can make some of its own Vitamin D

Needed for the normal development and maintenance of bones and teeth, especially in infancy and childhood

VITAMIN E
Wheat germ, nuts, green leafy vegetables

Contributes to the formation of normal red blood cells

VITAMIN B_1 (THIAMINE)
Whole grain/enriched bread and cereals, pork, poultry, peanuts

Helps maintain healthy nervous system

VITAMIN B_2 (RIBOFLAVIN)
Milk, cheese, meat, eggs, green vegetables, enriched bread and cereals

Aids in the conversion of food into energy; helps maintain healthy skin and eyes

VITAMIN B_3 (NIACINAMIDE)
Meat, poultry, fish, peanuts and peanut butter, whole grain/enriched bread and cereals

Helps maintain healthy nervous system

PANTOTHENIC ACID (a B VITAMIN)
Salmon, eggs, green vegetables, molasses

Helps the body convert food into energy

VITAMIN B_6 (PYRIDOXINE HYDROCHLORIDE)
Pork, whole grain cereals, potatoes, bananas

Aids in protein metabolism; helps nervous system to function properly

VITAMIN B_{12} (CYANOCOBALAMIN)
Liver, milk, eggs, meat, cheese

Helps produce red blood cells; helps maintain healthy nervous system

VITAMIN C (ASCORBIC ACID)
Citrus fruits and juices, strawberries, tomatoes, broccoli, cabbage

A factor in the normal development and maintenance of bones, cartilage, teeth and gums

VITAMINS

FOLIC ACID
Meat, kidney and lima beans, spinach, broccoli

Helps maintain healthy red blood cells; aids metabolism of other nutrients

BIOTIN
Meat, egg yolk, peanuts, grapefruit

Aids metabolism of other major nutrients

MINERALS

CALCIUM
Dairy products, leafy greens, dried peas and beans

Essential for the normal development and maintenance of healthy bones and teeth, especially in infancy and childhood

COPPER
Liver, nuts, whole grain cereals, fresh fruit, leafy vegetables

Important component of many enzymes

IRON
Meat, egg yolk, enriched bread and cereals, nuts

Helps red blood cells to carry oxygen; essential to prevent iron deficiency

IODINE
Iodized salt, shellfish, ocean fish

Helps the body use its energy

CARBOHYDRATES
Flour, cereals, bread, rice, noodles, potatoes, dried peas and beans, corn, sweet goods

Important energy source for the body; whole grains and beans also provide fibre

FATS
Butter, margarine, oils, fat from meat, poultry and fish; cream, milk; fried food, chocolate.

Provide reserve energy source for the body; delay hunger

PROTEINS
Meat, poultry, fish, eggs, milk, cheese, dried peas and beans, peanut butter, nuts

Important component of all body cells; can be used for energy if too little carbohydrate or fat is available

TAKE A CLOSE LOOK AT NEW SESAME STREET VITAMINS FROM JOHNSON & JOHNSON.

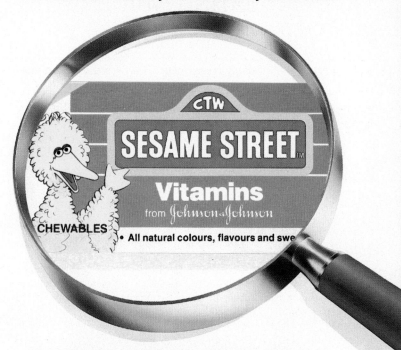

BECAUSE YOU CAN'T ALWAYS WATCH WHAT YOUR CHILDREN EAT!

Snacks, meals on the run, picky appetites – it's tough for parents to know if kids' nutritional needs are met every day. But now, you can be assured your kids are getting their vitamin needs, with new chewable SESAME STREET Vitamins.

Kids will love SESAME STREET character shaped vitamins. They contain **all natural colours and flavours.** Just what you'd expect from Johnson & Johnson.

And for kids who don't always drink their milk, there's new chocolate-flavoured SESAME STREET Calcium Supplement.

© 1990 Jim Henson Productions, Inc.

HEALTHY EATING GUIDE

	WHAT TO EAT FOR ENERGY AND BALANCE	**WHAT TO EAT FOR CONVENIENCE**
MILK AND MILK PRODUCTS Children (up to 11 years) 2–3 servings. Adolescents 3–4 servings. Pregnant and nursing women 3–4 servings. Adults–2 servings	Good milk choices such as: 2 per cent or skim milk; plain yoghurt; buttermilk; uncreamed cottage cheese; skim milk cheese.	All milk products are convenient: fluid milk; ice cream; yoghurt; milk-based soup; cheese.
MEAT, FISH, POULTRY AND ALTERNATES 2 servings. Examples include: Poultry, fish, liver, meat, peanut butter, dried peas, beans or lentils, nuts, cheese, eggs.	Choose small 90 g (3 oz.) servings of boiled, broiled, barbequed or roasted lean meats. Trim off visible fat. Pass up the gravy! Eat more poultry, fish, eggs and meat alternates.	Peanut butter; hamburgers; hot dogs; sliced luncheon meats; baked beans with pork; cheese; eggs; nuts and seeds.
BREAD AND CEREALS 3–5 servings of wholegrain or enriched products. Examples include; bread, cereals, rice, macaroni, spaghetti.	Remember to include these foods, they contribute important nutrients: plain rolls and biscuits; unsweetened cereals; bread (use less butter, jam, etc.)	Breads; ready-to-eat unsweetened cereals; muffin and tea biscuit mixes; ready-made or bake-and-serve rolls.
FRUITS AND VEGETABLES 4–5 servings. Include at least 2 vegetables. Choose a variety of both vegetables and fruits, cooked, raw or their juices. Include yellow or green or green leafy vegetables.	Choose these foods in their lowest energy form, e.g. an apple instead of apple pie; unsweetened juices; baked, steamed, boiled or raw vegetables; vegetables served without butter; sauces or gravy; green salads.	Choices requiring little or no preparation time: fruit and vegetable juices; fresh fruit; canned or frozen fruit and vegetables; dried fruit, e.g. raisins; tossed green salads; raw vegetables.

HOW TO CUT COSTS	NUTRITIOUS SNACKING	SELECTIONS FOR EATING OUT
Milk products are high in nutrients—a good buy; skim milk powder; fluid milk; yoghurt, which can be home made; cottage cheese.	Milk; cheese; eggnogs; yoghurt (plain or with fresh fruit or nuts and spices).	Milk; milkshakes; yoghurt; custard or rice puddings; cheese; soups; ice cream.
Consider cost per serving, not cost per pound, when buying meat. Watch for weekly specials. Use less meat; substitute macaroni and cheese; peanut butter; rice and kidney beans; baked beans; eggs.	Snacks for hearty appetites: cold meat slices; cheese; hard-cooked eggs; nuts; hot dogs; peanut butter and bread.	Pizza; lasagna; wieners; hamburgers; chicken; fishburgers; omelettes; other meat; fish, poultry; cheese; egg dishes.
Use breads and cereals to stretch protein foods in casseroles and meat loaves. Long-cooking rice; cooked cereals; day-old bread for toast; puddings; pasta dishes—macaroni, spaghetti, lasagna; home-made muffins.	Muffins; biscuits; ready-to-eat unsweetened cereals; breads; toast; crackers.	Pancakes; crepes; rolls, muffins; pasta dishes—macaroni, spaghetti, lasagna; bread; rice pudding.
Nutrients are about the same in fresh, frozen or canned fruits and vegetables. Buy fresh produce in season; frozen vegetables; unsweetened canned fruits (check prices). Use leftovers in soups and stews.	Fruit and vegetable juices; fresh fruit combinations such as fruit and cottage cheese or fruit and cheese kebobs; raw vegetable nibblers e.g. carrot sticks, green peppers, tomatoes, with yoghurt as dip.	Vegetable soups; fruit and vegetable juices; side salads; tossed salad; coleslaw; vegetables with the entrée; fruit cup; fruit salad plates.

Information supplied by the Ontario Ministry of Health.

COMMON EATING PROBLEMS

THE PROBLEM	AS YOUR CHILD SEES IT	AS YOU MAY SEE IT
Refusal to eat	I'm not hungry, I'm sick. I've found a new way to get attention.	I must make him eat; growing children need food.
Food jags: getting hooked on one food	I've found a wonderful new food. I've found a way to manipulate my mother.	I must make sure he eats a sensible diet.
Dislike of new foods	I don't like the taste of this food. I don't want to try anything new today.	I like this food. I think my child should learn to like it too, and should adjust to our family's eating patterns.
Rejection of vegetables	I don't like the texture or smell of cooked vegetables. Daddy never eats them. I'm bored with having the same one over and over again.	I think a child should eat cooked vegetables as part of a sensible diet.
Dawdling, or playing with foods.	I want to explore this food. I need time to get used to these utensils. I'm not hungry. I'm too tired.	I don't think children should play with their food.
Overeating	I get approval from the family when I eat a lot. Everyone else asks for seconds.	When he's good I reward him with a cookie. He'll outgrow his baby fat. A child should learn to clean his plate.

...AND
HOW TO COPE

Respect the wisdom of the child's own body. A skipped meal will not hurt a healthy child, so remove the food without fuss after a reasonable length of time (20–30 minutes). Involve your child in food shopping, preparation and serving... pouring milk, making sandwiches, setting the table.

Food jags aren't unusual in children or adults, and won't last long if no issue is made of them.

Children, like adults, will have a few dislikes. If you have time, a substitute food from the same food group may be offered. If the dislike is treated casually, the child will probably learn to like it at a later date.

It doesn't matter whether the vegetables are eaten cooked or raw. Just be sure they are not overcooked. Children often prefer the bright colors and crisp textures of raw vegetables. Vegetable juices are another alternative.

Remember children are the world's best imitators. Your likes are quickly noticed—and copied.

A child needs time to learn to use utensils. If you're a fast eater you might occasionally take the time to eat slowly with your child. You might begin feeding your child a few minutes before the rest of the family. Children learn by touching—give them time to explore food.

Reduce portion sizes. Don't force a child to take "just one more bite" or "clean his plate". Learn to prepare foods without adding extra calories—avoid sauces, breading or frying. Encourage more physical activity. Use a few kind words, a hug, a game, a toy, as rewards and comforters, rather than food.

Adapted from "Food for Little Folk" — a British Columbia Ministry of Health Publication

Fisher-Price

This Infant Car Seat keeps baby secure and comfortable in the car. And everywhere else too!

The Deluxe Nursery Monitor is a one-way, super-sensitive monitor that also lights up at baby's sounds.

We know that each and every baby is a new experience. Suddenly there are a lot of important decisions to make. And you depend on those you trust to help decide what's best for your baby.

We spend a lot of time watching babies, learning from their discoveries, and listening to their parents. Fisher-Price never loses sight of the little hands and curious, growing minds for whom our products are designed.

For more than half a century, parents have put their trust in Fisher-Price. As the world's leading manufacturer of infant and childhood products, we want to share our experience with you.

We know the toys babies love best are the ones that are cheerful, amusing and do surprising and funny things. And, we've learned that infant products parents love best are the ones that combine durability, ingenuity, comfort and time saving convenience.

Fisher-Price knows new babies are the source of exciting and wonderful moments. Trust us to help you enjoy them. Here are some of the products we make just right for baby and you.

This handy Bath Centre fits in the sink, the tub — even on a countertop. Helps make bathtime easy and fun.

A battery-operated Deluxe Port-A-Swing that's soft, gentle, quiet and very portable. Converts instantly to an Infant Seat too!

A Rock-A-Stack rainbow of rings and colourful Snap-Lock Beads provide babies with hours of discovery fun.

This Diaper Pail has an inner lid that keeps odours from sneaking out.

We know all about babies.

The Dancing Animals Music Box Mobile has our friendly farm animals that dance to Brahms' lullaby.

The Activity Links Gym features movable activities that can be rearranged or detached completely to go along with baby.

It's the Fisher-Price Hop Skip Jumper! Sturdy and secure...and lots of fun.

The easiest-handling Car Seat on the road today. Adjustable strap and shield breast plate keeps baby snug and secure.

The Three-In-One Travel Tender — a bassinet, portable crib and playpen that sets up fast, packs up small!

The Stay 'n Play Bath Ring, with non-skid pad, helps keep baby secure and makes bathtime easier for parents.

The Activity Centre. Ten fun things for baby all in one colourful toy.

Even the youngest baby will love Slumber Babies, the cuddly pillow-like companions designed for hugging and holding.

The High Chair has an extra-large tray you can operate with one hand while holding baby with the other.

The three-stage Activity Walker has lots of action and sounds to amuse infants to toddlers.

The Sure Grip Gate releases with one squeeze of the handle. So the other hand is free to hold baby.

The Toddler Kitchen. A child-sized kitchen that cooks up huge portions of fun.

Fisher-Price

Fisher-Price Inc., 5300 Tomken Road, Mississauga. Ontario L4W 1P2 © 1991 Fisher-Price Inc..

MAJOR NUTRIENTS IN VARIOUS TYPES OF MILK

ALL MILKS 250 ML (1 CUP)	CALORIES (kilojoules)	PROTEIN (g)	CARBOHYDRATE (g)	FAT (g)	CALCIUM (mg)	RIBOFLAVIN (mg)	VITAMIN A (RE)	VITAMIN D (IU)	FOLIC ACID (mg)
Whole Milk	159 (663)	8	12	9	308	.42	80	109a	13
2% Milk	128 (536)	9	12	5	314	.43	147a	106a	13
Chocolate Milk (partly skimmed)	189(790)	8	27	5	300	.43	150a	108a	13
Buttermilk (2%)	105 (438)	9	12	2	301	.40	21	2-7c	13
Evaporated (undiluted, 2%)	246 (1028)	20	30	5	738	.84	210a	232a	23
Condensed (sweetened, undiluted)	1036 (4335)	26	176	28	916	1.34	262	NA	36
Dry, Skim (instant, reconstituted)	90 (375)	9	13	tr	320	.36	178a	110a	13
Whole Goat's Milk	178 (743)	9	11	11	344	.36	144	2-7bc	2

NOTES

NA   Data not available
tr   Trace
a   Added to milk in accordance with Food and Drug Regulations.
b   May be enriched. Enrichment is voluntary.
c   These ranges are estimates from various sources.
Data compiled from Nutrient Value of Some Common Foods, 1987 and Canadian Nutrient File, 1985. Health and Welfare Canada.

The Ontario Milk Marketing Board, April 1989

FEEL THE MAGIC.
Baby magic®
Rich 'n Creamy
Riche et crémeuse
baby oil
huile pour bébés
by/par MENNEN®
FAST ABSORBING, NON-GREASY BABY OIL. Baby Magic Rich'n Creamy Baby Oil doesn't look or feel anything like ordinary baby oil because it's emulsified. So it absorbs faster and moisturizes your baby's skin without leaving a greasy feeling.
Feel all the magic with Baby Magic Rich'n Creamy Baby Oil and our family of Baby Magic hair and skin care products.
FEEL ALL THE MAGIC.
Baby magic®
baby powder
poudre pour bébés
250 g
Baby magic®
baby lotion
lotion pour bébés
240 mL
Baby magic®
baby bath
bébé bain
a cleanser · un nettoyeur
250 mL
Baby magic®
Rich 'n Creamy
Riche et crémeuse
baby oil & aloe
huile pour bébés avec aloés
240 mL
by MENNEN®
®Trade Mark(s) of The Mennen Company. Mennen Canada Inc R.U.

TOPPING AND TAILING

Topping and tailing concentrates on cleaning thoroughly the bits
that really need it: the eyes, nose and ears, the face, hands and bottom.

It keeps undressing (and re-dressing) to a minimum: therefore, it is a useful technique when baby is sick, when the care giver is in a hurry, or if the room temperature is cool.

Put the baby on a towel on a bed or changing table. Gather together a bowl of warm boiled water—this is for his eyes—another of ordinary warm water, cotton balls, washcloths, a soft towel, clean diapers and any cream, powder etc.

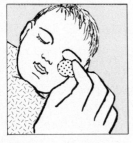

1. Wipe each eye with a separate cotton ball dampened in boiled water. Wipe always from inner corner outwards.

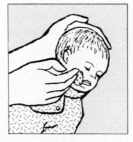

2. With another cotton ball, wipe around ears and neck to get rid of dried sweat which might cause soreness.

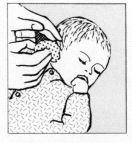

3. Use a further cotton ball to clean around his mouth and chin creases to remove dried milk and dribble.

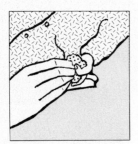

4. Use a clean washcloth dampened in warm water to wipe his hands, checking for any sharp fingernails.

5. Take off his diaper. If he is wet, wipe him with a damp washcloth. If he is soiled, get the worst off with the diaper, then use soap on one washcloth and rinse it off carefully with another.

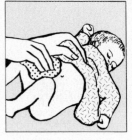

6. Dry every skinfold, not forgetting the crease between his buttocks; apply cream if you like, powder if you must!

2J

If You Haven't Chosen Baby Fresh Wipes, You May Have Made A Rash Decision.

Baby Fresh Wipes Are Hypo-Allergenic With No Alcohol To Dry Your Baby's Skin.

A mother has to make all kinds of choices about what's best for her baby. At least Baby Fresh can make one of those choices easy.

Pre-moistened Baby Fresh Wipes are hypo-aller-

Baby Fresh Wipes are bigger and thicker than pop-ups.

genic and alcohol free, so they're gentle on your baby's skin.

And, since they're bigger and thicker than pop-ups, they're more effective during the cleansing process – especially now, with the special fold

that lets you dispense with one hand.

Baby Fresh Wipes are available scented, unscented and now in Natural Formula with soothing Aloe Vera lotion.

Either way, you can be sure you aren't making a rash decision when it comes to the comfort of your baby.

The special fold means one-hand dispensing.

A Welcome Change For Fresher Babies.

SWADDLING

During the first month of life a newborn will feel more contented and secure if he is firmly wrapped up. A receiving blanket is ideal.

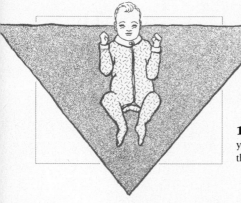

1. Fold the blanket into a triangle and lay your baby on top with his head aligned in the middle of the longest edge.

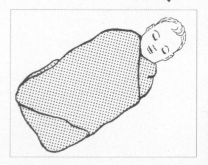

2. Fold one end across the baby and tuck it firmly underneath him. Repeat with the other edge.

3. Tuck the bottom of the blanket under his feet.

"New Pampers have two ways to help keep babies dry, ...and keeping babies dry is important for healthy skin."

Dr. John Blocker
Paediatrician
Phoenix, Arizona

New Pampers. Now the diaper that's already famous for dryness, doubles dryness.

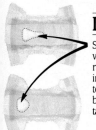

DRYNESS 1

Special absorbency zones where boys and girls wet most, to help lock wetness inside the diaper. This helps to keep wetness away from baby's skin which is important to skin health.

DRYNESS 2

New Pampers are designed with leak barriers – an additional pair of leg cuffs that gently curl up against baby's skin to help catch the other mess and keep it inside.

Now, more than ever, all the dryness a mother or father can give.

HIGH CHAIR SAFETY

Every year high chairs account for over 100 of the injuries
requiring emergency care or hospitalization that are reported to
Consumer and Corporate Affairs Canada.

WHAT TO LOOK FOR BEFORE BUYING:

1. Ensure that the seat belt is sturdy.

2. Make sure that the seat belt fastens securely.

3. Test, to make certain that it can be operated easily by an adult.

4. Make sure the chair is stable and has a wide base to prevent tipping.

FACTS AND FIGURES ABOUT HIGH CHAIR ACCIDENTS
○ In the United States high chair accidents result in at least two deaths each year.
○ Of all products for children, high chairs have been second only to walkers in reported injuries.
○ Most high chair injuries happen when children fall out of them.

SAFETY TIPS
○ High chair accidents can easily be prevented if the seat belt is used properly every time a child is placed in the chair.
○ Never leave a child unsupervised in a high chair.
○ Carefully follow the manufacturer's instructions or warning labels.
○ Never place a high chair where a child's legs can push against nearby furniture or a wall and tip the chair over.
○ Never allow older children to climb onto the chair even when it is unoccupied.

Text supplied by Consumer and Corporate Affairs Canada.

Fisher-Price
believes babies are their
own best teachers.

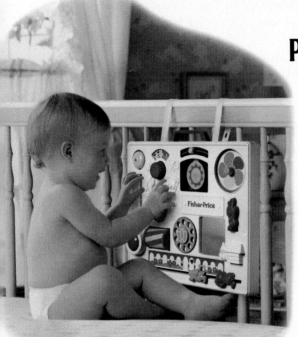

Put your baby near a
Fisher-Price Activity
Centre and you'll see.
Curiosity becomes
the driving force.
So there's a push that
rings a bell. A pat
that spins a colour
wheel. A pull that
makes a clickety
sound. With such
surprises and rewards,
a baby keeps
exploring.

Of course, no toy
takes the place of what
Mom and Dad pass
along; the name of red,
he feel of hugs, the sound of singing together.

Still, a baby with a stimulating
oy can find out a lot about the
world. So with toys like these,
here's no end to the learning.
And the fun.

Fisher-Price Inc., 5300 Tomken Road,
Mississauga, Ontario L4W 1P2 © 1991 Fisher-Price Inc..

CRIB AND CRADLE SAFETY

To be sure your crib or cradle complies with regulations
under the Hazardous Products Act, check that it meets
the requirements illustrated in these diagrams:

MATTRESS SUPPORT AT LOWEST POSITION AND DROP SIDE AT HIGHEST POSITION

drop side requires two separate, positive and simultaneous
actions to release the side, and engages automatically

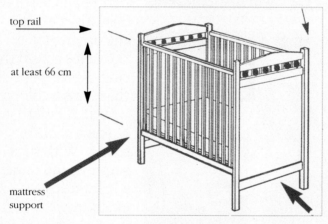

top rail

at least 66 cm

mattress
support

corner post no
higher than 3 mm

crib slats no more
than 6 cm apart

no gap between
lower edge of end
panels and upper
edge of mattress
support

MATTRESS SUPPORT AT HIGHEST POSITION AND DROP SIDE AT LOWEST POSITION

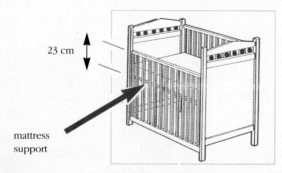

23 cm

mattress
support

Supplied by Consumer and Corporate Affairs Canada.

HEARING:
TURN DOWN THE VOLUME.
TURN DOWN THE RISK.

The noise of a chain saw or jet engine can damage hearing. So can loud music.

If you listen to music at a volume setting above halfway on your dial, you risk permanent hearing loss and, once the ear is damaged, it never recovers.

Do yourself a favor. Turn down the volume and turn down the risk. The chart below of sound levels and human response shows where loud music fits in.

COMMON SOUNDS	NOISE LEVEL (dB)	EFFECT
Jet engine (near)	140	
Shotgun firing Jet takeoff (100-200 ft.)	130	Threshold of pain (about 125 dB)
Thunderclap (near); Discotheque	120	Threshold of sensation
Power saw; Pneumatic drill Rock music band	110	Regular exposure of more than one minute risks permanent hearing loss
Garbage truck	100	No more than 15 minutes unprotected exposure recommended.
Average portable cassette player set above the halfway mark	?	Are you setting your volume too high? Don't play auditory suicide.
Subway; motorcycle; lawnmower	90	Very annoying
Electric razor, Many industrial work places	85	Levels at which hearing damage (eight hours) begins
Average city traffic noise	80	Annoying, interferes with conversation
Vacuum cleaner; hair dryer Inside a car	70	Intrusive, interferes with telephone conversation.
Normal conversation	60	
Quiet office, Air conditioner	50	Comfortable
Whisper	30	Very quiet
Normal breathing	10	Just audible

Courtesy Canadian Hearing Society Foundation

BABYSITTING REMINDERS

Important phone numbers in addition to where to reach parents

NEIGHBOR(S) ....

....

PHYSICIAN ....

FIRE/RESCUE...

AMBULANCE ....

POLICE..

POISON CONTROL CENTRE...

PARENTS SHOULD:
○ Check the baby sitter's references, training and general health in advance.
○ Allow the sitter to spend time with you before sitting to become acquainted with the children and their routine.
○ Show the sitter around the house pointing out fire escape routes and potential problem areas. Should be instructed to leave house immediately in case of fire and call fire department from neighbor's house.
○ Discuss feeding, bathing and sleeping arrangements for your children.
○ Write down and tell the sitter of any allergies or specific needs of your children.
○ Leave a flashlight available.
○ Write down and tell the sitter where you can be reached and your expected hour of return.

AS SITTER YOU SHOULD:
○ Always phone for help whenever you are concerned or in doubt.
○ Never open the door to anyone who has not been cleared by the parents.
○ Never leave the children alone in the house—even for a minute.
○ Never give any medicine or food unless instructed to do so.
○ Always remember that your primary job is to care for the children. Tender loving care usually quiets an unhappy child.

American Academy of Pediatrics

CHOKING

Call 911 or Emergency Ambulance for any severely injured child.

CHOKING

Begin the following if the child is choking and is unable to breathe. If the child is coughing, crying, or speaking, DO NOT do any of the following, but call your doctor for further advice.

FOR INFANTS UNDER ONE YEAR OLD (A)
- Call for emergency services or 911.
- Place infant face down over your arm with head lower than the trunk. Rest your forearm on your thigh.
- Deliver four blows with the heel of the hand, striking high between the infant's shoulder blades.
- If blockage is not relieved, roll the infant over. Lay the child down, face up, on a firm surface. Give four rapid chest compressions over the breastbone using two fingers. OR, SEE BOTTOM OF PAGE

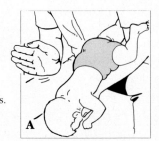

FOR CHILDREN OVER ONE YEAR OLD
- Call for emergency services or 911.
- Place child on his back. Kneel at the child's feet. Put the heel of one hand on the child's abdomen in the midline between the navel and rib cage. Place the second hand on top of the first. (B)
- The older, larger child can be treated in a sitting, standing, or recumbent position. (C)
- Press firmly, but gently, into the abdomen with a rapid inward and upward thrust. Repeat six to 10 times. These abdominal thrusts–called the Heimlich maneuver–should be applied until the foreign body is expelled.

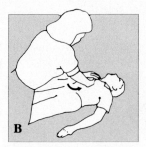

FOR CHILDREN OF ANY AGE
IF THE ABOVE MEASURES HAVE NOT REMOVED THE BLOCKAGE, open mouth with thumb over tongue and fingers wrapped around lower jaw.
- If you can see the foreign body, remove it with a sideways sweep of a finger. (Never poke your finger straight into the throat.) Be careful, though, because finger sweeps may push the object further down the airway.
- If blockage is not relieved and the child cannot breathe, begin the technique of pulmonary support (D) outlined on the next page.
- Rapid transport to a medical facility is urgent if these emergency first aid measures fail.

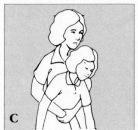

SAFETY AT HOME

Accidents at home cause 37 per cent of deaths in children between the ages of one and four plus a great many injuries. Most of them are avoidable so take the time to child-proof your home and safeguard your children.

GENERAL

•Buy all medicines in childproof bottles and always keep them out of the reach of your child in a locked medicine chest.

•Always keep medicines and chemicals in the clearly labelled containers they originally came in. Never put a poison into a bottle which previously held something harmless like lemonade or syrup.

•Store all drugs and chemicals as far away from food as possible.

•Don't leave aerosol cans lying around — your child could easily depress the nozzle and damage his eyes.

•Always keep a firescreen in front of a fireplace.

•Make sure the cords on electrical appliances are out of the reach of your child.

•All electrical cords should be in good condition and not frayed or otherwise damaged.

•Fit safety socket covers on all plugs.

•Cover hot radiators and pipes with towels or seal them off with pieces of furniture. Teach your child from an early age that radiators are hot and shouldn't be touched.

•Screen and bar all upper floor windows and never leave anything your child could climb up on near them.

•If you own a gun always store it, with its ammunition, in a locked cupboard.

•Keep pins, needles, matches, lighters, sharp knives and scissors out of the reach of your child, in a locked or childproof drawer.

•Buy flame-resistant clothing for your child.

•Your furniture should be too solid and heavy for your child to pull over.

BATHROOM

•Keep the toilet lid closed.

•Have a childproof lock on the medicine cabinet.

•Put safety handles on the bath.

•Have non-slip bath mats.

•Lock away all cleaning substances.

•All heaters should be wall-mounted.

•Put heated towel rails out of your child's reach.

KITCHEN

•Never leave a boiling pot unattended.

•Keep a fiberglass cloth near the stove.

•Always use a burner guard.

•Have childproof locks on dishwashers and washing machines.

•Don't leave long cords on electrical appliances.

•Put pets' bowls out of your child's reach.

•The floors should be non-slip.

•Keep doors and drawers closed and locked if possible.

•Always turn the handles of pans toward the back of the stove.

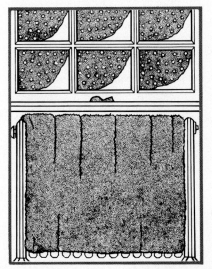

- Never reach across a heated burner.
- Don't use tablecloths.
- Keep plastic bags well out of reach of your child.
- Never leave a room with the iron on.
- Glasses that your child uses should be unbreakable.
- Keep your baby and his toys away from the immediate cooking area.
- If you put your child in a play pen in the kitchen make sure it's at least two feet away from your work tops.

LIVING ROOM
- Run electrical cords around the walls.
- Disconnect appliances when not in use.
- Don't place hot or heavy objects on low tables.
- All shelving should be securely fixed to the walls and well out of reach.
- Anything breakable should be out of the reach of your child.
- Never leave hot or alcoholic drinks sitting around within reach of your child.
- Make sure your houseplants aren't poisonous.

THE BEDROOM
- All furniture should have rounded corners; if they don't, put on special plastic safety corners.

- Store toys and games at a low level so your child doesn't have to stretch or climb up to get at them.
- Don't leave toys lying around on the floor.
- Don't put an electrical fire anywhere near your child's bed at night because he could throw off his blanket or quilt and cause a fire.
- If the bedroom is upstairs leave a safety gate at the top of the stairs.
- Buy non-flammable nightclothes.
- Wall-mounted lights are safer.
- Never leave your baby alone when the cot side is down.
- Never leave your baby alone on the changing table, even for a second.

HALLS/STAIRS
- Fit a safety gate to the top and bottom of the stairs.
- Never leave anything lying on or near the stairs.
- Bannisters should be secure and only have narrow gaps.
- Don't have open plan staircases.
- Stair carpets should be fitted well so that they don't slip. Any tears or holes should be patched immediately with heavy duty tape.

Babybotte, it's the first step that counts.

For several generations, Babybotte has been designing shoes to answer the exacting requirements of baby's feet and to help acquiring balance and confidence to discover the world. Protection of the ankle, natural formation of the arch, comfortable support of the feet, baby takes its first steps in a secure fashion. Today, Babybotte shoes are sold thru more than 500 children speciality shops across the country and because the first steps are also a game and a treat, Babybotte brings them colors  and attraction with a collection of over 100 styles each season.

babybotte

ALWAYS A SHOE AHEAD

SOME DANGEROUS HOUSEHOLD POISONS

This is not a complete list of potentially toxic products.
If in doubt contact your nearest Poison Information Centre.

CLEANING, BLEACHING AGENTS
Metal cleaners and polishers
Detergents
Ethylene glycol
Dry cleaning fluids
Amyl acetate
Benzine
Carbon tetrachloride
Ammonia
Copper and brass cleaner
Turpentine
Cleaning fluids
Alcohol
Oxalic acid
Kerosene
Methyl alcohol
Naphtha
Petroleum distillates
Window washing fluid
Drain cleaners
Typewriter cleaner
Aerosols
Oven cleaner
Bathroom bowl cleaner
Gun cleaners
Lighter fluid
Bleach

POLISHES AND WAXES
Furniture wax/polish
Car wax
Kerosene
Silver polish
Pine oil
Mineral oil
Turpentine
Naphtha
Paint

DRUGS AND MEDICINES
Home chemical testing agents
Narcotics

Antiseptics
Vitamins
A.S.A.
Iron medicines
Rubbing alcohol
Corn and wart remover
Iodine
Tranquilizers
Laxatives
Children's fever drops
Cough syrup
Pain killers
Clinitest tablets
Birth control pills
(Most of the items in this category are only
poisonous when taken orally by accident or
in excess.)

SOLVENTS
Paint remover
Wax remover
Grease spot remover
Lacquer remover
Paint thinner
Carbon tetrachloride
Kerosene
Methyl alcohol
Methanol
Turpentine
Lighter fluid
Petroleum products
Nail polish remover

COSMETIC PREPARATIONS
Nail polish remover
Nail polish
Corn and wart remover
After shave
Shaving lotions/creams
Hair lotions
Resins

Cuticle removers
Cologne
Permanent wave solution
Bubble bath
Hair dyes/tints
Hair remover
Neutralizers
Lacquers
Skin preparations
Plasticizers
Hair sprays
Dandruff shampoo
Eye make-up
Suntan lotions
Perfume

MISCELLANEOUS HOUSEHOLD PRODUCTS AND CHEMICALS

Epoxy glue
Model cement
Garden sprays
Insecticides
Pesticides
Strychnine
Herbicides
Rat killers (Rodenticides)
Fire extinguishing fluids
Rug adhesive
Antifreeze
Carburetor cleaners
Gasoline
Anti-rust products
Deodorizing tablets
Leather polishes and dyes
Shoe cleaners and polishes
Jewelry cleaners and cements
Laundry blueing
Inks
Plant food

HOUSE PLANTS

Hyacinth
Narcissus
Daffodil
Oleander
Arnica
Philodendron
Dieffenbachia

Calla lily
Dumbcane
Elephant's ear
Rosary pea
Castor bean
Mistletoe

FLOWER & VEGETABLE GARDEN PLANTS

Larkspur
Monkshood
Autumn crocus
Star of Bethlehem
Lily of the valley
Daffodil
Nutmeg
Sweet pea
Iris
Foxglove
Bleeding heart
Rhubarb leaves
Indian tobacco
Jonquil
Oleander

ORNAMENTAL PLANTS AND TREES

Daphne
Wisteria
Golden chain
Laurels
Rhododendron
Black locust
Azaleas
Jasmine
Lantana camera (red sage)
Yew
Oaks

PLANTS IN WOODS AND FIELDS

Jack-in-the-pulpit
Moonseed
Mayapple
Jimson weed (thorn apple)
Buttercup
Nightshade
Poison hemlock

This information is supplied by The Ontario Ministry of Health

PREVENTION OF FOOD POISONING

Keep perishable foods refrigerated. Ensure window in kitchen has a screen.

Wash hands after visiting the bathroom and handling garbage.

Fruit and vegetables should be thoroughly washed or peeled before eating.

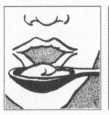

Spoons used for testing should not be put back in mixture.

Wash hands after using a facial tissue.

Clean dishes in hot soapy water and rinse well.

Always use the handle of cutlery when setting the table.

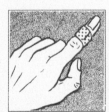

All cuts must be covered with waterproof dressing.

Tea towels should be clean daily.

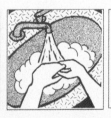

Wash counter, cutting board and hands after preparing meat, particularly chicken.

USE
BEFORE
MAY 15

Read and heed the expiry date on marked foods.

EMERGENCY NUMBERS

Post this list near the telephone so that it
is handy to anyone at any time

EMERGENCY ....

AMBULANCE ....

HOSPITAL ....

PEDIATRICIAN ....

FAMILY DOCTOR ....

DENTIST ....

POISON CONTROL CENTRE ....

POLICE ....

FIRE ....

PHARMACY ....

NEIGHBORS ....

....

....

BABYSITTERS ....

....

....

OFFICE ....

OFFICE ....

Review all numbers regularly to be sure that they still apply.

Supplied by CPS & Pampers

DENTAL CARE BRUSHING

 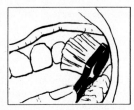 

Outside of front teeth: Hold your toothbrush at a 45° angle and place it where your teeth and gums meet. Move the brush back and forth in a gentle scrubbing motion to remove plaque from the outer surfaces of the front teeth, upper and lower.

Outside of back teeth: Continue brushing with short, angled strokes to remove plaque from the outer surfaces of the back teeth, upper and lower.

Inside of back teeth: Keep brushing with short, angled stokes to remove plaque from the inner surfaces of the back teeth, upper and lower.

 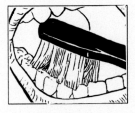

Inside of front teeth: Tilt the brush vertically and make up-and-down strokes to remove plaque from the inner surfaces of the front teeth, upper and lower.

Chewing surfaces: Hold the brush flat and use a scrubbing motion to remove plaque from the chewing surfaces of all teeth, upper and lower.

Information supplied by Crest Toothpaste.

The sooner the better.

By brushing your child's teeth with Crest from the very first, you can give him a head start on a lifetime of healthy teeth. That's because Crest's Fluoristat® strengthens teeth where they need it most. To make them more resistant to decay. And by helping prevent problems in baby teeth, you can help avoid problems in permanent ones.

Ask your dentist or hygienist what a difference it can make, or call Crest directly: 1-800-668-0150 (no charge)

 "Crest contains sodium fluoride which is, in our opinion, an effective decay preventive agent, and is of significant value when used in a conscientiously applied program of oral hygiene and regular professional care."

METRIC CONVERSION TABLES

Read the bold figures in the central column as either the metric or imperial measure. Thus 1 inch = 25.4 millimetres; or 1 millimetre = 0.039 inches

INCHES		MILLIMETRES	POUNDS		KILOGRAMS
0.039	1	25.4	2.205	1	0.454
0.079	2	50.8	4.409	2	0.907
0.118	3	76.2	6.614	3	1.361
0.157	4	101.6	8.818	4	1.814
0.197	5	127.0	11.023	5	2.268
0.236	6	152.4	13.228	6	2.722
0.276	7	177.8	15.432	7	3.175
0.315	8	203.2	17.637	8	3.629
0.354	9	228.6	19.842	9	4.082

FEET		METRES	PINTS		LITRES
			1.760	1	0.568
3.281	1	0.305	3.520	2	1.137
6.562	2	0.610	5.279	3	1.705
9.843	3	0.914	7.039	4	2.273
13.123	4	1.219	8.799	5	2.841
16.404	5	1.524	10.559	6	3.410
19.685	6	1.829	12.318	7	3.978
22.966	7	2.134	14.078	8	4.546
26.247	8	2.438	15.838	9	5.114

YARDS		METRES
1.094	1	0.914
2.187	2	1.829
3.281	3	2.743
4.374	4	3.658
5.468	5	4.572
6.562	6	5.486
7.655	7	6.401
8.749	8	7.315
9.843	9	8.230

OUNCES		GRAMS
0.035	1	28.350
0.071	2	56.699
0.106	3	85.408
0.141	4	113.398
0.176	5	141.748
0.212	6	170.097
0.247	7	198.446
0.282	8	226.796
0.317	9	255.146

TO CONVERT

To convert to metric, multiply by the factor shown. To convert from metric, divide by the factor. (Factors have been rounded.)

LENGTH	
miles: kilometres	1.6093
yards: metres	0.9144
feet: metres	0.3048
inches: millimetres	25.4
inches: centimetres	2.54
MASS	
tons: kilograms	1016.05
tons: tonnes	1.0160
pounds: kilograms	0.4536
ounces: grams	28.3495
CAPACITY	
gallons: litres	4.546
pints: litres	0.568

18

Development
and Care
of the Teeth

B y the sixth week of pregnancy tooth buds for the baby (primary) teeth are evident. Halfway through pregnancy, the enamel crowns of the baby's primary teeth are already calcifying (becoming hardened) deep down in his gums. Even the permanent teeth are beginning to form. By the fourth month, bud formation for the first molars are taking place. Shortly after his birth, the crowns of his permanent six-year molars begin to calcify.

Calcium, which a mother can obtain in generous amounts from milk and cheese, is essential for tooth development, and vitamin D helps her to use it efficiently. Experiments on animals have shown that vitamin A also plays an essential role in enamel formation. A good deal of this vitamin is found in yellow-fleshed vegetables and fruits, green vegetables, margarine, butter, eggs and especially in liver.

Other tests, this time on guinea pigs, have shown that the dentine-forming cells, which are located on the outer surface of the soft central pulp of each tooth, need vitamin C in order to make normal dentine. Thus vitamin C, which is found in abundant amounts in citrus fruits or their juices and in vitaminized apple juice, is helpful to mother and child during pregnancy.

A balanced diet also plays an important part in the development of a child's teeth during his first 12 years. The teeth continue to mature after they appear in the mouth and, unfortunately, recently erupted teeth are especially susceptible to decay.

The teeth all start developing deep in the gums. Most of the growth of the tooth occurs at its root. When the root becomes long enough, the crown is pushed through the overlying gum. Many people assume that teeth grow at their tops (the crown) rather than at their roots.

At first the cutting surfaces of the incisors of the permanent teeth are slightly scalloped. Within a few years these indentations disappear.

Reducing Tooth Decay

Most parents expect their children to develop cavities in their teeth. They think it is unavoidable. As a matter of fact, most and sometimes all of the decay can be prevented, although it is true that certain children are more susceptible to it than others.

Plaque, consisting of mouth bacteria and other substances, sticks to the teeth. It forms on the enamel continuously and the bacteria ferment or produce acids from carbohydrates (sweets and sugars) in the mouth. The acid breaks down the tooth enamel and the decay process continues unless cared for by a dentist.

Dentists have been investigating this problem for many years and have discovered four quite different ways of greatly reducing cavities.

Four Ways to Fight Cavities
1. Fluoridation
2. Elimination of sweets between meals
3. Brushing and flossing of the teeth
4. Regular dental care

Fluoridation

Fluorides make teeth more resistant to decay and may reverse the decay process. The enamel is made less easily eroded by the acid produced by mouth bacteria.Water fluoridation is one of the most effective methods of preventing tooth decay. Many communities have water sources which contain significant amounts of natural fluorides. Other communities have found it necessary and beneficial to fluoridate the water. Dental cavities reduction of 40-50 percent in primary and 50-65 percent in permanent teeth has resulted from community water fluoridation.

If your water supply does not have sufficient fluoride content (greater than .7 parts per million) then it will be necessary to use fluoride supplements suggested by your dentist.

In addition the use of a fluoride toothpaste helps to reduce decay as does a fluoride mouth rinse. Mouth rinses are available for weekly or daily use. These surface fluorides are not meant to be swallowed and so rinses are not recommended for young children. They are useful for children with dental appliances who have difficulty brushing their teeth.

Your dentist may apply a more concentrated form of fluoride to your child's teeth on his semi-annual visit.

Sweet Snacks

Sweets, such as cookies, cakes and candies, can cause tooth decay. Sticky candies such as toffee or caramel or foods such as raisins, or some cakes will remain in the mouth longer and also cause concern. Giving sweets only at meal time and at bedtime, prior to brushing the teeth, will help to prevent cavities.

Bottle-Related Cavities

Babies on a bottle can develop cavities if a large amount of sweet juice is given. Toddlers walking around with a bottle are constantly sipping at liquid that may contribute to tooth decay. A bedtime bottle can become a habit for such children which will be difficult to break. Try giving your child his juice from a training cup to break this habit. "Nursing bottle cavities" are common and a real concern as a young child needs his baby teeth for 10 years or so.

 Never put a child to bed with a bottle.

Brushing Teeth

Mouth germs and food in the mouth are necessary for the production of tooth decay. The main purpose of tooth cleansing is to starve the common acid-producing mouth bacteria. To be most effective, cleansing should be carried out as soon as possible after eating. (Brush your own teeth after you eat because imitation is a great aid in early training.)

The first baby teeth should be wiped with a damp piece of gauze square or cloth wrapped around your finger. A very small brush may be used but fabric is probably easier to manipulate in a small mouth. No toothpaste is necessary under one year of age.

Let your child brush his own teeth as soon as he is able to manage, often around three years. You will need to help him initially.

After the brushing routine is comfortable for the child, flossing where two teeth touch is a good practice and one that will help to prevent plaque developing.

The best type of brush has a straight edge at the top, is two or three tufts wide and only four to six tufts long. Scrubbing cross-ways merely shoves the food debris between the teeth and is therefore, a poor method. Putting the brush along the sides of the teeth (overlapping the gums a little) and giving it a slight to and fro movement as you move it towards the biting edge is most effective. The biting surface of the back teeth needs to be cleansed as well and the mouth should always be rinsed out with water after brushing. Your dentist or dental hygienist can demonstrate this technique.

If your child eats his lunch at school, he may not have an opportunity to brush his teeth. However, he can clean his teeth to a considerable extent by rinsing his mouth with water and then swallowing it – "swish and swallow."

Regular Checkups

Most children have all 20 of their baby teeth by 2 1/2 years. Plan to take your toddler to your dentist's office when all his primary teeth have erupted. From the age of three years, the best program is twice-yearly dental inspections. If your dentist should find a cavity in your child's tooth, it can be repaired in its early stages, when the damage to the tooth is minimal. Decay spreads more rapidly when it reaches the second, softer layer (the dentine). If the decay is allowed to progress well into the dentine towards the pulp (nerve), the tooth may be damaged beyond repair.

Also at these checkups, the dentist removes the hard, white deposit (tartar) from the surface of the teeth because if it is left on, it irritates the gums. She may also seal pits and fissures in the biting surface of the molars with a resin, to prevent bacteria and other substances forming a basis for decay.

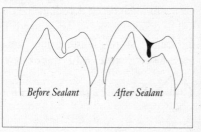

Before Sealant   *After Sealant*

Eruption of Teeth

Most babies cut their first tooth at six to seven months of age, but some perfectly healthy youngsters do not do so until they are several months older. Late teething is usually a harmless family characteristic – it is rarely due to any disease.

Baby's first tooth is one of his incisors, the sharp chisel-like teeth at the front. He may have been drooling and chewing things, preferably a firm rubber teething ring, for some weeks, or you may suddenly discover he has a tooth when it clicks against his feeding spoon.

FIRST TEETH	When teeth "come in"	When teeth "fall out"
Upper		
Central incisors	7-12 mos.	6-8 yrs.
Lateral incisors	9-13 mos.	7-8 yrs.
Canines (cuspids)	16-22 mos.	10-12 yrs.
First molars	13-19 mos.	9-11 yrs.
Second molars	25-33 mos.	10-12 yrs.
Lower		
Second molars	20-31 mos.	10-12 yrs.
First molars	12-18 mos.	9-11 yrs.
Canines (cuspids)	16-23 mos.	9-12 yrs.
Lateral incisors	7-16 mos.	7-8 yrs.
Central incisors	6-10 mos.	6-8 yrs.

Once he has started teething, he will continue to cut more teeth at intervals until he is 12-18 months old. During this time he will want to chew firm objects such as a teething ring or other firm pieces of rubber.

His teeth do not erupt in order from the front backwards. After he has cut his eight incisors, four above and four below, his next teeth will be his first baby molars. In other words, there will be a small gap between his outer incisors and his first baby molars. His rather sharp-pointed eye or canine teeth will later appear in this gap, and finally his second baby molars arrive behind his first molars. Twenty teeth make up his primary or deciduous set. It is true that he will eventually lose all these teeth, but some of them will serve him for 10 years or so, and thus they deserve good care.

Most babies are not disturbed by teething, but when they are cutting their molars they may be a little fretful, sleep less soundly and have depressed appetite. Medication is unnecessary for this normal event. This will not last more than a few days. Teething does not cause fever, convulsions, rashes or diarrhea.

As soon as your baby has cut his first tooth, give him a little toast or a teething biscuit to chew after at least one meal each day. He will enjoy gnawing it, and it will exercise his jawbones and muscles.

Permanent Teeth

The first permanent teeth to erupt are usually the six-year molars. At six to seven years of age they appear just behind the last primary teeth. They do not replace baby teeth and they should serve the youngster the rest of his life. These six-year molars are very

PERMANENT TEETH	When teeth "come in"
Central incisors	7-8 yrs.
Lateral incisors	8-9 yrs.
Canine (cuspids)	11-12 yrs.
First bicuspids	10-11 yrs.
Second bicuspids	10-12 yrs.
First molars	6-7 yrs.
Second molars	12-13 yrs.
Third molars	17-21 yrs.
Third molars	17-21 yrs.
Second molars	11-13 yrs.
First molars	6-7 yrs.
Second bicuspids	11-12 yrs.
First bicuspids	10-12 yrs.
Canines (cuspids)	9-10 yrs.
Lateral incisors	7-8 yrs.
Central incisors	6-7 yrs.

Upper

Lower

important teeth and unfortunately they are often allowed to become badly decayed. Your child's appearance, speech and even the level of his general health can be harmfully influenced by tooth decay.

Between six and nine years the primary incisors are replaced by permanent teeth. From nine to 12 years the cuspids (canine) and bicuspids are replaced. The second and third molars appear after 12 years of age. Sometimes the third molars never erupt or are extracted during the teenage period because of crowding. The full permanent set is composed of 32 teeth.

Later on, if your child plays rough or contact sports, insist that he wear a mouth guard. If your child breaks one of his teeth or has it knocked out, get him and the tooth to your dentist as soon as possible. Your dentist may put the tooth back in again, splinting it to its neighbors. Although the replaced tooth has been irreparably damaged, if it stays in place for a few years, it can help the other teeth to come through in the proper positions.

MOUTHGUARDS*

Mouthguards offer important dental protection for all young athletes. They not only lower the incidence and severity of injuries to teeth, they act as a buffer against jaw fractures, neck injuries and concussions by absorbing some of the blow.

There are three kinds available: custom-fitted latex, mouth-formed and stock. They vary in cost, comfort and protection. Today's enthusiastic athlete doesn't have to sacrifice his or her front teeth to the sport.

Sports that require mouthguards include hockey, football, boxing, squash and lacrosse. Other sports that involve risk for teeth are volleyball, martial arts, wrestling, racquetball, skiing, skate-boarding and bicycling.

These suggestions are from the Canadian Dental Association

1. Editor's Note: The Canadian Dental Association recognizes toothpaste brands it deems effective in fighting tooth decay.

Quick Reference

Four Reasons to Take Your Child to the Dentist Right Away

1. Broken tooth
2. Knocked-out tooth
3. Swelling, sores or bleeding of gums or tongue
4. Toothache, even a mild or sporadic one

Four Reasons to Take Your child to the Dentist as Soon as Possible

1. Tooth sensitive to heat, cold or sweets
2. Brown spot on tooth
3. Tooth out of normal alignment
4. Discolored tooth

What to Do In Case of:

- **Broken tooth:** Gently clean any dirt or debris from the injured area with warm water. Apply cold compresses or ice to the face over the injured tooth to keep swelling down. Take the child to the dentist.

- **Knocked-out tooth:** A permanent tooth can be replanted if you move quickly. If the child is old enough, the tooth is a permanent one, it appears clean and it's not too painful, place the tooth back in the socket. If that's not possible, place the tooth in a container of milk.
  Now take the child – and the tooth – to the dentist or emergency dental clinic. If you get there within 30 minutes the chances of successful replanting are fair.

- **Toothache:** If the area is swollen, apply cold compresses to the face over the tooth. Do not put aspirin directly on the tooth or gum tissue. Take the child to the dentist.

- **Bitten tongue or lip:** Apply direct pressure to the bleeding area with a clean cloth. Use cold compresses if the lip is swollen or may swell. If you can't stop the bleeding, go to a hospital emergency room for medical care. Then go to the dentist.

- **Teething troubles:** Gently rub the gums with a clean finger or the back of a small, cool spoon.

- **Fever with teething:** Consult your physician

- **Loose "baby" teeth:** Don't use force to pull them.

Reproduced with the permission of the Canadian Dental Association from its "First Teeth" booklet.

19

Holidays and Travelling

Handle all foods with extra care during the hot summer months. Babies are particularly susceptible to diarrhea so be sure to keep his food cold (refrigerated if possible) after preparation. Breast-fed babies are much better protected against these viral infections. Hot weather, especially if it is also humid, is hard on everyone but it is particularly hard on infants. He will perspire and thus will require more water to replace the fluid he has lost, and yet he is not able to ask for it. Remember to offer him cooled boiled water, although he may refuse it.

If pasteurized milk is not available wherever you may travel, then use formula or evaporated milk for your baby and powdered skim milk for your older children. It may be advisable to leave a baby on formula or evaporated milk until you return from a holiday.

Summer Clothes

A newborn will need a shirt and nightgown to keep him warm even during hot weather. After the first couple of months, dress him according to the weather and feel his body to make sure that he is comfortable. On hot days just a diaper may be sufficient, and extra baths will help to keep him cool. Think of him when you put on a sweater or pull up a blanket to keep yourself warm, and you will probably have him suitably dressed.

When you are outside, keep him on a screened porch or put a large mosquito netting "bag" over his carriage with the top up. Flies carry germs, and some babies have pronounced reactions to mosquito or black fly bites. Calamine lotion will soothe itchy bites.

With so much concern over the damaging affect of the sun's rays on skin, some dermatologists advise no exposure of a baby's skin to the direct rays of the sun under one year of age. This will require light weight clothing to cover arms and legs and a sun hat. It will also mean choosing areas of shade for baby in which to play or sleep while outdoors.

Over a year of age, keep your children out of the direct rays of the sun in the middle of the day, when the rays are strongest; plan indoor activities if possible.

In the sun, always apply a sun screen with a protective factor between 15 and 30. A child's skin is very sensitive to the sun's rays and over time unprotected skin may develop skin changes leading to cancer in adult life.

Extra Precautions

In the summer, boil your water if you are visiting a camp or cottage. If you have any concern about the safety of your drinking water the local department of health will test a sample – call the department in your area and enquire about its testing procedures.

Whenever possible, peel raw fruits and vegetables before eating them – otherwise wash them carefully. Except for peeled bananas and apples, and possibly scraped celery, a young toddler is given only cooked fruits and vegetables.

Camps

If your family takes holidays together during the summer, your child is probably better with you for most of the time. If your holiday is brief, a supplementary holiday for your youngster at one of the many camps is worth considering. A few weeks at camp will provide opportunities for skills and social development that are not available at home.

Camps vary greatly both in their programs and in the skill and experience of their staff. Before you decide to send your child to a camp, investigate it adequately. Also plan, if possible, to visit the camp after your youngster has been there awhile.

Some children work too hard or relax too little at camp. They are the ones that come home tired out and lighter in weight than when they went. It is evident that such a holiday is not suitable for them, at least at their age. Most youngsters, on the other hand, enjoy the community life and benefit by the opportunity of learning new sports and skills.

Travelling with a child will add many complications to what might be a leisurely holiday for his parents. However, more families are travelling together in cars or planes, and restaurants and hotels are catering more to young families.

Children who visit different countries are enriched by the experience. Changes in climate, food and culture are met early in life.

During the planning stages of a trip, check with your doctor to see if additional immunization will be necessary.

If travelling outside the country, consider additional health insurance such as Blue Cross for the family. If your child has an ongoing (chronic) health problem, discuss your holiday plans with your own doctor. Also determine what health care resources are available en route and at your destination.

On the Road

A small baby usually travels well. If he is kept dry, fed regularly, given sufficient opportunity to sleep and the usual warmth and attention from his parents, he will scarcely notice changes in his surroundings. Disposable diapers (with accompanying small plastic garbage bags) are handy.

Nursing mothers usually have no problem supplying adequate food. If you are bottle-feeding, make the formula ahead and carefully pack his bottles in a well-insulated container which is kept cold constantly with an "ice-pack". Be sure to refreeze the "ice-pack" when necessary. Thermos bottles cannot be sterilized, so do not carry baby's formula in them. Don't hesitate to ask permission to use kitchen facilities to warm bottles and other food, as most places are very co-operative when you are caring for a baby.

Arrange to have about twice the average resting time when you have a small baby to care for en route.

Around six to eight months, a child becomes more aware of his surroundings. He will take more time to settle in an unfamiliar room. It is wise to take along a few of his favorite toys. Often the excitement of travelling will have made him so tired that, although he is restless, sleep will take over before too long. At this age avoid as many changes in location as you can; otherwise no one will enjoy the holiday.

To travel with a toddler is to explore the world anew. Be prepared for extra soiling and wetting and more frequent spills, as the excitement of travelling seems to set him back weeks in his routines. Stick to small, simple meals – don't try to give him complete dinners. Powdered skim milk and baby cereal keep well without refrigeration and can be made up readily; so carry them with you.

Boil any water not supplied by a city or large town – you can take along an electric kettle for this purpose.

Carry a sheet or blanket and a pillow so that he can sleep when he feels like it. Give him an opportunity to exercise before a plane flight or a long drive in the car. When driving, stop at intervals of an hour or so to allow him to run about. A few little books and special travel toys will help to occupy some of his time.

By school age he will be able to learn from travel, and it is a wonderful family adventure. The trip should not be too extensive until he has learned to adjust reasonably quickly to changes in his surroundings. Plan simple menus. In restaurants order foods that are served hot and require minimal handling by staff. Prepare tinned soups, hot dogs (in preference to hamburger) and poached eggs are among the safest. Hamburg can go "bad" quickly in hot weather unless it is kept frozen.

When travelling it is wise to carry simple remedies for common ailments – damp packaged tissues for cleaning dirty hands, sun screen to protect against sunburn, band-aids for scrapes and cuts, and jellies to ease the tickle of a cough. It is useful to carry some acetaminophen to treat a fever. If your child is on any regular medication, be sure to carry an adequate supply for the duration of your holiday.

Many children get car-sick, but keeping the car well-ventilated and feeding them only light, easily digested food may reduce this tendency. Have paper towels and plastic bags readily available. Anti-nausea pills are usually unnecessary. For a child who becomes motion sick easily, anti-nausea pills may be recommended by your doctor. Sedating children for long trips is usually unnecessary and is actually counterproductive resulting in hyperactivity.

Take along some medicine for treating a bout of diarrhea, should it develop on your trip.

Waiting rooms in airports and railway stations expose your children to the diseases of other travellers. The hazard of coming into contact with new infections is one of the dangers of travelling – keep your child away from other children as much as you reasonably can.

Cars and Planes

Car accidents are the leading cause of death to children after the first few months of life. Most accidents occur when the car is travelling at moderate speed and is within 30 miles of home. Car seats and belts are necessary and legally required whenever you take your child on the road. Seat belts should be worn by passengers of any age.

 Safety lock devices for doors and driver-controlled door and window locks are excellent safeguards when young children are in the car.

Car Seats

Infants in car seats must face the rear of the car. Parents have the choice of buying two seats – an infant seat followed by a standard seat, or just buy a convertible seat. This dual functioning convertible seat is used facing backward in the car for the infant; the reclining position gives good support to the large head and small body. The driver of the car is able to keep an eye on the baby. As the child becomes older and can sit

Direction of Travel

Infant car seats should face the rear of the car.

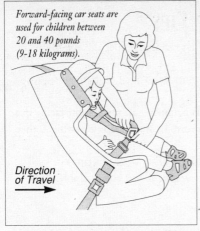

Forward-facing car seats are used for children between 20 and 40 pounds (9-18 kilograms).

Direction of Travel →

and stand readily, (around 10-12 months) the seat is positioned upright in a forward position in the car. Baby can now look outside, his head and back firmly supported in his own seat.

The safest place for his seat is the middle of the back seat of the car. When the middle of his ear comes to the top of his seat, he will need another change in car seat.

As your child grows, special adaptation of seats and belts must be made to hold him securely and to adjust to this growth.

A special car booster seat will be necessary for the three to four year old so that the seat belt will be low enough to avoid the abdominal area and yet hold the child securely. As the shoulder straps are not positioned for a child's size, do up the lap belt first, then place the shoulder belt behind the child's back.

Currently car seats are being upgraded to protect the infant on planes as well as in cars. Look for such a seat if your are shopping for a new car seat.

Most airlines now recommend carry-on infant car seats provided the measurements do not exceed those of carry-on luggage and you have bought a ticket for the child. There is no standard legislation for all airlines as yet so it is wise to call ahead and enquire of the airline about its policy.

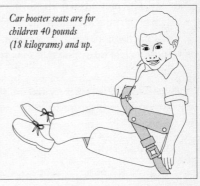

Car booster seats are for children 40 pounds (18 kilograms) and up.

IMPORTANT *Whatever model you choose, have it properly installed and use as recommended. Car seats in the forward position are required by law to be bolted to the car.*

DANGEROUS PRACTICES

1. Travelling with a baby or small child in your arms.
2. Letting a child stand up in a car, especially in the front.
3. Allowing a child to kneel on the back seat.
4. Letting a child lie on the back "parcel shelf".
5. Permitting a child to lie, stand or sit in the back section of a station wagon.

CAR SEAT TIPS**

The driver is responsible for ensuring that children, under the age of 16, are buckled up. This is what is required:

Infants: Up to 20 pounds (nine kilograms) must travel at all times in an approved rear-facing car seat.

Toddlers: From 20-40 pounds (nine to 18 kilograms) must travel front-facing in a car seat in their parents' or guardians' car. In someone else's vehicle, they must be in a lap belt.

Preschoolers: From 40-50 pounds (18-23 kilograms) must be in a lap belt.

Older Children: Up to 16 years old, must wear the full seat belt assembly.

Important Reminders:

- Push the child safety seat well down into the upholstery before securing it with the lap belt.
- Always thread the lap belt exactly according to the manufacturer's instructions.
- Keep the car safety seat held in place with the lap belt at all times whether in use or not. This prevents it from moving inside the vehicle.
- When purchasing a secondhand safety seat make sure it meets federal safety standards and has not been in an accident.
- Choose a child safety seat that suits your needs, protects your child and fits your vehicle.

*** This information has been provided by the Onario Ministry of Transportation and Communications*

20

Care of the Sick Child

U p to now, much advice has been given on how to keep your child well. However, every child is exposed to infection and becomes sick at least occasionally.

Bed rest is best for an acutely ill child. When he begins to feel better and wishes to get up, it is wise to dress him and move him from his bedroom. When he is again ready to rest he will go to bed willingly.

Encourage him to drink small amounts of clear fluids frequently and if he wishes to eat give him a little light food.

Keep a list of the medications and the times they were administered.

Fortunately, children recover almost as suddenly as they become ill. A child who has seemed very ill when he went to sleep may feel so well the next day that you cannot keep him in bed.

 Never hesitate to contact your child's doctor if you have any health concern.

Treating a Fever

Fever may be the first sign of an acute infection such as a cold. Crankiness or decreased appetite may precede it by a few hours. Young children tend to run high fevers – even as high as 104 Fahrenheit (40 Celsius).

Fevers usually are not harmful, do not cause brain damage and in fact are considered by many to be beneficial to the body as they increase the activity of the immune system. Treating a fever will make the child feel more comfortable. The child should not be awakened for treatment of a fever and the aim should not be to reduce the temperature to normal, but rather to a level that will make the child feel more comfortable. Acetaminophen is the drug of choice and is usually given by mouth. (If the child is vomiting it may be given rectally in suppository form.)

Dress the child lightly and give clear fluids to replace losses that will occur when a child has a fever.

Taking a Temperature

The preferred site for taking a temperature is under the arm although it is more accurate if taken rectally. The oral route should only be used for a co-operative child older than five years. A rectal thermometer has a blunt, thick bulb at its lower end. An ordinary mouth thermometer has a long, thin end which might easily break. As thermometers vary, check the recommended instructions.

A digital thermometer can be used rectally, orally or under the arm. There is a "beep" when the temperature of the child is reached and this usually occurs in less than a minute. It is durable but more expensive.

Before using a thermometer, shake the mercury down to 96 Fahrenheit (35.5 Celsius), or lower. To do this, hold the thermometer firmly between your thumb and forefinger and give it a few sharp, quick wrist snaps. Read it to see that the mercury is down to the desired level. If not, shake it again.

When you are taking a rectal temperature, hold your baby with his face downward on your lap or lay him on his left side on a table or cot and stand facing his back. Put a diaper underneath him, as the thermometer may stimulate him to have a bowel movement. Separate his buttocks and place the bulb end of the thermometer lubricated with petroleum jelly gently into the rectum with a screwing motion. Hold the ther-

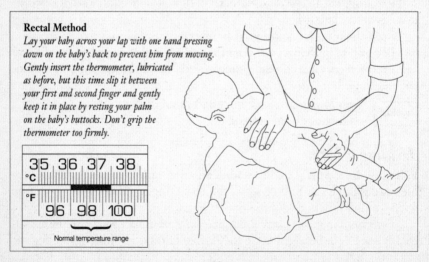

Rectal Method
Lay your baby across your lap with one hand pressing down on the baby's back to prevent him from moving. Gently insert the thermometer, lubricated as before, but this time slip it between your first and second finger and gently keep it in place by resting your palm on the baby's buttocks. Don't grip the thermometer too firmly.

Normal temperature range

mometer with your fingers approximately 1 inch (2.5 centimetres) from the end, pressing the fingers against the anus or the hand against the buttocks so that the thermometer cannot move in or out of the rectum (see diagram on previous page). With your other hand hold the child securely. Leave it in for exactly two minutes. Then remove it, read it and write down the reading.

> **NOTE** *A rectal temperature of 100.4 Fahrenheit (38 Celsius) or higher is considered a fever.*

To take an armpit (axillary) temperature the thermometer should be placed in the armpit, and secured in place by the arm being held firmly against the infant's side for four minutes. A temperature of greater than 99 Fahrenheit – 37.2 Celsius – is considered a fever.

To clean the thermometer, rub it off with a piece of toilet paper or absorbent cotton and then wash it with soap and cold water, using a fresh piece of cotton. Do not use hot water because that will break the bulb.

Settling the Stomach

Vomiting may occur at the onset of any acute infection in children. If the infection is in the bowel your child may vomit repeatedly. Indeed it may be difficult to control the nausea and settle his stomach. There are many causes of vomiting so be sure to consult your doctor.

When your child is nauseated, hold him to reassure and comfort him. Have a bowl handy by his crib/bedside. When he throws up, support his head with one hand on his forehead. When the vomiting has stopped, sponge his face and wipe around his mouth. Give him a few chips of ice to freshen his mouth. Then let him rest or sleep. Wash the bowl and replace it, in case he is sick again.

Wait an hour or so to let his stomach settle. Then offer him only three to five teaspoons of clear fluid, juice or ginger ale every five to 10 minutes. Larger amounts may cause him to vomit. As he becomes better he will retain more and the interval may be lengthened. When he asks for food, start with clear soups and gelatine jellies.

If vomiting persists, call your doctor for further advice and care.

Giving Medication

Oral

There are several methods of administering liquid medicine – a medicine spoon, dropper, tube-spoon or oral syringe.

• Have a favorite drink ready to use as a "chaser" to take away the taste of the medicine.

• It helps to tell the child, if he is old enough,

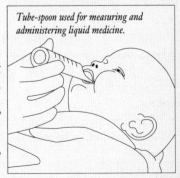

Tube-spoon used for measuring and administering liquid medicine.

why he has to take the medicine and that it will eventually make him feel better.

- If you find it impossible to get your child to swallow the medicine, call your doctor and she may prescribe one with a different flavor or form.

Nose Drops

Preschoolers

- Have your child lie down and place a small pillow beneath his shoulders. His head will now tilt back. (Another person can steady the head if your child is likely to wriggle.)
- Put the tip of the dropper just above your child's nostril and squeeze out the prescribed number of drops.
- After the drops are administered, ask the child to remain lying down for about a minute.

Babies

Giving nose drops to an infant is very disturbing to him and can be difficult to do. Oral medication is preferred by many physicians. If you must give nose drops follow the directions below.

- Wrap baby snugly in a blanket and lay him on his back across your knee. His head should tilt back slightly. Keep one hand under his head to support it and with the other administer the drops as instructed for the preschool child.

 The dropper should not touch the nose. If it does, wash it immediately before using it again.

Ear Drops

Preschoolers

Ear drops are easier to administer because following their use there is often considerable relief from pain.

- Ask your doctor if you can warm the drops. To do this place the bottle in a bowl of warm water for a few minutes, then check the temperature on the inside of your wrist.
- Have the child lie on his side with the affected ear uppermost, then squeeze the prescribed number of drops into the ear. The child should remain in this position for about a minute.

Babies

- Wrap baby snugly and lay him on your lap with the affected ear uppermost. Support his head with one hand, then administer the ear drops as instructed for a toddler.

Eye Drops and Ointment

Preschoolers

- Position the preschool child so that he is lying with his head in your lap.
- Clean around you child's affected eye with a cotton ball dipped in warm boiled water.
- Place one arm around you child's head with your palm against his cheek then tilt the head so that the affected eye is a little lower than the other.
- Draw the lower eyelid gently down with your thumb.
- The dropper should be positioned over the gap, between the lower lid and the eye, angling it so that it is out of your child's sight. (If necessary, another person could hold the head steady.)
- Squeeze out the prescribed number of drops into the outer corner of the eye being careful not to touch the eye or the lid.

Babies

Eye drops or ointments are almost impossible to administer to a young child or baby. Oral medication is preferred by many physicians.

- Attempt administering drops only when baby is relaxed.
- Wrap baby snugly and lay him on a firm surface or across you knee. Administer drops or ointment as you would to a toddler.
- If necessary, administer the drops into the inner corner of the closed eye. When the infant opens the eye, the drops will roll in.

Steaming

Croup often appears suddenly at night. Your child may have gone to bed quite well and then awakened with a barking cough. Go into the bathroom with him and fill the bathtub with hot water. A hot shower will also steam the bathroom but don't lose all your hot water! Sit with him until the coughing stops and his breathing becomes easier. Meanwhile, your partner can put a vaporizer in his room that will provide moisture for the remainder of the night. For simple croup, a cool or warm mist vaporizer will likely be recommended by your doctor.

If his breathing does not become easier, call your doctor. Your child may have to be admitted to hospital, where he will be placed in a "Croupette" which will provide cool moist air.

Convulsion

A febrile convulsion in a young child usually comes on suddenly, associated with the fever of an acute infection. Typical febrile seizures do not cause brain damage or have any long-term after effect. Usually a febrile convulsion does not last long. Be sure to turn the child on his side so that breathing will be easier and secretions will run out of his mouth. Sponge the sick child and when possible, give him acetaminophen to help bring down his temperature. Contact your doctor.

Sponging

- When your child has a fever over 104 Fahrenheit (40 Celsius), try reducing it by sponging his body with tepid water.
- Remove the child's bedding and bed clothes.
- Place towels under him so that the crib/bed does not get wet.
- Fill a bowl with tepid water and wring out a sponge or cloth in it.
- Gently wipe you child's face, neck , arms and legs in turn.
- Sponge until cool (approximately 15-30 minutes).

21

Accidents: Prevention & Treatment

Every year accidents kill and cripple more children than all diseases combined. Nearly all these serious accidents could have been prevented, although many minor ones are unavoidable. If you can, take a first aid course, where, amongst other training, you can learn how to carry out artificial respiration (see action charts). Accidents are unintentional acts. Many occur without injury, damage or harm. Your main effort is to prevent accidents without overprotecting your child and stifling his curiosity. This involves teaching him how to do innumerable things safely, both by your own example and by simple explanations.

You can protect against hazards. Post a list of telephone numbers by your phone including those of your doctor, the hospital emergency department, poison control centre, taxi company, fire department and police department (see action charts).

Prepare a first aid kit containing the following :
- Gauze bandage rolls – 1 inch and 2 inch
- Absorbent cotton
- Sterilized gauze pads (ready to use)
- Adhesive tape – 1 inch
- Band Aids
- Rubbing alcohol
- A recommended antiseptic ointment
- Baking soda (sodium bicarbonate)
- A thermometer, digital, mercury, (rectal and/or oral)

Swallowing Foreign Objects

Be on guard to see that your small child can find no small objects with which to play. Youngsters have swallowed all kinds of things – wooden beads, rings, the button eyes of stuffed animals, prune pits, small coins, safety pins, pieces of chewed-up plastic toys and much more.

If the child is choking and having difficulty breathing, hold him upside down and slap between the shoulder blades vigorously. If this fails to dislodge the object, hail a passing car and get him as quickly as possible to the nearest hospital or doctor.

If the object swallowed is small and has no sharp edges, it will not likely cause further trouble. Even if your child has swallowed an open safety pin, it may still pass through without causing any damage, but the child needs to be carefully watched. Consult your doctor.

Examine his bowel movements carefully during the next week – usually the object will be passed within two or three days. If the youngster vomits or complains of pain in his abdomen or if the object is not found in the first week, tell your physician about it again. If there is much delay in the passage of the swallowed object, your doctor may recommend that an X-ray be taken.

Never give a laxative or laxative food to a child who has swallowed a hard object even though it might seem logical. It is dangerous because a laxative stimulates the intestines to contract vigorously. This increases the pressure on the swallowed object, and as a result, the lining of the intestines may be injured or even perforated.

If, after swallowing an object, a child experiences difficulty in swallowing or breathing, if there is pain on swallowing or if the child drools or spits up blood, immediate medical attention should be sought.

Foreign Objects in the Lungs

Serious lung disease may be caused by breathing small pieces of peanut or seeds into the lung. Therefore, don't ever give young children peanuts or other "hard" foods, and warn older youngsters not to "fool around" when they are eating them.

If your youngster chokes on a peanut, hold his head and chest down over the side of a bed and try to get him to cough it out. Even if this is successful, tell your physician about the accident.

Foreign Objects in the Ear or Nose

Small youngsters sometimes shove beans, beads, shells and other small objects into their ears. If they are projecting from the surface and can be securely grasped with a pair of tweezers, you may remove them yourself. Someone else will be needed to hold the child's head absolutely still while you are doing this. You want to avoid pushing the object further down the ear canal, so unless you can get a really good grip on the object, don't try to get it out. Let an expert do it.

Do not try to syringe out a bean or pea with water or even oil, as it swells when it is wet and that makes it harder to get it out.

If your child pushes something up his nose, it is best to have it removed by a doctor.

If your child develops a foul odor from the nose, especially together with a yellow/green discharge, it may indicate that there is a small object or remnant left in the nose that must be removed. Therefore, the child needs to be examined by a physician.

Foreign Objects in the Vagina, Rectum or Penis

These are unusual places for a child to place a foreign object. If you believe that your child has a foreign body in the vagina or penis, the child should be seen by a physician for its removal and so that any behavioral implications can be explored. The same is true for foreign objects in the rectum. Specifically, these occurrences may be an indication of sexual molestation.

Puncture Wounds

It is usually very hard, even for a physician, to remove a needle that has broken off in the foot or any other part of the body without the assistance of an X-ray machine. Limit your efforts to putting an antiseptic over the puncture wound. Take your child to your doctor or the hospital at once, while you still know where the needle went in.

Cuts and Scratches

A neglected wound may become infected, which of course delays healing and may possibly lead to serious trouble. Clean the area around the injury thoroughly with warm water and absorbent cotton. An antiseptic wipe or a small amount of soap with warm water on absorbent cotton may be used on the injury. Rinse with warm water. Lay a piece of sterilized gauze over the wound and bandage it. If the cut is small, a band-aid is enough. Keep the band-aid or bandage dry, and change it once a day to see how the wound is healing.

If it is large or deep (such as that caused by a nail) consult your doctor. She will want to know when your child received his last booster of tetanus toxoid.

Splinters need to be removed promptly with a sterilized needle.

Falls and Concussions

A baby falls a lot when he is learning to walk, but he has not far to go before he hits the floor. Often he will learn to pick himself up without crying. Using a harness in his carriage and high chair, keeping the sides of his crib up, and never leaving him alone on a table or adult bed after he has learned to roll over help to avoid falls. Installing safety gates at the top and bottom of stairs until he has learned to negotiate them safely, and bars across low windows are similarly useful.

Most falls are not serious and if the child after his bout of crying seems normal

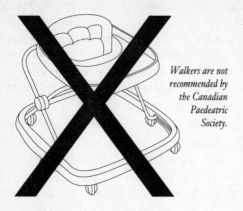

Walkers are not recommended by the Canadian Paedeatric Society.

and bright, there is no cause for alarm. If there is minor bruising apply cold compresses for about a half-hour. If the fall is more serious, with a change in consciousness or with painful movement, call 911. When there is a great deal of pain and you are suspicious of a fracture, do not move the affected area until a splint has been applied. If the back or neck is involved, wait for medical assistance. Call 911.

If the child is not breathing, cardiopulmonary resuscitation (see action charts for CPR technique) immediately and have someone call 911.

 The use of a walker may result in serious injury and is, therefore, not recommended

Burns and Scalds

These accidents are much too common and are often serious. The kitchen is the main site of danger, and many mothers keep their crawling or toddling youngsters occupied elsewhere when they are cooking or serving a meal. Your baby can watch you from his pen set up at a safe but sociable distance.

With preschool children in the home, always turn pot handles towards the middle of the stove, and when you are serving hot drinks or dishes, set the containers in the middle of the table. Avoid table clothes that hang down temptingly over the side.

 Keep matches and lighters where they cannot be reached by your child.

If your child gets a mild burn (skin is unbroken and there are no blisters), immerse the burned area in cold water or apply towels soaked in cold water to the affected area until the pain stops.

If the burn is more severe, call 911 or take the child immediately to the hospital. If possible, remove smouldering or chemically contaminated clothing. Do not break blisters or try to clean the burn. Wrap the area loosely in clean fabric. Keep him warm.

If acid or lyes or other potentially corrosive substances come in contact with a child's skin, brush off the dry material gently. Wash him with large quantities of water and remove contaminated clothing wearing rubber gloves, if possible. Seek immediate medical attention.

Electricity can also cause painful burns – for example, if a baby sucks the free end of an extension cord that is still connected to a wall plug, he may fill it with saliva which causes a short circuit and a bad electrical burn in his mouth. Disconnect extensions at the "power" end. You would also be wise to cover any unused wall plug with a safety plug-cover or by moving a heavy piece of furniture in front of it. A curious toddler could push some metal object into the plug, and receive a shock or burn.

Do not touch the injured child until the current is broken. Pull him from the contact using wood, rubber or thick, dry cloth. Apply CPR (see Action Chart) and have someone call 911.

Suffocation

Plastic bags, commonly used to cover dry-cleaned clothing, can suffocate a baby if he gets his head in it. It clings to his face and he does not know how to remove it. In fact, while your youngsters are small, dispose of this plastic immediately.

Quite a number of young children have climbed in and been suffocated in discarded refrigerators. If you have one around, remove the door or the catches while waiting for garbage pick-up. If your child cannot be roused or if his breathing is labored and noisy, or shallow or absent check his airway.

If breathing is absent, apply CPR (see Action Chart) if indicated. Call 911.

If your child is breathing turn him on his side to maintain an adequate airway. Loosen all tight clothing.

Drowning

Only a few inches of water can drown a baby! Never leave him alone, even for a minute, when he is in his bath. Be very cautious about wading pools. Until he can swim well, always have him wear a life preserver when he plays on the edge of a river or lake or when he is in a boat. Young children are attracted by water. Ensure that any nearby pools or bodies of water are safely fenced in.

In the event that a child does get into trouble in the water call 911 and apply CPR if indicated (see Action Chart).

Poison Prevention

It is a challenge to foresee the curiosity and imagination of a child. Go through your home, from top to bottom, and sort, with little people in mind. Throw out, or securely package or put well away, what is not suitable to leave about. It is much easier on everyone if this is done before something happens.

Poison prevention is important. Throw out all of the following materials entirely – rat poisons, mouse seed, roach powder, moth balls, oil of wintergreen, boracic acid, borax, carbolic acid, bichloride of mercury, lye, caustic soda, or potash, and strong acids. Reduce to a minimum strong cleansers in your home and keep the few cleansers that are really necessary in a special cupboard, inaccessible to your child, not under the sink. Baking soda, soaps, sponges and scouring pads with water clean most of the spills that occur while the children are small.

Preschool children are of the greatest concern. A toddler needs to be watched by someone all the time, because he has no understanding of what might happen to him as he explores. A child of four to five years has had a little more experience with many accidents, but will still get into the forbidden, if not supervised.

Medicines

Choose a high cupboard for medicines and put a lock on the door. Keep only the ones for which you have a use. Try to remove and return medicines to this cupboard when the children are not around. When you give a medicine be sure that you are able to see the label and the instructions. At night, with fatigue and sometimes unwell yourself, it is easy to make a mistake. Children's medications are better not to be treated as a sweet, or in anyway made too desirable. They can work wonders, but when used incorrectly can make your baby very ill.

Always put medicine away promptly. Never leave pills on a table or in a purse, even for a few moments. Most home poisonings involve drugs.

Many products in the home are considered hazardous because of toddlers putting most things in their mouths, drinking any available liquid, and reaching for any object. Try to limit the bottles and tubes on your dresser, on the counters in the kitchen and bathroom, in the garage and home workshop. Keep bottles and tubes tightly capped (some have safety caps).

Do not use drinking containers or empty food jars for household chemicals. Mix-ups have resulted!

Be Prepared

Have the phone number of your nearest Poison Control Information Centre on hand to call for advice at once if an accident has occurred (see Action Chart). It is recommended that Syrup of Ipecac, (obtainable at the drug store) be kept in your medicine cupboard. It will cause vomiting if given; but give it only on the recommendation of your doctor or the Poison Control Centre.

CHOKING**

If the Choking Victim is an Infant (Younger Than 1 Year of Age)

1. (a) Place the infant face down on the rescuer's forearm at a 60° headdown position with the head and neck stabilized. Rest the forearm firmly against the rescuer's body for additional support. (b) For the choking large infant, an alternate method is to lay the infant face down over the rescuer's lap, with the head firmly supported and held lower than the trunk.
2. Administer four back blows rapidly with the heel of the hand high between shoulder blades.
3. If obstruction is not relieved, turn the infant over to a supine position resting on a firm surface and deliver four rapid chest thrusts (similar to external cardiac compressions) over the sternum using two fingers.
4. If breathing is not resumed, open the victim's mouth by grasping both the tongue and the lower jaw between thumb and finger and lifting (the tongue-jaw lift technique); this draws the tongue away from the back of the throat and may help relieve the obstruction. If the foreign body is visualized, it may be manually extracted by a finger sweep. However, blind sweeps may cause further obstruction and thus should be avoided.
5. If no spontaneous breathing occurs, attempt ventilation with two breaths by mouth-to-mouth or mouth-to-mouth and nose technique.
6. Repeat steps 1 to 5 and persist in performing the above techniques as needed while rapidly seeking aid from emergency medical services.

If the Choking Victim is a Small Child (Older Than 1 Year of Age)

1. Apply a series of six to ten abdominal thrusts (the Heimlich maneuver) until the foreign body is expelled. The child should be placed on his or her back. The rescuer should kneel at the child's feet if the child is on the floor, or stand at the child's feet if the child is on a table. The astride position is not recommended for small children. The heel of one hand should be placed in the midline between navel and rib cage and the second hand placed on top of the first and pressed into the abdomen with an upward thrust. In small children, the maneuver must be applied gently. It should consist of a rapid inward and upward thrust.
2. If the obstruction is not relieved using the Heimlich maneuver, open the airway using the tongue-jaw lift technique and attempt to visualize the foreign body. No blind finger sweeps should be used.
3. If no spontaneous respirations result, attempt to ventilate the victim. If unsuccessful, repeat a series of six to ten abdominal thrusts.
4. Repeat steps 1 to 3 and persist in performing the above sequence while rapidly seeking aid from emergency medical services.

** *Canadian Pediatric Society recommendations*

Poison-Proofing Checklist**

Drugs
- Go through the medicine chest and return out of date or old medications to your pharmacist for safe disposal.
- Protect medication labels by covering with transparent tape to keep them legible. Always pour liquid away from the label side to prevent smearing or staining.
- Do not take medicine in front of a child. He may decide to imitate you.
- Never refer to medication as candy to get a child to take it. Do not make the giving of medicine a game.
- Ask your pharmacist to put all prescriptions and non-prescription drugs in containers with safety lids.
- Before leaving the doctor's office or pharmacy be sure that you understand why you or your child is to take the medicine, the amount, how often, and the length of time you will need to continue the medication.
- Read labels carefully before taking any medication. Never give medications in the dark.
- Always leave medicine in its original container. Do not mix different drugs, vitamins, or other tablets in the same container.
- Do not medicate yourself or child with another person's medication.
- Some people carry medication in their purses which could be harmful to a child, so be careful to keep all purses out of reach of children.
- Be extra cautious when the household routine is disrupted (i.e. holidays, when visiting, personal crisis) as this is when the likelihood of an accidental poisoning increases.

Household
- Store food, medication and household cleaning products separately.
- Keep all cleaning products out of children's reach. Use safety catches on cupboards and use safety containers.
- Never leave cleaning products and medication unattended.
- After a party, empty ashtrays and unfinished drinks.
- Make sure that toys, the crib and other "chewable" objects have non-toxic paints. The lead-based paint that is still present in some older homes may be harmful if ingested by children.
- Check areas such as the garage, laundry room and basement that may become catchalls for insecticides, paint products, gasoline, bleaches, rust removers etc.
- Do not mix cleaning products together – chemical reactions can cause toxic fumes.
- When painting, spraying, using oven cleaners or other volatile products, keep the

area well ventilated.
• Many house plants are poisonous. (Check the appendix for them.)

Insecticides
• All insecticides and pesticides are potentially dangerous. Buy only the amount needed for the job.
• Wear protective clothing to avoid skin contamination. Leather absorbs insecticides and should not be worn.
• To avoid inhaling pesticides, do not spray or dust on windy days and wear a protective mask if directed on the label.
• Contact the ministry of environment for information on local collection days or depots for insecticides/pesticide containers.

Food Poisoning
• Never taste food from a can that is bulging or leaking. Canned food that has a "funny" odor or is "off color" or that spurts out when the can is opened may cause trouble.
• Leftovers should be wrapped tightly and be well spaced in your refrigerator. They must be promptly stored after being allowed to cool for approximately one hour.
• Food that is warm when placed in the freezer will partially thaw those foods next to it, also allowing for bacterial growth.
• A build up of frost in your freezer does not allow for proper freezing of foods.
• Never stuff a turkey and then store it in the refrigerator before cooking. The dressing in the dark cavity of the fowl is an excellent place for bacteria to grow.
• Frozen foods should not be thawed on the kitchen counter. Foods should be thawed by one of the following three methods:
a) Wrap food in paper and leave on counter
b) Place in refrigerator
c) Place wrapped food in cold water
• Make a tour of your kitchen to check for proper food storage in cupboards.
a) Do not store cans under the sink where moisture or heat can cause the can to rust or leak.
b) Do not store food products near cleaning products.
c) Check product labelling to see if the product should be refrigerated after opening.
d) Place newly purchased containers behind older containers on your shelves.
• On picnics, ensure that foods are kept properly chilled in a cooler.
• In case of power failure, keep the freezer door closed as foods will stay frozen for up to 48 hours. Open your refrigerator door as infrequently as possible.

** The above is a condensed version of "Poisons – Not Just Kid Stuff."

22

Ailments and Diseases of Concern in Childhood

ABDOMINAL PAIN

Abdominal pain is a common complaint in children. An upset or anxious child may complain of abdominal pain. If it is not too severe, comfort the child. The pain may be forgotten if attention is diverted elsewhere – to a book or a game. Sometimes, you never discover what caused the upset.

The onset of an acute infection, in some children, may be marked by abdominal pain followed by vomiting and/or fever. The most common site for an infection in childhood is the respiratory tract. A bowel infection, with vomiting and/or diarrhea, may cause pain which is not as severe or persistant as that which occurs in appendicitis.

Cramping, abdominal pains may be evident when a child is constipated. A constipated bowel movement is dry, firm and may be painful to pass. If your child eats a balanced diet, (this includes generous amounts of fruits and vegetables and at least some whole grain cereal); if he has a regular time for his bowel movement and is not hurried in the process; if he drinks a fair amount of fluid and gets sufficient exercise, he will rarely need even a mild laxative.

The regular use of laxatives, enemas or even suppositories is a habit to be avoided. Never give a laxative to a child who has a pain in his abdomen because it causes the muscles both in his bowel and appendix to contract strongly. If the pain is due to an inflamed appendix, the laxative may cause the appendix to rupture which will make the child acutely ill.

Appendicitis

Appendicitis (inflammation of the appendix) is rare in the first year of life, infrequent in the second, but quite common from then on, especially after six.

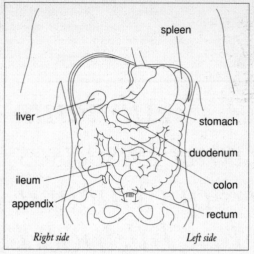

Right side   *Left side*

The appendix itself is a narrow hollow sac, usually about the size and shape of a short fat earthworm, attached to the cecum or first part of the large intestine. Intestinal contents from the cecum can flow in and out of the appendix through the opening where the appendix is attached. The appendix has no function in humans.

Appendicitis is more common when respiratory diseases are prevalent.

A small amount of intestinal contents (feces) may remain inside the appendix and become dry and hard, almost like a small stone – a fecolith. A fecolith, is often found in an inflamed appendix that has been removed by a surgeon.

The symptoms of acute appendicitis vary a great deal. If your youngster has a pain in his stomach (abdomen) which lasts two hours or more, have your physician see him. The pain need not be severe. Often it begins around the navel or in the upper abdomen and later shifts to the lower right side of the abdomen. It may be lower or higher or more towards the middle if the appendix is not in its usual position.

Often the child vomits once, twice or even more; but he may not vomit at all. He may have a moderate fever. His bowel movements may be normal, or he may be constipated. Diarrhea is less common, but can occur. Often the pain is worse when he pulls up his right knee or walks around.

Have your child seen early in the attack by your doctor. The abscess-like inflammation of the appendix may spread through the wall and rupture, causing peritonitis (inflammation of the lining of the abdomen). It is far safer to have the appendix removed before it ruptures.

 If abdominal pain is persistent and/or severe, do contact your doctor.

AIDS (Acquired Immunodeficiency Syndrome)

When a child's immune system becomes disturbed, he will suffer from many illnesses that he would normally be able to resist. AIDS has become a feared illness, caused by the Human Immunodeficiency Virus or more commonly, HIV.

Babies may become infected from a mother who has AIDS. It can be acquired before, during the birth, or after the birth from breast milk.

Anyone, regardless of age, who shares needles is subject to the risk of picking up infections, including the HIV which causes AIDS.

Fortunately, AIDS is not prevalent in Canada and efforts are being made to stop the spread of HIV through education. It is important to remember that blood, semen, and vaginal fluids of infected persons spread the HIV. Your child is not at risk of acquiring AIDS should he require a blood transfusion as blood donors are rejected if tests are positive for HIV infection.

ALLERGY

What lay people talk about as an allergy, the experts call atopy. Here we will use the term "allergy" in its lay sense.

The five common forms of allergy are hay fever, asthma, eczema, perennial rhinitis and hives, but there are also several other less common types. In addition, asthma, eczema and hives (urticaria) are often due to other causes than allergy.

An allergic person is one who reacts in an abnormal way to substances that do not bother normal people – they have substances in their blood, antibodies and/or lymphoid cells, which interreact with the material to which they are sensitive. Histamine or histamine-like substances are liberated. An involved process occurs, which is not completely understood, resulting in the various forms of allergy.

Inheritance plays a large part in allergy. If you suffer from hay fever, do not be surprised if one or more of your children develop allergic signs. If there is allergy on both sides of your family tree, the chance of it occurring in your children is high. Very often the kind of allergic disease varies in different generations.

Some kinds of allergy are more common at certain ages. Eczema is most common in babies, asthma usually appears after the age of two years (although it can occur as early as one month of age), and hay fever is more frequent after puberty.

The history of the attacks and the study of the patient's environment, help to determine the cause of the allergy.

Food sensitivity is identified by using a diet with foods to which few children are sensitive. Foods are added at intervals, and if an attack occurs, the suspected food can be tested separately and eliminated, if necessary.

A series of skin tests, often done by an allergist, will help to determine the causes of a child's allergy and the degree of sensitivity.

Vials, containing suitable dilutions of the allergens to which the child reacted most strongly, can be made. Your child is then given regular injections of this material. This hyposensitization nearly always greatly reduces the frequency and severity of the allergic attacks. Sometimes it even stops them completely.

Many allergies can be controlled by newer medications and the removal of offending substances. However, in some severe cases of asthma and/or those cases which are not well controlled by medication, hyposensitization is an alternative.

Asthma

An asthmatic child has an airway that is hyperreactive to various causes. In an attack of asthma the small tubes or bronchioles of the lung become blocked, and as a result the patient has difficulty in breathing, particularly breathing out. This experience is frightening. If you can stay calm and divert your child it will help him. The child wheezes when he breathes and is more uncomfortable when he lies down. Inhalants, oral medicines or injections can be given which relieve the attack. The attack is nearly always followed by some bronchitis, which causes coughing.

Asthma can occur in sensitive children with a viral infection of the respiratory tract. It may be due to horse, cat, or dog hair, feathers in pillows or to other materials in the child's environment. Less frequently it follows the eating of certain foods such as eggs, nuts or wheat. In a few cases the cause can be easily discovered – for instance, when the child develops it a few weeks after adopting a kitten. Giving the kitten away and avoiding cats generally will prevent further attacks due to this cause.

Eczema

Eczema usually appears first on a baby's face as small red spots. These soon run together and become moist and covered with crusts. It is extremely itchy and is almost invariably scratched, with the result that it often becomes infected.

As soon as you see such a rash, take your baby to the doctor. It may be caused by contact with certain materials such as wool, soap or household pets or by some foods. Your physician will likely enquire about this and prescribe suitable ointments, and make any necessary changes in your baby's diet.

The condition usually persists for a considerable period of time but much can be done to keep it from becoming severe. It may involve other areas, such as the front of the elbows or behind the knees. In most cases it clears up in the second or third year but the child may later develop asthma or hay fever. Eczema is not contagious.

Hay Fever

The sneezing, the watery nasal discharge, and the itchy eyes and nose of hay fever are too familiar to need comment. The season of the year at which it occurs indicates strongly which types of pollen are responsible. Skin tests can confirm one's suspicion as to the offending allergen(s).

Hives (Urticaria)

Hives are flat, raised, irregularly-shaped, red or whitish areas on the skin, surrounded by a patch of redness. They are extremely itchy, but applying cold compresses may help to relieve the discomfort.

They are sometimes due to a sensitivity to a certain food, most often one that is not eaten frequently. For example, a big feast of fresh strawberries may cause hives in the occasional individual. Very often the cause cannot be discovered. Fortunately, unless the skin is broken by scratching, the hives leave no trace when they disappear.

Rhinitis

Perennial or allergic rhinitis (inflammation of the nose) often produces symptoms similar to hay fever, but the sneezing and itchy eyes are usually less prominent. In other words, it may seem likc a persistent or frequently recurring cold. The cause is usually something in the house, such as cat or dog hair, house dust or feathers.

Treatment of the Allergic Child

Your doctor is the person to recommend investigation and treatment for an allergic child. Antihistaminic drugs are widely used for the milder forms – hay fever, rhinitis and sometimes hives.

Asthma and eczema are best treated on an individual basis.

ANEMIA

Anemia is a physical condition, a pallor, due to fewer red blood cells in the blood stream than normal, or a reduction in the haemoglobin in the red blood cells. There are many causes of anemia.

Skin color – from fair to dark – requires judgment, to be sure of pallor. Many red-haired or blond children have fair skin that is not necessarily pale. With dark skin the pallor is sometimes difficult to assess. Looking at the lining of the lower lid of the eye or the palm of the hand will often help to decide whether or not the child is indeed pale.

It is important to see your doctor and have blood tests done to determine the degree and possible cause of an anemia.

Causes of Anemia

Lack of an essential substance in the diet will prevent the formation of haemoglobin (the red oxygen-carrying pigment in the red blood corpuscles).

Iron deficiency anemia is the most frequently seen blood disease of infancy and childhood. It is important, particularly in the rapidly growing infant, to give iron rich foods. These are infant cereals for babies and meat, egg yolk, vegetables, whole grain cereals, and legumes (beans) for the older child.

Repeated loss of blood in excess of the body's ability to replace it will also produce an iron deficiency anemia.

Too few red blood cells may be produced if there is a depressed red blood cell formation in the bone marrow when a child has a chronic infection or a cancer. Leukemia is the most common form of childhood cancer.

A haemolytic anemia is a breakdown of the child's red blood cells. Thalassaemia

(Mediterranean anemia), a genetic disorder, haemolytic disease of the newborn (Rh incompatibility) and some toxins will cause a haemolytic disease. These are less common.

CONVULSIONS

Convulsions can occur at any age but they are commonest in babies six months to four years of age. In fact, 50 out of every 1,000 children (5 percent) have one or more convulsions by the time they reach maturity. They are serious at any age, and any child who has a generalized convulsion should be seen by his physician as soon as possible.

A febrile convulsion may occur when the child develops an acute infection that causes a rapidly rising temperature. Meningitis also gives rise to convulsions, but it is fortunately not common. There are other less common causes of convulsions.

There seems to be great variation in children as far as convulsions are concerned. Some develop them during the course of relatively slight illnesses – while others never have convulsions, no matter how sick they are.

A convulsion is very frightening to a parent. The child becomes unconscious and then trembles all over, sometimes quite violently. The convulsion itself is practically never fatal, but it is an unmistakable warning that the child is seriously ill. If your baby has a convulsion, put him in bed, turning him on his side. If he seems feverish, you can give him a sponge bath with tepid water.

Usually the convulsion lasts only a very short time.

Your doctor will try to determine the cause of the convulsion so that she can treat it adequately. Tests may be necessary at the hospital.

Rarely, a convulsion lasts longer than a few minutes; in which case, arrangements should be made to transport the child to a hospital emergency at once.

Epilepsy

In older children (and adults), epileptic seizures take a variety of forms. The most common type, grand mal, produces a generalized seizure. There may be a feeling or awareness or sign that a seizure is imminent. This is called an aura. The child becomes unconscious and falls down, and then the stiffening and jerking follow. Often he will give an unnatural cry, the sequel to a spasm of his throat. Frothing may be evident. He neither suffers pain nor is he aware of the seizure.

The child is usually tired after the seizure and may be dazed or sleep for an hour or so.

The other common type of epilepsy is called petit mal or absence seizure. This generalized seizure last a few seconds and the patient does not fall. The seizures are often called staring or nodding spells, and there may also be a flickering of the eyelids. During the spell the child is unconscious, but he comes to very quickly and continues with what he was doing. Many spells may occur during a day and cause learning difficulties at the time.

Partial seizures affect only a side or portion of the body and there is no loss of consciousness.

Spells are relieved with drugs. However about half of the children go on to have other types of seizures. It is important for epileptics to be monitored by a doctor for adjustments in medication.

All children subject to seizures should carry a card or wear a wrist tag.

DIARRHEA

Diarrhea means frequent loose bowel movements, often with an offensive or different odor from the usual. In babies it may be caused by an indigestible food, by an infection in the intestinal tract, by an infection elsewhere in the body, by an allergy to a certain food or by a defect or deficiency in the functioning of the digestive system.

In older children, the eating of an indigestible food or an infection in the digestive tract are the commonest causes. The infection may be caused by a virus – such as rotavirus, coxsackie virus or adenovirus, bacteria – such as Campylobacter jejuni Shigella, Salmonella or some forms of E. coli, or protozoa – such as Giardia lamblia. A rotavirus is felt to be the cause in over half of the attacks of acute diarrhea in children.

Many intestinal infections can be prevented by washing the hands after using the toilet and before preparing and eating food. All fruits and vegetables that are to be eaten raw should be washed before eating.

An acute attack of diarrhea will usually last two to three days. It is one of the commonest ailments of babies and children. When a child has diarrhea, it is important to replace the liquid that is lost in the stool. Giving clear fluids that will not upset the stomach and bowel is important. If the diarrhea is severe and/or persistant, then your doctor may wish to add liquids that will replace the salts which are also being lost. A culture of the stool may be necessary to identify the cause of the infection.

If the child refuses to drink, vomits repeatedly, becomes listless or whimpering – seek medical advice. These signs suggest a more severe attack and dehydration may be the result.

EARS

The ear consists of three main parts – the outer canal, the middle ear and the inner ear. The outer canal, which you can see from the outside is closed off by a tough small membrane called the eardrum. On the inner side of the eardrum is the middle ear. It is a box-shaped cavity about the size of a large pea, filled with air and connected by a passage, called the Eustachian tube, with the throat. Arching across the top of the chamber of the middle ear is a chain of three tiny bones which connect the eardrum on the outer side with the inner ear on the inside. If these bones are damaged by an infection, the hearing becomes impaired.

The lining of the throat is continuous with the lining of the eustachian tube. When the throat is red and swollen, the lining of the Eustachian tube and middle ear may become affected. This is more apt to happen in babies than in older children, as the eustachian tube is shorter and straighter in an infant.

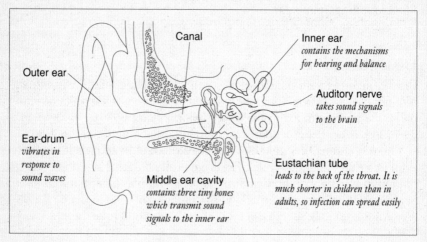

Canal

Outer ear

Inner ear
contains the mechanisms for hearing and balance

Auditory nerve
takes sound signals to the brain

Ear-drum
vibrates in response to sound waves

Middle ear cavity
contains three tiny bones which transmit sound signals to the inner ear

Eustachian tube
leads to the back of the throat. It is much shorter in children than in adults, so infection can spread easily

Earache

Otitis media, an infection of the middle ear, usually causes earache. If a baby with a cold cries for some time, as though in pain, it is likely that he has an earache. He will probably be restless and feverish as well. Older babies sometimes pull the sore ear and children, of course, complain of a painful ear. Do consult your doctor. From the appearance and shape of the eardrum the doctor can tell a good deal about the middle ear.

For an acute ear infection antibiotics will probably be prescribed. If there has been a build up of pressure in the middle ear because of the infection or other cause, it may be necessary to relieve this pressure by minor surgery to the eardrum. If fluid in the middle ear causes recurrent build up of pressure, then tubes may be inserted in the eardrum to allow drainage.

 It is necessary to protect the small bones in the middle ear from damage, so as to preserve the child's hearing.

Excessive wax

The lining of the outer canal produces a protective wax, which occasionally forms in excessive amounts, causing a hearing loss. The wax may need to be softened by ear drops for a few days, before being syringed out by the doctor.

With moisture, dryness, or injury to the skin of the ear canal, the protective wax, may be altered and infection may occur. This is seen in swimmers, especially if they have been in rivers or lakes. The ear canal will be very painful and may be badly swollen.

Ear drops are usually necessary to clear the infection.

Deafness

Deafness can be due to a variety of causes. An infant may be born with an inherited hearing impairment, or with developmental damage to the ear which has occurred in utero. Fluid in the middle ear can cause a hearing impairment. If you are suspicious that your child is not hearing, have an assessment made as soon as possible.

Anyone with normal hearing should turn to a ticking clock or the crunch of paper or other similar noise that is new and out of sight. There may be other reasons why the child does not turn to the sound but the presence of a response should assure you that he is hearing.

Children with defective hearing will have difficulty in learning, unless assisted in a manner to minimize this problem. With a severe loss of hearing, the handicap may necessitate special schooling with sophisticated amplification of sound.

Medical management over a period of time will resolve more minor problems.

HEPATITIS

Infectious or catarrhal hepatitis is an inflammation of the liver caused by hepatitis A virus (HAV or enterovirus 72) that can be passed from one person to another. It is quite rare in children under three years, and it is not common in older children.

At the onset, the child feels tired and cross. There is fever and loss of appetite. Pain or discomfort is present in his upper abdomen due to the increase in size and tenderness of his liver.

The liver makes bile, which normally drains into the digestive tract. Due to the swelling and other changes in the liver, bile is dammed up in the liver and cannot escape as usual. The brownish color of normal bowel movements is due to the bile – in infectious hepatitis the stools become a pale clay color. The bile also gets into the blood and this causes the patient's skin to turn a greenish-yellow color – jaundice. The bile passes from his blood into his urine, making it darker.

A child with infectious hepatitis must be kept quiet, under the supervision of your doctor. Rest is important. Infectious hepatitis will last approximately two to three weeks.

Hepatitis B is the other common form of viral liver infection and is caused by hepatitis B virus (HBV or hepadnavirus 1). It was initially known as serum hepatitis because it was proved to be transmitted through blood products, such as blood transfusions. After the virus was identified, it became possible to identify those who had the disease or had had it and those who had never had it. The prevalance of the disease became recognized.

The incubation period for hepatitis is between 60-150 days. Those who develop the clinical infection will show signs of jaundice and liver enlargement. Many acquire the infection without becoming ill. The virus may be carried for an indefinite time in both situations. The carrier state is prevalent in certain races, such as Orientals, and it can be associated with impaired liver function.

Because all blood and blood products are now screened for the presence of HBV, the main source of the infection in the paediatric group is the transmission of the virus from the carrier mother to her newborn.

The infant is now protected from acquiring the infection by the use of 3 hepatitis B vaccine injections and an intramuscular administration of a specific anti-hepatitis B globulin.

There are many other causes of hepatitis but they are not commonly seen.

HERNIAS

A hernia is a weakness in the support of the abdominal wall. The most common site is in the inguinal area where a loop of intestine bulges through the weak area and produces a hernia that may appear and disappear or remain.

Hernias usually don't bother babies. Crying, straining or standing will make the hernia more evident, but does not produce it.

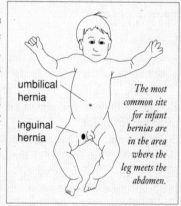

An operation repairs this weakness, with little upset to the child. The surgeon sews the tissues together to make the weak spot stronger. The hernia is cured but sometimes recurs at a later date.

Umbilical hernias may occur after the cord falls off. Loops of intestine may slide in and out of the rupture without causing discomfort. Usually the lump becomes progressively smaller and is no longer noticeable by eighteen months of age. A few persist, become larger and require surgical correction.

umbilical hernia

inguinal hernia

The most common site for infant hernias are in the area where the leg meets the abdomen.

INFECTIOUS MONONUCLEOSIS (MONO)

Infectious mononucleosis (glandular fever) can appear in anyone over the age of four months but is commonest between the ages of 17 and 25 years. Boys are more likely to develop it than girls. The patient feels sick, has a sore throat and a fever. Lymph glands (nodes) become enlarged, especially those in the neck. The spleen may be enlarged.

The patient's blood contains an increased number of white blood cells (lymphocytes), many of them unusual in appearance. A positive heterophile antibody test confirms the diagnosis.

The disease is caused by the Epstein-Barr virus. It is not very infectious and isolation is not necessary.

Symptomatic treatment – that is, treatment that is indicated by whatever symptoms the child displays – is all that is necessary, and there is usually a complete recovery, although fatigue may continue well after the acute illness for some weeks.

MENINGITIS

An inflammation of the thin membranes (meninges) that surround the brain and spinal cord is called meningitis. It is relatively uncommon.

Except in young babies, the most typical signs of this disease are painful stiffness of the neck, fever, severe headache and vomiting. The baby or child looks and feels sick, is irritable and may develop a purplish rash. Call your doctor at once. This disease must have prompt and expert treatment in hospital.

Several different bacteria cause meningitis. By obtaining a small amount of spinal fluid from around the spinal cord (a safe procedure) the physician can usually discover which bacteria are causing the disease. With the use of adequate amounts of suitable antibiotics and other treatment, most patients make excellent recoveries.

A number of different viruses can cause aseptic meningitis. This illness is milder and there is usually complete recovery.

NOSEBLEEDS

Nosebleeds are nearly always minor ailments. Usually the bleeding comes from a tiny vessel on the inner wall near the tip of the nose. Once it has been broken, it is apt to break again, causing recurrent nosebleeds.

Apart from injury, they may occur most frequently during a respiratory infection such as a cold. If there is a weak blood vessel, stooping over or lifting weights, both of which increase the flow of blood to the nose, may cause the vessel to rupture.

When a child has a nosebleed, have him sit, preferably with a basin on his lap, holding his head bent forward a little but held up, to prevent the blood from running down his throat. You can put a cold compress over his nose to reduce the size of the blood vessel and lessen the bleeding. Pressing his nostrils firmly together between your thumb and forefinger may control the bleeding.

Tell your child to wipe his nose gently and not blow it at all for the rest of the day. Do not be in a hurry to

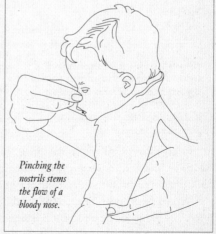

Pinching the nostrils stems the flow of a bloody nose.

remove the clotted blood from the lower part of his nose, as that, too, is apt to start the bleeding again.

If, despite all your efforts to stop it, the nosebleed persists for more than 10 minutes, get in touch with your doctor.

PARASITIC INFECTION
Worms

Any family can be affected by common pinworms. If one child has them, his brothers and sisters will probably be infected too, and often his parents.

The female worm looks like a tiny white thread about 1/2-inch long (1.27 centimetres); the male is even smaller. The invisible eggs of these worms are swallowed inadvertently. They hatch out in the intestinal tract. After they have stayed there for some weeks, the female worms become mature. Then they migrate to the anus (the lower opening of the digestive tract) and lay thousands of eggs.

Often the child infected with worms experiences no discomfort. In some cases, the female when laying her eggs produces a tickling sensation or even severe itching or pain around the anus. Some children are also troubled with restlessness, sleeplessness, loss of appetite and weight and occasionally abdominal pain, nausea and vomiting. In girls some of the worms may wander into the vagina and cause a vaginal discharge.

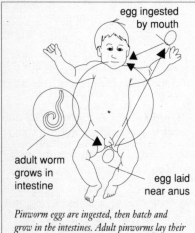

egg ingested by mouth

adult worm grows in intestine

egg laid near anus

Pinworm eggs are ingested, then hatch and grow in the intestines. Adult pinworms lay their eggs in the skin around the anus, where children may pick up eggs on their finger-tips and then ingest them. (Egg and worm are not drawn in proportion)

All of these symptoms may be due to other conditions, but if you suspect pinworms, you may be able to see them by examining the anus in daylight or with the aid of a flashlight after the child has gone to sleep. The live worms move about in a jerky way. Special swabs may be examined to identify the characteristic eggs . The use of these swabs causes no pain or discomfort to your child.

If your family has pinworms you can prevent the eggs from spreading. Soap and hot water are effective in removing and destroying the eggs. All the family should wash their hands well, especially after using the toilet and before preparing or eating food. Keep fingernails short and clean. Showering is probably more efficient in getting rid of the eggs than bathing.

As you can imagine, one can pick up the eggs from contaminated clothes, taps, furniture and so on. While treatment is under way, wash night clothes, underwear, towels and washcloths every day in hot water. As the eggs can be scattered about in the air, use a damp cloth, which can be discarded, for dusting or to cover your mop or broom. Vacuum rugs and bedding. The eggs are very resistant to chemical disinfectants.

Your doctor will prescribe medicine for the entire family, which will be effective against the worm.

A few popular misconceptions about pinworms are prevalent. It is not necessary or wise to give worm medicine periodically. Kittens and puppies are not infested by pinworms. Too many sweets will not produce worms. If your child is whining and tired, it is not a "sure sign" of pinworms.

Giardia Lamblia

Giardia lamblia is a protozoa that is worldwide and common. It is one of the causes of diarrhea in children.

The cysts of the protozoa are swallowed and mature in the upper intestine. Mature forms and cysts are passed in the stool where they may be identified. Infection is spread, from person to person, water borne or food borne. Epidemics do occur. Dogs, beavers and man are infected by Giardia lamblia.

The infection may present as diarrhea, weight loss and failure to thrive. However, 20-60 percent of those infected do not have any symptoms.

Most cases respond to prescribed treatment.

Other kinds of worms may be found in children, but they are much less common than those described above.

 Teach your child to wash his hands before eating and after using the toilet.

RESPIRATORY TRACT INFECTIONS

Respiratory tract infections are most frequently caused by a virus. Identification of the virus is possible but is usually not done for a particular infection. Infections are usually mild, inevitable and part of growing up and developing one's own immunity to the viral agents.

However the location of the infection in the respiratory tract produces a different problem because of the passageway's size, location and response.

As many, literally hundreds of viruses, cause respiratory tract infections, an identified group is mentioned only as interest, as the general handling of these infections is the same, with perhaps some change in the medication.

Viruses are not affected by antibiotics. Slowly a few antiviral agents are surfacing, but they are not generally available.

Common Cold

Preschool children, especially with older siblings, develop more colds, coughs and sore throats than anyone else in the family. It is some encouragement to know that as they grow older, they will also have fewer and less severe infections as their bodies' ability to handle infections improves.

Colds are caused by a large number of different viruses, most commonly the rhinoviruses. A cold virus causes the lining layer of the nose (mucosa) to swell and to produce an excessive amount of watery mucus. During the course of the cold, the superficial cells of the mucosa are shed with replacement occurring. The fever is usually not too high.

Unfortunately, many colds do not stop there. After the virus has lowered the resistance of the nose, the secondary invaders, this time bacteria such as streptococci or pneumococci, may take over. These cause the nasal discharge to become thicker and greenish-yellow in colour. The bacteria may be present in the nose and throat normally; others are acquired, and they are more likely to cause serious trouble.

The lining of the nose is continuous with the lining of the sinuses, the throat, and the Eustachian tubes – the upper respiratory tract. In an ordinary cold the sinuses become involved and heal as the cold evolves. The Eustachian tubes run from the throat to the middle ears. As they are shorter and straighter in a baby, he is more likely to develop an ear infection with a cold than an older youngster.

Certainly for two hours and possibly 24 hours before your cold becomes obvious it may be spread to others. To prevent colds, avoid taking your baby or small child into crowded places, especially during the "cold seasons"—September, late January and April. These areas often have poor ventilation. Nearly always some one has a cold. Avoid them.

Do not let anyone with a cold visit your infant.

In many homes the humidity is extremely low when the furnace is on and the dryness irritates the lining of the nose and throat. Therefore, another precaution you can take against colds is to humidify the air in your home during the winter months. Keep the temperature in your home at about 68 to 70 Farhenheit (20-21 Celcius).

There is no specific treatment for a cold. Antibiotics are ineffective against the cold viruses. The acute stage of a cold will last two to four days, and it will take a week for the cold to resolve. Your doctor may recommend nose drops or medicine to relieve obstruction of the passages.

If a baby's nose is blocked with mucus, sleeping on his side will help secretions drain. A brief warm bath in a warm room is often of value in clearing the mucus from a small child's nose.

Tonsils and Adenoids

The tonsils, adenoids, lymph glands (nodes), thymus gland and some other small areas in the walls of the digestive tract and elsewhere in the body are made of lymphoid tissue.

This tissue has two main functions: it traps bacteria that are carried to it by the lymph (which is much like colorless blood) in the lymph vessels, and it produces many of the white blood cells, some of which can produce antibodies.

The amount of lymphoid tissue in the body increases up to the age of about twelve years and then it decreases. Thus it is not surprising that the tonsils are normally quite large in a child 10-12 years of age. The adenoids are located in the nasopharynx.

Normally the tonsils and adenoids catch and kill most of the harmful germs that reach them. Some of the glands in the neck may become enlarged and tender during an attack of tonsillitis. This is an indication that the infection is more severe. There is often an associated high fever.

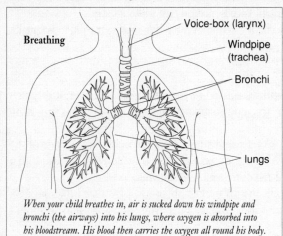

Breathing

Voice-box (larynx)

Windpipe (trachea)

Bronchi

lungs

When your child breathes in, air is sucked down his windpipe and bronchi (the airways) into his lungs, where oxygen is absorbed into his bloodstream. His blood then carries the oxygen all round his body.

Tonsillitis may be treated with an antibiotic.

Sometimes, the tonsils are not too efficient and a chronic or recurrent inflammation (tonsillitis) occurs. Diseased tonsils are usually harmful, and most children are better off without them.

Enlarged adenoids may cause partial deafness or mouth breathing and for these reasons, their removal may be recommended.

A surgeon can take out all of the tonsils, but it is neither possible nor desirable to remove all the adenoid tissue.

Spasmodic Croup

Croup is an inflammation of the throat and windpipe, commonly due to a parainfluenza virus, causing a hoarse cough and possibly difficult breathing. It usually affects a child six months to three years of age. The child may have a slight cold or a little hoarseness and cough, during the day, but wakens during the night with a spasm of sharp barking cough, noisy breathing and difficulty in catching his breath. His face is usually flushed and he is, naturally, frightened. He has little, if any, fever. Always call your doctor if your baby develops croup.

Warm or cool moist air helps to relieve his distress. Carry him into the bathroom and get the air full of steam by filling the tub with hot water. Before he goes back to his bed, many physicians recommend humidifying the air in his room also. If a warm mist humidifier is used be sure that it is safely positioned where your child cannot burn himself. A cold mist is also of benefit and there is no risk of a burn. Stay in the room with him while his breathing is a concern. Remove the vaporizer when not in use.

Usually after an hour or two the child will fall asleep; although he may have another attack later during the night.

There is also a much less common but much more severe kind of croup, which is often called laryngo-tracheo-bronchitis. The child has a more severe cold, a barking cough with noisy and difficult breathing. The child looks and acts sick; he has a fever, and his face may be ashen. Hoarseness with fever or difficulty in breathing with fever are danger signals. Your child needs medical care without delay.

Call your doctor at once and if you cannot reach him take your child to hospital.

Bronchiolitis

This disease of the winter months is caused by a respiratory syncitial virus, RSV, and seen in infants under a year of age, most commonly under six months. This virus also causes pneumonia.

The baby becomes sick with a running nose and pharyngitis, (inflamation of the pharynx), almost like a cold. After one to three days the baby develops a cough with a wheeze that can be quite loud and distressing. Consult your doctor.

With some babies the infection is over in about a week; other babies become sicker with considerable distress in breathing. They require constant nursing care in hospital.

Pneumonia

In pneumonia, patches of lung tissue of various sizes become inflamed. It frequently occurs in the winter and early spring when colds and other respiratory infections are at their peak.

If your child has a cold and then develops a fever, is breathing rapidly and appears more ill, contact your doctor. Older children may have a shaking chill, high fever, cough and chest pain at the onset of pneumonia.

Pneumonia caused by bacteria is usually controlled by suitable antibiotics. Under favorable conditions, older children may be treated at home. Babies are frequently treated in hospital.

Viral pneumonia occurs most commonly in the first year of life. The onset is similar to a cold, but the infant develops a high fever with a more severe cough. Food is refused and the child is listless and looks much sicker. Your doctor will want to see your child.

SCARLET FEVER

The bacteria called beta hemolytic streptococci (strep) can cause several different diseases, most often severe sore throat, less commonly scarlet fever.

Symptoms of the disease usually appear a few days after the child has been exposed to someone with a "strep" throat. Typically, after a day or so of fever, sore throat, headache and possibly vomiting, the child develops the characteristic rash. Three or four days after the onset, the tongue is usually heavily coated. In mild cases (often called scarlatina) the child may show only a slight elevation of temperature before the rash appears.

The rash appears first on the neck or chest and soon spreads over the entire body with the exceptions of the face, (which is flushed with a circumoral pallor), and the scalp. At this time the white coating on the tongue disappears, leaving the tongue red and shiny. If the rash is examined closely, it is seen as minute red points on a pink-ish background. It fades within a week, often leaving a flaking skin – particularly the finger tips. This process may take several weeks.

If your child develops a rash with a sore throat, have him examined by your physician. Penicillin or other antibiotics given for 10 days, are effective against beta haemolytic strep and will prevent later complications.

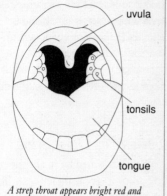

A strep throat appears bright red and there are often dots of pus on the back of the throat and the tonsils.

SKIN PROBLEMS
Boils

A boil is much like a very large pimple. It is swollen, red, painful and contains pus. Take a careful look at the leg or arm or other area where the infection is located and note any red streaks on the skin spreading from the infection. Check for tender lymph glands in the nearby area such as the groin, armpit or neck.

Your doctor may tell you to soak or apply hot compresses to the boil. This helps to relieve the pain, keeps the center of the boil open, and promotes the discharge of the pus. Half a cup of table salt or Epsom salts (magnesium sulphate) in two quarts of warm water, may be used as a compress, or soak.

A large, dry, sterile gauze pad makes a good cover for the boil between soakings. Do not put adhesive tape near it until it is healed, as the slight injury caused by removing the tape may result in another, probably smaller, infection.

It may also be necessary to place the child on an antibiotic.

A great many skin infections can be avoided if your children report their scrapes to you when they occur. Quickly wash them with soap and warm water. If your child is old enough to keep the cut clean without a covering, it will heal faster if left exposed to the air. If, because of its location or the age of the child, a covering is needed, be sure to replace it if it becomes wet or dirty.

Impetigo

This relatively common ailment usually occurs on the face, especially near the nose and mouth. It begins as little water blisters, but soon golden crusts appear with practically no reddening of the surrounding skin. It is caused by beta haemolytic streptococci or staphylcoccus aureus and it is very infectious. It can be spread from one area to another in the same child, or from child to child. It may be spread by scratching, shared towels or direct contact.

Your doctor will likely prescribe an antibiotic ointment for the skin. It may be necessary to prescribe an antibiotic by mouth as well, if the deeper layer of the skin is involved.

Poison Ivy Dermatitis

This rash is caused by an allergic reaction to the oil of the wild poison ivy plant which affects most people if they come in contact with it. The plant grows in shady, wooded areas, spreads by the roots running under the ground, with shoots appearing at intervals from the roots. These shoots are identified by glossy green compound leaves of three leaflets. In autumn the leaves may turn red. White berries may be noted. Show your child and teach him to avoid it.

The dermatitis is acquired by direct contact of the skin with the plant, the oil of the plant on clothing, the fur of animals that have run through it, or occasionally smoke fumes of the plant burning. Once the oil is in contact with the skin, it soon produces itchy, red spots that often become weeping watery blisters. There may be a linear appearance from scratching and spreading the oil.

If you know or suspect that your child has been in contact with poison ivy, as soon as possible, lather the area with soap and water thoroughly, and then rinse it off. Contaminated clothing needs to be thoroughly washed or if dry-cleaned, it should be labelled as having been exposed to poison ivy. Otherwise the plant oil will remain on the clothing for months.

If the lesions are watery, compresses of a drying solution, (Burow's) may be applied until the moist areas have become crusted. Corticosteriod ointments are usually used and an antihistaminic, orally, may help to relieve intense itching. Occasionally, oral steriods are required with severe involve-

Poison Ivy

ment. Your doctor should be consulted to confirm the diagnosis and treat the condition adequately.

Scabies

This is caused by an itch mite which is transmitted (passed) directly from an infected person or contaminated clothing. The mite creates small burrows in the skin which are extremely itchy. The common sites are between the fingers, wrists, elbows, groin and axilla. In babies, burrows are not seen and the palms, soles, face and scalp are usually affected.

The itching is extreme, especially at night, and this leads to secondary infection from scratching – boils or impetigo – which hide the original problem.

Your doctor will recommend a specific lotion to be applied to the body.

Lice

Also known as pediculosis, lice are seen in children, most commonly on the head. The lice are found occasionally but usually the nits are more easily seen. The scalp becomes very itchy and some infection may occur from scratching.

Look at the hair at the back of the head and around the ears for nits on a hair shaft. The tiny white grain or nit (egg) is firmly attached to the hair shaft close to the root and cannot be removed by scraping.

Other members of the family may be infected also.

Head lice are too small to see, but their shiny white egg cases are visible sticking to hairs close to the head.

All bedding, hats, combs and brushes should be cleaned at the same time as treatment, recommended by your doctor, is being given.

STINGS AND BITES

Numerous mosquito bites can upset a baby or small child. Screens on the windows and veranda or netting over his carriage when he is asleep will protect him from bites.

If your child does get a bite, dab calamine lotion on it to relieve the discomfort. Secondary infection can occur as a result of scratching.

Bee stings are painful, and are soon followed by redness and firm swelling. Wild bees, wasps and hornets do not leave their stingers behind, but the honeybee may leave its stinger in the skin. It should be removed.

Dabbing moistened baking soda on the sting relieves the soreness.

The venom that an ant deposits in its bite also contains acid like the bee's poison, and baking soda helps to relieve the irritation of ant bites, which are usually quite painful.

Spider bites are relatively painless, but can cause considerably more swelling than mosquito bites. Antihistaminics, if given early enough, can prevent some of this reaction.

Tick Bites

If you live in an area where there are ticks, check your youngsters daily for tick bites. Ticks are slow feeders and can take up to 20 hours to feed on blood. Look for them, especially in hair and folds of skin. Remove any you find with tweezers, being sure to get the head out as well as the body. If it clings, loosen its hold by smearing with grease, or oil. Crush it, but not with your fingers. Clean the wound with soap and water or a mild antiseptic.

Wearing long sleeves and pants in wooded areas will protect much of the exposed skin. Check the skin after a walk for bites and evidence of a small tick which will swell with blood.

Most ticks are harmless, but some carry Colorado tick fever, Rocky Mountain spotted fever, Lyme disease, and others. Lyme disease has been in the news because of the identification of deer ticks, which carry the bacterium causing the illness, in south-western Ontario. A few deer tick have been found in Manitoba, Prince Edward Island,and Quebec. There have been about 30 confirmed cases of Lyme disease reported in Canada.

The flu-like illness may occur (incubate) two to 35 days after the tick bite. If identi-fied and treated with antibiotic, later complications such as arthritis, will be avoided.

WARTS

Warts are caused by viruses. Different kinds of warts are caused by different viruses. The virus causes a growth of the skin or mucous membrane.

Warts are very common in children. They are acquired from others with warts either directly or through contaminated clothing or other substance. It may take from 1-8 months for the wart to form.

The common warts appear on the fingers and hands but may appear on the face, knees or elbows. They are painless, ugly looking lumps of hard dry skin.

Planter warts occur only on the soles of the feet and appear flat because of the pressure of weight bearing. They become painful with the build-up of skin and the pressure on nerve endings in the skin. Frequently they are picked up at swimming pools. Keeping the foot dry and cool discourages the development of these warts.

Most warts disappear in time on their own. However, it is worthwhile treating the painful planter warts. Your doctor may remove the dead skin by paring it. She will recommend a solution to be applied to the wart.

URINARY TRACT INFECTIONS

Infections of the urinary tract occur more often in girls than boys and are most com-mon in the 7-11 year old girl. The majority of the infections are caused by an E. Coli, which is a bacterium ever present in the stool. As the infection is introduced from the perineum and goes up the urinary tract, it is important to prevent the bacteria from moving forward from the anus to the urethra (urinary tract). Teach your daughter to wipe from behind after passing a bowel movement.

There are other factors which come into play as well as the location of these two openings, as some girls never get infections and others may have recurring bouts. For this reason further tests are carried out. Some children may have had a low grade infection before the acute attack. It is important to assess the state of the kidney and adjoining structures.

Occasionally a urinary tract infection occurs in a newborn. It may become a blood-borne infection and occurs more often in boys.

Often fever, without an identifiable cause, will make your doctor suspicious of a urinary tract infection and she will want a specimen to examine.

In older children, frequency, pain or burning on voiding, great urgency, or abdominal pain may be present.

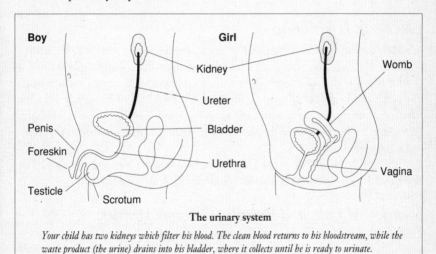

The urinary system

Your child has two kidneys which filter his blood. The clean blood returns to his bloodstream, while the waste product (the urine) drains into his bladder, where it collects until he is ready to urinate.

VIRAL INFECTIONS COMMON IN CHILDHOOD
MOST WITH AN ASSOCIATED RASH
Pharyngo-conjunctival fever

Pharyngo-conjunctival fever (caused by an adenovirus) is an illness which occurs year round but most frequently in the spring or early summer. There is usually a high fever which lasts four to five days. The throat (pharynx) and whites of the eye (conjunctiva) are inflamed.

Specific medication is not required and there is complete recovery.

Chickenpox

Chickenpox is a very common, highly infectious disease of infancy and childhood. It is caused by a specific virus and results in lifelong immunity. It is acquired from an infected person as there is no carrier state. The incubation period is from 12-21 days.

Although your child may feel out-of-sorts for a few hours before the rash appears, usually the rash is the first intimation that he is ill. A few scattered red spots, on the trunk, abdomen or less often the face, appear marking the onset of the rash. These develop into water blisters within a few hours and become itchy. Within a few days the blisters dry up, leaving a crust or scab, which will persist for another few days. Other fresh spots keep appearing for about a week. Lesions at all stages of development will be evident. During this time, there may be spikes of fever with the appearance of new lesions.

Treatment consists of keeping the child at rest if fevered or in the home until all the crusted areas have cleared. Calamine lotion or tepid baking soda baths may relieve the itch.

Erythema Infectiosum

A human parvovirus causes this illness which is unusual in that there may be little or no fever. The rash associated with it sometimes causes alarm. It first appears on the cheeks, giving a "slapped-cheek" appearance. It is puzzling as there is not a high fever, nor is the child sufficiently upset to produce the "flush". Most frequently after but sometimes before, a blotchy rash appears on the trunk and extremities – similar in appearance to the eruption of measles. Usually medical advice is sought at this point and a diagnosis is made.

As the rash fades, it develops a lacy appearance, which is very characteristic. The rash may last two days to several weeks but eventually heals completely.

Measles, Mumps and Rubella (German Measles)

A child today should be protected by immunization against the viruses causing the following illnesses. Occasionally, breakthrough cases are seen, but it is usually a modified form of the illness.

Measles

The early stage of measles is very infectious and is much like that of a bad cold. The child sneezes, his nose runs, and he often has a cough. Usually his eyes are red and watery, and he has some fever. After three or four days of this, a blotchy red rash appears, on his forehead or behind his ears. When the rash is at its peak, his face becomes somewhat swollen and he develops a higher fever. The rash gradually spreads over the entire body. As the rash fades the fever drops.

Mumps

This is most common between the ages of five and 15 years, but does occur in adults too. It is not very infectious. The incubation period is rather long – usually between two and three weeks.

Pain is noticed near the angle of the jaw, below the ear. Moving the jaw or swallowing sour food makes the pain worse. Fever, headache and poor appetite may precede the pain. Then one or more of the salivary glands begins to swell. The largest glands, the parotid glands, (situated below and in front of each ear) are most commonly involved. The swelling increases for a few days, then becomes stationary and finally decreases in size.

Rubella

This is nearly always a mild disease. Usually the first thing noticed is the rash, which appears on the face around the ears and spreads over the body within a day. The rash varies considerably and often is hard to distinguish from measles or scarlet fever. It usually lasts about three days. Nearly always the glands at the back of the neck are enlarged and tender – sometimes those below the ears and elsewhere are larger than normal. Often the patient is a little feverish but the rash may be the only sign of the illness.

Roseola (Exanthem Subitum)

This is an unusual disease in which the child, between six months and three years of age, is feverish for three to four days and as the fever falls, the rash appears. The infection is caused by herpes virus 6.

The child's fever may be high and he may seem quite sick, but the doctor cannot find cause for his fever. The child may even have a convulsion. The fever disappears and a fine red rash appears on the body and face within 24 hours. The child continues to improve over the next few days.

WHOOPING COUGH

Whooping cough is a highly contagious illness, with severe paroxysms (severe, sudden attacks) of coughing, caused by a bacterium called Bordetella pertussis. The episodes of coughing may be so severe that the child will vomit with the paroxysms. It is particularly severe in infants. Children up to the age of seven should receive protective immunization.

A full course of immunization with pertussis vaccine produces immunity in about 80-90 percent of recipients. Children who acquire whooping cough in spite of full immunization have a less severe infection and fewer complications.

Severe complications from pertussis vaccine are very unusual.

Index